W9-CDM-714

A Third Course

More Cooking with Class
from Charlotte Latin School

Copyright 2003
by Charlotte Latin School

1st printing   April 2003   10,000 copies

ISBN: 0-9615616-2-9

About the artist: The illustrations for *A Third Course: More Cooking with Class* are taken from original watercolors by Charlotte Latin School parent, Champagne Maker.

WIMMER
COOKBOOKS

ConsolidatedGraphics

1-800-548-2537

History

About Charlotte Latin School......

Founded in 1970, Charlotte Latin School is an independent college preparatory day school for students in transitional kindergarten through grade twelve. Located on a 122-acre campus in Charlotte, North Carolina, Charlotte Latin is accredited by the Southern Association of Colleges and Schools and the North Carolina Department of Public Instruction. The School is a member of the National, Southern, and North Carolina Associations of Independent Schools. Charlotte Latin's Lower, Middle, and Upper Schools have been named "Blue Ribbon Schools of Excellence" by the United States Department of Education.

The School was named for America's early public schools, called "latin schools," in which colonial children pursued a traditional, liberal arts curriculum, including studies in the classical languages Latin and Greek. With an educational approach that is traditional in design, yet progressive in implementation, Charlotte Latin School today remains true to its founding parents' vision as a place where a stimulating academic environment is united with a vibrant family community to create an ideal setting for the education of children.

Charlotte Latin School
9502 Providence Road
Charlotte, North Carolina   28277
(704) 846-7250
www.charlottelatin.org

Charlotte Latin is an independent, non-sectarian, coeducational, college preparatory day school for students in grades transitional kindergarten through twelve. Charlotte Latin School does not discriminate on the basis of sex, race, color, religion, or national origin in the administration of its educational program, admissions policies, financial aid policies, employment practices, or other school-administered programs.

Orientation

The Charlotte Latin Parents' Council welcomes you back to class! After 20 successful years of tremendous praise and demand for our first and second Cooking with Class cookbooks, we invite you to enroll again for *A Third Course, More Cooking with Class*.

Parents, alumni, faculty, staff, and family friends did their homework to help us develop the curriculum for this course by turning in some 1,000 recipes. Our cookbook faculty devoted countless hours this semester reviewing and testing recipes. At final exam time, about 350 recipes graduated with honors for inclusion in *A Third Course*.

Some recipes score high in taste and appearance for the educated palate, while others offer to tempt the taste buds with a simple preparation approach tailored for our busy lives. We think you'll find many selections that will stir your senses and complement your cooking style.

And, just as we encourage our children to fine-tune their study skills, we cooks can earn extra credit in the culinary department when we add new or timeless cooking tricks and food tips to our repertoire. So, *A Third Course* includes a sampling of these to help you earn high marks at the kitchen table.

Finally we would like to thank everyone who completed their assignments in order to provide you with a culinary curriculum that dishes out savory recipes sure to please all. We hope you enjoy the flavor of *A Third Course* as you prepare and share the best from the halls of Charlotte Latin School.

To order additional copies, please contact
CLS Parents' Council
9502 Providence Road
Charlotte, North Carolina 28277
(704) 846-7250
www.charlottelatin.org

Class Officers (Section Leaders) – Suzette Buchan, Karen Taylor, Martha Player, Anita Griffin, Barbara Monckton, Kelli McAlister, Kristi Foxgrover, Mary Tanneberger, Barbara Chase, and Celeste Rudolph

Faculty (Cookbook Committee) – Cam Wester, Teresa Carroll, Kathy Gately, Champagne Maker, Donna Burdick, Kathy Rowan, Win Register, Parkie Thomas, Laura Shwedo, Wandra Mackie, and Doris Barahona-Burton

Honor Roll

Meg Adams
Anne Alexander
Betty Gray Anderson
Marion Andrews
Elizabeth Arnall
Jean Asinger
Lilla Austin
Elizabeth Ayers
Laura Baragona
Madia Barber
Elsie Barnhardt
Kim Barnhardt
Patty Barnhardt
Marsha Barry
Anne Barry
Katie Bates
Marcia Beare
Susan Beatty
Suzanne Beatty
Maralee Beck
Sarah Lee Beck
Anne Belk
Marge Berglund
Allison Berkowitz
Beth Beuley
Ellen Bickett
Bebe Blake
April Booe
Mona Booe
Cindy Booke
Beth Bowen
Mary Helen Bowman
Maurya Boyd
Rachel Brazell
Beth Breeney
Jamie Brown
Shelly Brown
Linda Brown
Susan Buchanan
Robyn Budelli
Judy Buening
Leigh Bullard
Ann Burton
Libby Cable
Lisa Dulin Cagley
Cheryl Carson
Terry Casto

Carol Caudill
Ruth Cecil
Christie Chaconas
Michelle Challis
Brandon Chapman
Karen Chapman
Stacey Chapman
Mary Catherine Chesney
Nan Clarke
Susan Claytor
Gina Clegg
Bobbie Cloud
Debbie Cockerham
Ginny Collett
Dianne Cowart
Linda Crawley
Alice Ann Creasey
Beth Crigler
Pam Critz
Adele Daniels
Rosemary Davenport
Becky Davis
Laurie Davis
Lynn Davis
Anne Denton
Jessie Derham
Leslie Bibble
Karen Dickinson
Denise Dixon
Jean Dixon
Marilyn Dougherty
Sarah Douglas
Brenda Dunaway
Cecily Durrett
Ashley Dyson
Mimi Earley
Sharon Edge
Mary Edwards
Judy Emken
Carolyn Eskridge
Barbara Finn
Meredith Finnen
Susan Floyd
Carol Lomax Fortenberry
Betsy Fox
Dee Foxgrover
Amy Franklin

Tonia Fuller
Terry Gaffney
Beth Gage
Carol Gamble
Carla Gambrell
Ruth Gammon
Nancy Gaskin
Beth Gates
Alma Gay
Daryl Gerber
Tammy Golder
Martha Goodwin
Carole Goodwin
Jane Gordon
Debbie Gourley
Sally Graves
Mary Gregory
Alice Grier
Julie Griffin
Shirley Griffin
Laura Grooms
Edith Hall
Ann Hallett
Patsy Hallett
Meg Hancock
Bryan Hanson
Margaret Hardage
Nancy Harris
Debbie Hartnett
Gracey Loftin Hayes
Emily Hensley
Barbara Henson
Linda Hinson
Lynn Hodges
Suzanne Holmes
Dianne Hoover
Shelley Hulihan
Marcia Hurd
Jouete Hutchins
Annette Imbrogno
Bonnie Isaacson
Ann Jamieson
Mindy Jones
Jayne Kaiser
Hanna Kane
Peggy Kane
Susan Karp

Barbara Kellmann
Jill Kelly
Beth Koonce
Jill Krieger
Manetta Latham
Ellen LeBlanc
Beth Lee
Dee Lewis
Mary Lewis
Rachel Lewis
Valerie Lewis
Link Litaker
Mary Ann Little
Mary Loftin
Jane Loftin-Gray
Mary Louise Lowe
Jane Lucas
Anne Lupo
Rob Maccubbin
Frances Magee
Holly Maurer
Lib McAlister
Marsha McCrory
Liz McDowell
Page McEachern
Tammy McFalls
Jennifer McIntosh
Patricia McLendon
Maureen Meacham
Pam Metcalf
Emily Metz
Trudy Mills
Barbara Milner
Stuart Milton
Virginia Milton
Pam Misle
Verna Cole Mitchell
Noreen Moody
Patty Moody
Lisa Moreland
Denise Morrison
Lanier Morrison
Maxine Nance
Stuart Nance
Susan Noble
Debbie O'Hare
Julie O'Korn
Linda Oelschlaeger

Sally Olson
Winnie Owings
William Painter
Susie Papadopulos
Gay Pappin
Vickie Payne
Julie Peters
Penny Pezdirtz
Harriet Pharr
Amy Philipp
Susan Pollan
Katherine Pollard
Mary Ann Poteat
Donna Preddy
Teresa Prichard
Janice Privette
Ingrid Rand
Martha Rand
Anne Ratcliffe
Gay Reames
Beth Reigel
Leigh Revels
Marsha Rich
Vivian Ritter
Suzanne Robards
Pam Roberts
Carol Robinson
Suzy Robison
Sara Lynne Roettger
Laura Roselli
Chris Ryskiewich
Quentin Salerno
Carolyn Samson
Dabney Sanders
Donna Sassano
Christine Schaeffer
Angela Schellpfeffer
Sharon Schmidt
Ann Sellers
Nancy Sharma
Medora Sheehan
Susan Sheild
Mary Sheridan
Donna Short
Margaret Sigmon
Jean Skidmore
Susan Skipper
Dorothy Smith
Maxine Starner

Marsha Stiegel
Posey Stitcher
Patty Stone
Michelle Stover
Kerry Strayhorn
Melissa Stroup
Betsy Strowd
Lou Anne Stucky
Pat Summers
Jan Swetenburg
Lil Swindell
Kathleen Taddonio
Trudy Tanneberger
Janet Taylor
Julie Taylor
Nancy Taylor
Sally Teden
Kathy Tennyson
Elaine Thigpen
Ellen Thomas
Lori Thompson
Susan Tome
Lisa Tomlinson
Jane Townell
Janet Trusty
Cathlean Utzug
Elizabeth Vaughn
Erin Vorhoff
Susan Walker
Veta Wall
Bennett Waters
Amy Watson
Laura Weisner
Jane Wester
Mary Ann Wexler
Debbie Whelchel
Nancy Whitmore
Julie Allen Whittington
Cheri Wiles
Marilyn Williams
Nancy Williams
Donna Willis
Cindy Wilson
Hannah Wilson
Kari Wimbish
Brenda Wing
Jenny Lou Wright
Virginia Wynn
Sara Zollicoffer

- *Every attempt was made to acknowledge all of our contributors and testers. We regret any omissions to our Honor Roll.*

Syllabus

Table of Contents

Admissions
Appetizers & Beverages 9

Pre-Requisites
Soups & Salads 45

Required Courses
Meat, Poultry & Seafood 91

Electives
Vegetables & Fruits 167

Extra Credits
Pasta & Rice 195

Extra Curricular
Breads & Brunches 223

SAT's
Sweets & Treats 253

Curriculum
Index 303

APPETIZERS

Gougères 9

Hot Crab Bites 10

Sun-Dried Tomato Toasts 11

Spinach Parmesan Toasts 12

Dijon Chicken Tidbits 12

Romano Shrimp
    Stuffed Mushrooms 13

Bacon-Wrapped Water Chestnuts 14

Wing Dings 14

Carolina Shrimp 15

Hatcher Crackers 16

Artichoke Truffles 17

Salmon Roll-Ups 18

Basic Bruschetta 18

Tortilla Roll Appetizers 19

Oven-Dried Grape Tomatoes 20

Parmesan Glazed Walnuts 20

Prissy Pecans 21

Orange Toast 21

Cheesy Corn Dip 22

Hearts of Palm Spread 22

Light Spinach Artichoke Dip 23

Vidalia Onion Dip 24

Fabulous Mexican Dip 24

Apache Cheese Bread 25

Salmon Spread 25

Crawfish Dip 26

Havarti Cheese Pastry 27

That Ranch Stuff 27

Pecan Praline Brie with Fruit 28

Avocado & Corn Salsa 29

Gran's Fresh Tomato Salsa 30

Black Bean Salsa 31

McClellanville Caviar 31

Apple Cheese Ball 32

Blue Cheese & Walnut Dip 33

Colorful Crabmeat 34

Shrimp & Caper Dip 34

Vegetable Cheesecake 35

Swiss & Chive Spread 35

Bacon & Tomato Dip 36

BEVERAGES

Mary Ann Little's Creek Water Tea 37

Old-Fashioned Lemonade 38

Purple Cow Shake 38

Beach Weekend Fizzies 39

Favorite Party Punch 39

Cranberry-Apple Limeade 40

Mr. James' Margaritas 41

Cosmopolitans 41

Bourbon Slushes 42

Swamp Water 43

Peach Fuzzies 43

Chocolate Martini 44

Homemade Irish Cream Liqueur 44

GOUGÈRES

*An impressive yet simple hot cheese puff, originally from
the Burgundy region of France. Serve straight from the oven.*

Yield: about 20 puffs

1 cup milk	5 eggs, divided
1 stick (½ cup) butter	1½ cups grated Parmesan cheese,
1 teaspoon salt	plus an additional ½ cup to
1 cup sifted all-purpose flour	sprinkle on top, if desired

- Preheat oven to 375°. Lightly spray large baking sheet with nonstick spray.
- Combine milk, butter, and salt in small saucepan and bring to a boil.
- Remove saucepan from heat and add flour all at once. Whisk vigorously for a few moments, then return pan to medium heat and cook, stirring constantly, until batter has thickened and pulled away from sides and bottom of pan. NOTE: This may take a few minutes or may happen almost instantly, depending on your pan and stove.
- Remove saucepan from heat again and stir in 4 (not all 5) eggs, one at a time, making sure each egg is incorporated before adding the next.
- When all 4 eggs are incorporated, stir in 1½ cups Parmesan.
- Drop batter by tablespoonfuls onto prepared baking sheet, spacing puffs at least 1 inch apart.
- In small bowl, beat remaining egg. Brush tops of puffs with beaten egg and sprinkle with additional Parmesan, if using.
- Set baking sheet on center rack of oven and reduce heat to 350°. Bake 15 to 20 minutes or until gougères are puffed and well-browned. Serve immediately.

HOT CRAB BITES

These are great to have in the freezer and always the first thing to go at a cocktail party. Try to have someone serve them hot from the oven while you broil the next batch!

Yield: 48 appetizers

1 (6¾-ounce) can crabmeat, drained and checked for shell
1 jar Old English sharp cheese spread
1 stick (½ cup) butter, softened
1½ teaspoons mayonnaise
¼-½ teaspoon garlic salt
6 whole English muffins

- Mix crabmeat, cheese, butter, mayonnaise, and garlic salt.
- Split each muffin and cut each half into four quarters. Spread each quarter generously with crab mixture.
- Place on cookie sheet and freeze. When frozen, put in Ziploc freezer bags and freeze until needed. These must be frozen before cooking.
- To serve, remove from freezer and broil on cookie sheet until bubbly.

Serve hot!

When a recipe calls for canned crabmeat, soak it in ice water for a few minutes to freshen the flavor. Drain well and blot dry.

SUN-DRIED TOMATO TOASTS

Looks like a long recipe, but each step is very simple. If you are a fan of sun-dried tomatoes, this will be your new favorite appetizer.

Yield: 24 appetizers

1 (16-ounce) jar sun-dried tomatoes in oil
¼ cup chopped green onion
2 teaspoons minced garlic
½ teaspoon salt
¼ teaspoon red pepper flakes
1 teaspoon dried basil

¼ cup chopped fresh parsley
1 (8-ounce) package cream cheese, softened
¼ cup grated Parmesan cheese
24 (or more) thin slices French bread, toasted

- Drain 2 teaspoons oil from tomatoes and heat oil in heavy skillet over medium heat.
- Add green onions and sauté 3 minutes or until soft. Add garlic and sauté 1 minute.
- Add ½ cup chopped tomatoes (reserve remaining tomatoes and their oil), salt, red pepper flakes, and dried basil. Cook 2 minutes.
- Remove from heat; stir in parsley.
- Blend cream cheese and Parmesan in small bowl. Add 2 teaspoons oil from sun-dried tomatoes and mix well.
- Drain and chop remaining tomatoes.
- Add skillet mixture and chopped tomatoes to cheese mixture; mix well. Mixture may be refrigerated or frozen at this point.
- To serve, spread toasted French bread generously with tomato mixture and broil. Watch carefully!

SPINACH PARMESAN TOASTS

A different presentation for well-loved spinach dip.

Yield: 24 appetizers

1 (10-ounce) box frozen chopped spinach, thawed, drained, and squeezed dry
1 (8-ounce) package cream cheese, softened
½ clove garlic, minced
¼ cup mayonnaise

5 tablespoons finely chopped onion
Dash of white pepper
Dash of red pepper flakes
About 24 thin slices French bread
1 cup freshly grated Parmesan cheese

- Preheat oven to broil.
- Stir together spinach and cream cheese until well blended.
- Stir in garlic, mayonnaise, onion, white pepper, and red pepper. Mix very well.
- Spread mixture on French bread slices and sprinkle with Parmesan. Arrange on cookie sheet.
- Broil until browned and bubbly. Serve immediately.

DIJON CHICKEN TIDBITS

Great to pass with toothpicks at a cocktail party.

Yield: 16 appetizer servings

2 whole skinless, boneless chicken breasts
½ stick (¼ cup) butter
2 teaspoons Dijon mustard

1 teaspoon minced parsley
1 teaspoon lemon juice
¼ cup dry bread crumbs
¼ cup Parmesan cheese

- Cut chicken into ¾-inch pieces.
- Melt butter in skillet and add mustard, parsley, and lemon juice.
- Add chicken to skillet and sauté 5 to 10 minutes or until lightly browned.
- Sprinkle with bread crumbs and Parmesan cheese and toss lightly. Serve warm.

ROMANO SHRIMP STUFFED MUSHROOMS

Yield: 20 appetizers

20 large fresh mushrooms
(2 to 2½-inch diameter)
1 (4½-ounce) can shrimp, drained, rinsed, and chopped
1 (4-ounce) container whipped cream cheese with chives

½ teaspoon Worcestershire sauce
Dash of garlic powder
Dash of Tabasco sauce
Grated Romano cheese

- Remove stems from washed mushrooms.
- Simmer mushroom caps in boiling water for 2 minutes. Drain and invert on paper towels to dry thoroughly. Allow to cool.
- While mushrooms are cooling, stir together shrimp, cream cheese, Worcestershire, garlic powder, and Tabasco.
- Spoon shrimp mixture into mushroom caps with small teaspoon. Place in shallow baking pan or dish and sprinkle with Romano cheese.
- Cover and refrigerate for 3 to 24 hours.
- When ready to serve, preheat oven to 400°. Bake, uncovered, at 400° for 15 minutes.

Store mushrooms in a paper bag to absorb moisture and keep them fresh.

BACON-WRAPPED WATER CHESTNUTS

Follow baking directions and chestnuts will not be greasy — just delicious!

Yield: about 24 appetizers

1 can whole water chestnuts
1 pound bacon, slices cut in half
  (may not need whole package)
1 cup Miracle Whip salad dressing

1 cup chili sauce (may use entire
  12-ounce bottle for spicier sauce)
½ cup brown sugar

- Preheat oven to 325°.
- Wrap each water chestnut in ½ slice of bacon, securing with toothpick if necessary. Place on rack of broiler pan.
- Bake at 325° for 40 minutes.
- While chestnuts are cooking, mix together Miracle Whip, chili sauce, and brown sugar to make sauce.
- After 40 minutes, drain drippings from pan, return chestnuts to pan without rack, and pour sauce over chestnuts.
- Bake at 325° for 25 minutes.

WING DINGS

4-5 pounds chicken wings
  Salt
  Black pepper
  Poultry seasoning

  Paprika
  Garlic powder
1 (1-pound) box dark brown sugar
1 (10-ounce) bottle soy sauce

- Preheat oven to 300°.
- Season chicken generously with salt, pepper, poultry seasoning, paprika, and garlic powder.
- Whisk together brown sugar and soy sauce until smooth.
- Pour over chicken and bake, uncovered, at 300° for about 3 hours, basting often.

CAROLINA SHRIMP

Never lasts long at a cocktail party.

1 pound medium shrimp, peeled,
   deveined, and cooked
1 large sweet onion, thinly sliced
¼ cup ketchup
½ cup cider vinegar
½ cup salad oil
2 teaspoons sugar

2 teaspoons salt
2 tablespoons Worcestershire sauce
1 tablespoon peppercorns
½ teaspoon dry mustard
2-3 bay leaves
2-3 dashes Tabasco sauce
   Fresh dill and parsley for garnish

- Layer shrimp and onions in deep glass bowl.
- Whisk together ketchup, vinegar, oil, sugar, salt, Worcestershire, peppercorns, mustard, bay leaves, and Tabasco. Pour over shrimp and onions.
- Cover and refrigerate for at least 10 to 12 hours.
- Drain and garnish with fresh dill and parsley sprigs. Serve with toothpicks.

To cook shrimp, drop raw shrimp in boiling water with seasonings of your choice and cook just until shrimp turn pink – do not overcook.

HATCHER CRACKERS

Loved by all who try them! Be sure to line saltines tightly in pan and grate cheese directly onto crackers. We don't know why — but it works!

Yield: 40 crackers

40 saltine crackers
 Ground red pepper to taste

1 (8-ounce) block New York State sharp or extra sharp Cheddar cheese

- Line 11x16-inch rimmed baking sheet with foil. Place crackers side by side in a single layer on baking sheet. If last row doesn't fit, break carefully or trim with scissors. Crackers must fit tightly in pan.
- Sprinkle crackers lightly with red pepper to taste.
- With coarse grater, grate cheese directly onto crackers as evenly as possible. Be sure to use all of cheese.
- Place pan on bottom shelf of oven and turn on broiler. Leave oven door open and watch carefully!
- After about 10 minutes, cheese will begin to bubble. When cheese stops bubbling and bubbles are firm on top, remove from oven. Turn off broiler and set oven to 150°.
- Place pan on top rack of oven and close door. Leave crackers in 150° oven for several hours or overnight to dry. Store in airtight containers.

ARTICHOKE TRUFFLES

*Messy to prepare — fabulous to eat! Serve with
toothpicks on a platter lined with whole flat-leaf parsley.*

Yield: about 24 truffles

½ cup freshly grated Parmesan
    cheese
2 tablespoons chopped fresh parsley
½ (8-ounce) package cream cheese,
    softened
3 ounces goat cheese, softened

2 teaspoons grated lemon zest
1 teaspoon dried tarragon
⅛ teaspoon black pepper
2 (6½-ounce) jars marinated
    artichoke hearts, drained and
    cut into bite-sized pieces

- In small bowl, mix Parmesan cheese and parsley. Reserve.
- In medium bowl, combine cream cheese, goat cheese, lemon zest, tarragon, and pepper.
- Add artichoke pieces to cream cheese mixture and mix gently, being sure to coat each artichoke liberally with mixture.
- Roll each coated artichoke in Parmesan mixture, covering completely. You may need to put some Parmesan in your hands and roll each truffle individually, patting to cover well.
- Place truffles on baking sheet lined with parchment or waxed paper. Refrigerate until firm, about 1 hour. Let stand at room temperature for 30 minutes before serving.

*Cream cheese mixture may be prepared and refrigerated up to 3 days before
serving, then brought to room temperature before coating artichokes. Truffles
may be prepared up to 1 day ahead and refrigerated.*

SALMON ROLL-UPS

Slicing the cucumber may be a bit challenging, but the taste is great.

Yield: as many as needed

Cucumber
Cream cheese with onions and chives

Flour tortillas
Thinly-sliced smoked salmon

- Peel cucumber. Using vegetable peeler, make long, thin slices of cucumber (do not use seedy part).
- Spread cream cheese on tortillas, covering very close to edges.
- Alternate rows of salmon and cucumber on top of cheese.
- Tightly roll up tortillas, wrap rolls in plastic wrap, and refrigerate.
- When ready to serve, slice into 1-inch pieces.

BASIC BRUSCHETTA

Perfect with a pasta meal — also makes a great appetizer.

Yield: 24 slices

8 ripe plum tomatoes, seeded
¼ cup olive oil, plus more for
   brushing on bread
1 tablespoon minced fresh garlic or
   to taste
Salt to taste

2 baguettes, or 1 loaf Italian or
   French bread
12 large fresh basil leaves, chopped
½ tablespoon balsamic vinegar
   Freshly grated Parmesan cheese

- Light grill or preheat oven to 325°.
- Dice tomatoes into fine pieces. Add olive oil, garlic, and salt to taste; reserve.
- Slice bread about ½-inch thick. Dab each piece with small amount of olive oil and grill until lightly browned, or bake in single layer in oven for 10 minutes.
- Add basil, vinegar, and salt to taste to tomato mixture. Spread on toast rounds, sprinkle with Parmesan, and serve at room temperature.

Tomato mixture may be made ahead and refrigerated. Bring to room temperature before spreading on toast.

TORTILLA ROLL APPETIZERS

These may also be served, unsliced or cut in half, as a tasty sandwich with soup.

Yield: 10 appetizer servings

1 (8-ounce) container sour cream	1 teaspoon Worcestershire sauce
1 (8-ounce) package cream cheese, softened	1 clove garlic, minced
	2 tablespoons chopped black olives
1 (4-ounce) can chopped green chiles, drained	1 jalapeño pepper, diced
	Salt to taste
1 green onion, sliced	8-12 large flour tortillas
2 tablespoons picante sauce	

- Mix together sour cream, cream cheese, chiles, green onion, picante sauce, Worcestershire, garlic, olives, and jalapeño pepper until well blended. Add salt to taste.
- Spread mixture over tortillas, being sure to spread to edges. Roll tortillas loosely, wrap in damp paper towels, place in baking dish, and refrigerate several hours.
- Just before serving, slice tortillas into 1-inch thick slices, discarding end pieces (a sharp serrated knife works best).
- Serve with additional picante sauce.

To reduce the heat of chile peppers, scrape out the veins that line the inside of the chile flesh. This is where capsaicin, the heat source of a chile pepper, is concentrated. The seeds do not contain capsaicin, but are often quite hot because of their close proximity to the veins.

OVEN-DRIED GRAPE TOMATOES

Like homemade sun-dried tomatoes in oil — fun to make!

1 (2-pound) box grape tomatoes	White vinegar
Salt	Garlic cloves, minced
Black pepper	Basil leaves, chopped
Sugar	Olive oil
Ground thyme	

- Preheat oven to 225°. Spray cookie sheet with nonstick spray.
- Slice tomatoes in half lengthwise. Place cut side up on greased cookie sheet. Sprinkle with salt, pepper, sugar, and thyme.
- Bake at 225° for 2½ to 3 hours depending on dryness desired.
- Remove from oven and let cool completely.
- Dip each half in vinegar and place layers in large glass jar, alternating tomatoes with garlic and basil. Layer until all ingredients are used, then cover with olive oil. Seal and store in refrigerator for up to 3 months.

To serve, spread goat cheese on crackers and top with tomatoes.

PARMESAN GLAZED WALNUTS

Great for a cocktail treat or sprinkled into a green salad.

Yield: 1½ cups

1½ cups walnut halves	¼ teaspoon smoked salt
1 tablespoon butter or margarine, melted	¼ teaspoon salt
	¼ cup grated Parmesan cheese

- Preheat oven to 350°.
- Spread walnuts in jelly roll pan and bake at 350° for 10 minutes.
- Mix butter and both salts. Toss butter mixture with walnuts.
- Sprinkle cheese on top and bake another 3 to 4 minutes.

PRISSY PECANS

Serve in nut dishes for a party or package for gifts.

Yield: 1 pound

1 pound unsalted pecan halves
   (Georgia Stuarts, if possible)
1 stick (½ cup) butter

¼ cup sugar
1 teaspoon freshly grated nutmeg
Pinch salt

- Preheat oven to 325°.
- Place pecans in shallow glass baking dish. Roast at 325° for 20 minutes, turning frequently with fork.
- While pecans are roasting, melt butter in small saucepan with sugar, nutmeg, and salt.
- Remove pecans from oven, pour butter mixture over pecans, and stir well. Return to oven for 3 to 4 minutes.
- When pecans have absorbed most of the butter, turn out onto paper towels and let dry.

ORANGE TOAST

A sweet, crispy pick-up, perfect for showers, teas, and even cocktail parties.

Yield: 24-32 pieces

1 stick (½ cup) butter, softened
½ cup sugar
Finely grated zest of 1 orange

12-16 slices Pepperidge Farm very
   thin white bread

- Preheat oven to 300°.
- In small bowl, cream together butter, sugar, and orange zest.
- Trim crusts off of bread and cut each slice in half. Spread generously with creamed mixture.
- Place bread on cookie sheet and bake at 300° for 30 to 45 minutes or until crisp and golden brown. Let cool before serving.

May be prepared ahead and stored in airtight container.

CHEESY CORN DIP

This recipe lends itself to several variations — all delicious!

Yield: 2 cups

1 (8-ounce) package cream cheese
1 (8-ounce) bag frozen white shoe
   peg corn

1 (10-ounce) can Rotel tomatoes
   with chiles, drained (mild or hot
   according to your preference)
Tostitos tortilla chips

- Preheat oven to 350°. Spray small baking dish with nonstick spray.
- In saucepan on low to medium heat, warm cream cheese until softened.
- Add corn and tomatoes; mix well.
- Place in prepared baking dish and bake at 350° for 10 minutes or until bubbly. Serve hot with tortilla chips.

Variations: For sausage dip, substitute ½ pound cooked and crumbled sausage for corn and bake as directed. One cup of shredded Cheddar cheese may be added to either dip before baking. Doubles easily.

HEARTS OF PALM SPREAD

Yield: 2 cups

1 (14-ounce) can hearts of palm,
   drained well and chopped
1 cup shredded mozzarella cheese
¾ cup mayonnaise

½ cup grated Parmesan cheese
¼ cup sour cream
2 tablespoons minced green onion
Paprika to garnish

- Preheat oven to 350°. Lightly spray 9-inch quiche dish with nonstick spray.
- Combine hearts of palm, mozzarella, mayonnaise, Parmesan, sour cream, and green onion. Spoon mixture into prepared dish and sprinkle with paprika. May be made several hours ahead to this point and refrigerated, covered.
- Bake at 350° for 20 minutes or until bubbly.

Serve with crackers.

LIGHT SPINACH ARTICHOKE DIP

A lighter version of a favorite hot dip.

Yield: 8-10 appetizer servings

1 (10-ounce) package frozen chopped spinach, thawed, drained, and squeezed dry
½ cup shredded part-skim mozzarella cheese
½ cup fat-free sour cream
¼ teaspoon black pepper
1 tablespoon minced garlic

1 (14-ounce) can artichoke hearts, drained and chopped
1 (8-ounce) package low-fat cream cheese, softened
Dash of cayenne pepper
4 tablespoons grated Parmesan cheese, divided

- Preheat oven to 350°. Grease 1½-quart baking dish or pie plate with cooking spray.
- Stir together spinach, mozzarella, sour cream, pepper, garlic, artichokes, cream cheese, cayenne, and 2 tablespoons Parmesan.
- Spoon mixture into prepared dish and sprinkle with remaining 2 tablespoons Parmesan cheese.
- Bake, uncovered, at 350° for 20 to 30 minutes or until bubbly and lightly browned.

Serve with tortilla chips or Wheat Thins.

After working with pungent ingredients such as garlic, onions, or fish, many cooks use a little lemon juice to wash away any lingering odors from their hands. But sometimes the smell is stronger than the citrus. For those tough cases, try washing your hands with a couple of tablespoons of mouthwash. Any inexpensive brand is fine.

VIDALIA ONION DIP

Guests have been known to go after this dip with a serving spoon!

Yield: 5 cups

4-5 Vidalia onions, coarsely chopped
½ stick (¼ cup) butter
2 cups mayonnaise

2 cups shredded Swiss or Cheddar cheese, or mixture of both

- Preheat oven to 325°.
- In large skillet, sauté onions in butter over medium-low heat until translucent.
- Mix onions with mayonnaise and cheese and put into pie plate.
- Bake, uncovered, at 325° for 25 to 30 minutes.

Good served with Ritz crackers or your favorite variety.

FABULOUS MEXICAN DIP

Perfect for a casual get-together or tailgating party.

Yield: enough for a crowd

1 (14½-ounce) can refried beans
½ packet taco seasoning
1 (8-ounce) container sour cream
½ (8-ounce) bottle green goddess dressing
1 bunch green onions, chopped (include plenty of green part)

1 (2¼-ounce) can chopped or sliced black olives, drained
2 tomatoes, peeled, seeded, and chopped
1 (8-ounce) package Monterey Jack cheese, shredded

- Mix together refried beans, taco seasoning, sour cream, and dressing. Spread mixture in 9x13-inch serving dish. Cover and refrigerate 1 hour.
- Layer onions, black olives, tomatoes, and cheese on top of bean mixture.
- Serve with tortilla chips or Fritos.

APACHE CHEESE BREAD

Yield: serves a crowd

1 (2-pound) round loaf rye or other bread (use 2 1-pound loaves if preferred)
1 (16-ounce) block sharp Cheddar cheese, shredded
1 (8-ounce) package cream cheese, softened

1 (8-ounce) carton sour cream
½ cup minced green onion
1 teaspoon Worcestershire sauce
2 (4½-ounce) cans chopped green chiles
1 cup chopped ham (about ⅓ pound)

- Preheat oven to 350°.
- Cut off top of bread, reserving top. Scoop out inside of bread (save insides for dipping, if desired).
- In large mixing bowl, combine Cheddar cheese, cream cheese, sour cream, green onion, Worcestershire, chiles, and ham. Mix well (mixture will be stiff).
- Fill bread with cheese mixture and replace top. Place on cookie sheet and bake at 350° for 1 hour and 10 minutes.

Serve with tortilla chips, crackers, or reserved bread cut into cubes.

SALMON SPREAD

Yield: 1 cup

1 can salmon, bones removed
1 (8-ounce) package cream cheese, softened
2 tablespoons liquid smoke

2 tablespoons grated white onion
2 tablespoons creamy horseradish
2 tablespoons lemon juice

- Mix together salmon, cream cheese, liquid smoke, onion, horseradish, and lemon juice until creamy.
- Cover and chill at least 4 hours.

Serve with crackers.

CRAWFISH DIP

This rich dip tastes incredible, but it does make a lot! Serve to a crowd or halve the recipe — you'll just need to use half-cans of the soup and tomatoes. In our area, crawfish tails are sold cooked, peeled, and frozen in 8-ounce packages.

2 pounds peeled crawfish tails
  (4 8-ounce packages)
  Salt
  Black pepper
  Garlic powder
1 stick (½ cup) butter
1 green bell pepper, chopped
½ red bell pepper, chopped
1½ cups chopped green onions

1 (10¾-ounce) can condensed cream of mushroom soup
1 (2-pound) box Velveeta cheese, shredded
1 (10-ounce) can Rotel tomatoes with chiles (mild or hot according to your preference)
1 tablespoon Worcestershire sauce
  Dash Tabasco sauce

- Sprinkle crawfish with salt, pepper, and garlic powder to taste. Sauté crawfish in melted butter (until pink if raw; just until heated through if already cooked) and remove from pan with slotted spoon.
- Sauté green and red bell peppers and onions in same pan on low heat for about 20 minutes.
- Add crawfish, soup, and cheese. Mix well.
- Add tomatoes, Worcestershire, and Tabasco. Stir well until cheese is melted.
- Serve warm with crackers or toasted bread rounds.

If you can't find crawfish, shrimp may be substituted.

HAVARTI CHEESE PASTRY

Yield: 10-12 appetizer servings

1 can Pillsbury crescent rolls
1 (8-ounce) block Havarti cheese
   (with dill, if desired)

2-3 tablespoons honey mustard
1½ tablespoons lemon-herb
   seasoning, divided

- Preheat oven to 350°.
- Unroll crescent roll dough onto ungreased cookie sheet, pinching seams together to keep dough in one big piece.
- Place cheese in middle of dough. Spread honey mustard on top of cheese.
- Sprinkle 1 tablespoon lemon-herb seasoning on top of cheese.
- Bring up edges of dough to cover cheese completely and form a package by twisting two longer ends together. Shapes may be cut out of excess dough and used to decorate pastry.
- Pinch seams together again if necessary, and sprinkle remaining lemon-herb seasoning on top.
- Bake at 350° for 15 to 20 minutes until lightly browned.
- Let stand for 5 minutes before transferring to serving platter. Garnish with grapes and serve with crackers.

THAT RANCH STUFF

You'll be glad you tried this instead of buying another bottle of the ready-made dressing!

Yield: 3 cups

1 (16-ounce) carton sour cream
½ cup mayonnaise

1 packet original Ranch powdered
   salad dressing mix
½ cup milk

- Combine sour cream, mayonnaise, dressing mix, and milk.
- Whisk until smooth, cover, and store in refrigerator.

Serve as a dip for vegetables or as a topping for tacos or baked potatoes.

PECAN PRALINE BRIE WITH FRUIT

The individual wedges look very pretty, but another way to present this appetizer is to pour the praline mixture over the unsliced Brie, garnish with fruit and crackers, and let guests serve themselves with a spreader.

Yield: 8 appetizer servings

1 pound red or green seedless grapes, or any seasonal fresh fruit
¾ cup dark brown sugar
4 teaspoons butter

2 teaspoons light corn syrup
1 tablespoon water
2 ounces pecans, chopped
1 (1-pound) round Brie cheese

- Rinse, drain, and cut grapes or fruit into small clusters or pieces; refrigerate.
- To make praline, combine brown sugar, butter, corn syrup, and water in small saucepan over medium-low heat. Bring to boil, then reduce heat and simmer 3 minutes. Remove from heat and stir in pecans.
- Cut Brie into 8 wedges and arrange on round serving platter or 8 small cocktail plates. Spoon 1 teaspoon praline mixture over each wedge and garnish each portion with fruit.

AVOCADO & CORN SALSA

In the winter or in a hurry, substitute a bag of John Cope's frozen white corn for fresh corn. Replenish leftover salsa with more fresh avocado to serve again the next day — salsa will keep covered in the refrigerator for 2 to 3 days.

Yield: 5 cups

4 ears fresh corn, husked
1 large red onion, diced
1 red bell pepper, diced
⅓ cup olive oil
¼ cup red wine vinegar
1 tablespoon minced garlic
 Pinch of sugar
4-8 drops Tabasco sauce
1 tablespoon ground cumin

1 teaspoon chili powder
¼ cup chopped fresh oregano
 (or 4 teaspoons dried)
½ cup lime juice (about 4 limes)
 Salt and freshly ground black
 pepper to taste
2 ripe avocados
 Tostitos tortilla chips

- Blanch corn in generously salted boiling water for 3 minutes.
- Drain, cool under cold water, and cut kernels off cob.
- Mix corn with onion, bell pepper, oil, vinegar, garlic, sugar, Tabasco, cumin, chili powder, oregano, lime juice, salt, and pepper in medium bowl. May be made ahead to this point and refrigerated.
- Just before serving, peel and dice avocado and add to salsa.
- Especially good served with lime-flavored tortilla chips.

Instead of trying to peel a ripe avocado, cut it in half, twist to remove the pit, and scoop out the flesh of each half with a large metal spoon. Start at the wide end of the avocado and keep the spoon close to the peel.

GRAN'S FRESH TOMATO SALSA

Make this after summer tomatoes arrive at the farmer's market!

Yield: 3 cups

2 cups peeled, chopped fresh tomatoes (about 2 large tomatoes)
1 fresh jalapeño pepper, seeded and finely chopped
½ cup thinly sliced green onions

¼ cup chopped fresh cilantro
½ teaspoon salt
½ teaspoon oregano
⅛ teaspoon black pepper
2 tablespoons fresh lemon juice

- Combine tomatoes, jalapeño pepper, green onion, cilantro, salt, oregano, pepper, and lemon juice in glass or pottery bowl.
- Cover and refrigerate for several hours.
- Serve with pita chips or homemade roll croutons (see recipe below).

Roll croutons: Slice stale rolls about ½ inch thick. Arrange on cookie sheet and spray slices with nonstick spray. Sprinkle with Jane's Krazy Salt, oregano, and garlic salt. Bake at 375° for 10 minutes.

BLACK BEAN SALSA

This chunky salsa may also be served as a cold side dish.

Yield: 3 cups

1 (16-ounce) can black beans, rinsed and drained
1 (16-ounce) can corn, drained
½ cup chopped fresh cilantro
¼ cup chopped green onion
¼ cup chopped red onion
⅓ cup fresh lime juice
3 tablespoons olive oil
1 tablespoon cumin
Salt and black pepper to taste
½ cup peeled, seeded, and chopped tomato

- Combine beans, corn, cilantro, green onion, red onion, lime juice, olive oil, cumin, salt, and pepper (do not add tomato). Cover and refrigerate several hours to allow flavors to blend.
- Add tomato just before serving.

Serve with tortilla chips.

McCLELLANVILLE CAVIAR

Must be made ahead — and takes about five minutes if you use frozen shrimp!
McClellanville is a small, coastal town in South Carolina.

1½ pounds cooked shrimp, peeled and chopped (may use frozen peeled and cooked shrimp, thawed and chopped)
1 (16-ounce) can black beans, rinsed and drained
¼ cup finely chopped bell pepper
½ cup chopped Vidalia onion
⅔ cup salsa (hot or mild according to your preference)
¼ cup fresh lime juice
2 tablespoons honey
2 tablespoons vegetable oil

- Toss together shrimp, black beans, bell pepper, onion, and salsa.
- In small bowl, whisk together lime juice, honey, and oil. Pour over shrimp mixture and mix well.
- Cover and refrigerate for 8 hours, stirring occasionally.

Serve with Fritos scoopers and plenty of napkins!

APPLE CHEESE BALL

There's no apple in this cute appetizer — it looks like an apple!
A colorful addition to an autumn party table.

Yield: 10-12 appetizer servings

1 (8-ounce) block white Cheddar
  cheese, shredded
1 (8-ounce) package cream cheese,
  softened
1 teaspoon garlic powder

⅛ teaspoon ground red pepper
  Paprika
1 (½-inch) cinnamon stick
1 bay leaf

- Process Cheddar cheese, cream cheese, garlic powder, and red pepper in food processor until smooth, stopping to scrape down sides. Chill 30 minutes.
- Shape cheese mixture into a ball. Make an indentation in top to resemble an apple. Chill ball 30 minutes.
- Coat ball heavily with paprika; cover and chill 1 hour.
- Insert cinnamon stick and bay leaf into indentation to resemble apple stem and leaf. Serve with assorted crackers.

It's easy to shred semisoft cheeses such as Swiss, mozzarella, or Cheddar in the food processor – until, of course, a big chunk sticks in the feed tube or gums up the shredding disk. You can avoid this problem by spraying the feed tube, disk, and work bowl of the food processor with a light coating of nonstick spray before you begin.

BLUE CHEESE & WALNUT DIP

A very good combination of favorite flavors.

Yield: 1¼ cups

1 (8-ounce) container sour cream	¼ cup walnuts, toasted
1 (3-ounce) package cream cheese, softened	(see instructions below)
4 ounces blue cheese, crumbled	1 small shallot, quartered
	½ teaspoon sugar

- In food processor, process sour cream, cream cheese, blue cheese, walnuts, shallot, and sugar until smooth.
- Pour into serving bowl, cover, and refrigerate at least 1 hour before serving.
- Serve with apple wedges, baby carrots, celery sticks, and crackers.

Toasting nuts brings out their flavor! To toast nuts, place a rack in the middle of the oven and preheat to 375°. Spread nuts in a single layer on a rimmed baking sheet and toast, stirring once or twice, until crisp and fragrant (8 to 10 minutes). Do not overcook or nuts will be bitter. Transfer toasted nuts immediately to a bowl to cool.

COLORFUL CRABMEAT

The red, green, and white colors make this especially pretty at Christmas, but it's tasty any time of year.

Yield: about 3 cups

2 (8-ounce) packages cream cheese, softened
⅓ cup minced onion
1 tablespoon mayonnaise
1 tablespoon Worcestershire sauce
½ teaspoon garlic powder

2 (6¾-ounce) cans crabmeat, drained and checked for shell
1 (12-ounce) bottle chili sauce
Chopped fresh parsley
Assorted crackers

- Mix cream cheese, onion, mayonnaise, Worcestershire, and garlic powder in medium bowl.
- Press into bottom of 8-inch quiche dish.
- Smooth mixture evenly and spread crabmeat over cheese mixture. Cover with chili sauce.
- Just before serving, garnish heavily with fresh parsley.
- Serve with assorted crackers.

SHRIMP & CAPER DIP

Especially good served with toasted baguette slices.

Yield: 1 cup

½ pound shrimp, peeled and cooked
1 (8-ounce) package cream cheese, softened

1 teaspoon garlic salt
3 tablespoons sour cream
½ jar capers, drained

- Chop shrimp into bite-size pieces.
- Mix cream cheese with garlic salt and sour cream.
- Stir in shrimp and capers.
- Spread dip in serving dish, cover, and refrigerate until serving time.
- Serve with crackers.

VEGETABLE CHEESECAKE

Without the crust, this mixture also makes a
delicious sandwich spread for thin-sliced bread.

Yield: 8-10 servings

½ (10-ounce) box thin vegetable crackers
5 tablespoons butter or margarine, melted
2 (8-ounce) packages cream cheese, softened
½ cup finely chopped broccoli florets
½ cup finely chopped carrots
¼ cup finely chopped red bell pepper
¼ cup finely chopped green onion
⅓ cup grated Parmesan cheese
2 teaspoons Ranch powdered salad dressing mix
¼ teaspoon garlic powder
Dash of Worcestershire sauce

- Process crackers in food processor until fine crumbs are formed.
- Stir together crumbs and butter. Press into springform pan.
- Beat cream cheese until smooth. Add broccoli, carrots, bell pepper, green onion, Parmesan, dressing mix, garlic powder, and Worcestershire.
- Spread mixture over crust.
- Cover and chill for 8 hours. Remove sides from pan and place on platter. Serve with crackers.

Best served with water wafer crackers or any light, thin cracker.

SWISS & CHIVE SPREAD

Yield: about 3½ cups

3 cups finely shredded Swiss cheese (about 12 ounces cheese)
¾ cup mayonnaise
¼ cup chopped chives
½ teaspoon salt
¼ teaspoon ground white pepper

- Stir together cheese and mayonnaise in bowl.
- Add chives, salt, and white pepper, mixing well.
- Cover and refrigerate until ready to serve.
- Place in serving dish and serve with buttery crackers.

BACON & TOMATO DIP

Tastes like a BLT!

12 slices bacon
1 large tomato, peeled, seeded, and chopped (see instructions)
1 (8-ounce) package cream cheese, softened

1 tablespoon mayonnaise
1 teaspoon Dijon mustard
Dash of Tabasco sauce (optional)

- Dice bacon (easiest to do while bacon is very cold or frozen) and cook in large skillet until crisp.
- Bring small saucepan of water to boil. If you are using a fresh, ripe summer tomato, dip tomato briefly (10 to 15 seconds) into boiling water, remove with tongs, and hold under cold water. Peel, seed, and chop tomato. When "real" tomatoes are out of season, let tomato cook in boiling water for 2 to 3 minutes before peeling to soften texture.
- Mix bacon, tomato, cream cheese, mayonnaise, and mustard in food processor or blender. Add Tabasco, if using.
- Serve with crackers.

Want an easy, low-fat container for a dip or salad that's both decorative and edible? Press an 8- to 10-inch soft tortilla into a 10-ounce heatproof glass bowl, letting the edge ruffle above the bowl. Microwave, uncovered, on High for 1½ to 2 minutes, rotating the bowl at halftime, until tortilla is dry and lightly browned. Remove the tortilla, dry upside-down, and store in an airtight container until serving time.

MARY ANN LITTLE'S CREEK WATER TEA

We are honored to publish this recipe in loving memory of Mary Ann Little, for 15 years the "angel" of Charlotte Latin School. Mary Ann was our lower school counselor and a guiding light to hundreds of young children. Our children were blessed to know her ... and so were we.

Yield: 1 gallon

3 cups water
6 regular-size tea bags
1½ cups sugar
1 cup chopped fresh mint leaves

1 cup orange juice (fresh or store-bought)
1 (6-ounce) can frozen lemonade concentrate
Water to make 1 gallon

- Bring 3 cups water to boil, take off heat, and steep tea bags for 15 minutes. Remove tea bags.
- Add sugar and stir until dissolved.
- Put mint in 1-gallon pitcher and pour hot tea over mint.
- Add orange juice, lemonade concentrate, and enough water to make 1 gallon. Serve cold over ice.

Looks like creek water — but tastes like great iced tea!

OLD-FASHIONED LEMONADE

The real thing. Garnish with lemon slices and mint sprigs.

Yield: 7 cups

3 cups cold water
2 cups sugar syrup
   (see instructions below)

1¾-2 cups fresh lemon juice (from
   about 2 pounds of lemons)

- Stir together water, sugar syrup, and lemon juice until well blended.
- Serve cold over ice.

❧ Sugar Syrup ❧

Essential for old-fashioned lemonade and many other drinks.

2 cups sugar, 1 cup water

Stir together sugar and water in a small saucepan. Bring to boil over medium heat, stirring often. Reduce heat and simmer 1 minute or until sugar is completely dissolved. Cool before using in recipes. Makes 2 cups syrup.

PURPLE COW SHAKE

"I never saw a purple cow …" — but your kids will love this shake!
This recipe is from Latin's first grade classes.

Yield: 2 servings

½ cup milk
1 (6-ounce) container frozen grape
   juice concentrate

2-3 cups vanilla ice cream

- Combine milk, juice concentrate, and ice cream in blender and mix well.

BEACH WEEKEND FIZZIES

Add 1 cup of club soda after you blend if you like it "fizzy"
— or a touch of rum or vodka if you like it "dizzy!"

Yield: 6-8 servings

2 cups fresh orange juice
2 cups pineapple juice

1 pint peach frozen yogurt or
   sherbet

- Blend all ingredients in blender.
- Serve in wine glasses, garnished with mint leaves, cherries, and colorful straws.

You can make this ahead and put blender container in freezer. Defrost slightly and blend again before serving.

FAVORITE PARTY PUNCH

Very simple, yet so refreshing — not too sweet! The powdered mix makes it extra-easy.

Yield: 18 servings (about 5 ounces each)

4 scoops (½ cup) powdered
   lemonade mix (like Country
   Time)
1 (46-ounce) can pineapple juice

1 (2-liter) bottle Sprite
   Lime and lemon slices and mint
   sprigs for garnish

- Mix lemonade mix and pineapple juice together and chill until serving time.
- When ready to serve, add Sprite and ice.
- Garnish with lime and lemon slices and mint sprigs.

CRANBERRY-APPLE LIMEADE

Refreshing and pretty.

Yield: about 3 quarts

¼ cup fresh lime juice
2 (6-ounce) cans limeade
   concentrate, thawed
1 (48-ounce) bottle cranberry juice
   cocktail, chilled

1 (32-ounce) bottle apple juice,
   chilled
Lime slices for garnish

- Combine lime juice, limeade concentrate, cranberry juice, and apple juice in large pitcher. Stir well and refrigerate.
- Serve cold over ice, garnished with lime slices.

It takes about 6 limes to get 1 cup of fresh lime juice.

MR. JAMES' MARGARITAS

This recipe, from a Latin grandfather, is not for the faint of heart!

Yield: 6 servings

3 cups tequila
1 cup triple sec

16 ounces sweet and sour mix (may use one 16-ounce or two 8-ounce cans limeade concentrate or Bacardi margarita mixer)
1 cup fresh lime juice

- Mix together tequila, triple sec, sweet and sour mix, and lime juice. Pour into glass jars (must be glass), leaving room at top for expansion.
- Place in freezer overnight or longer.
- Take out of freezer when ready to serve.

COSMOPOLITANS

Very sophisticated!

Yield: 1 drink (multiply ingredients to make as many as needed)

Juice of ½ lime
1 jigger Cointreau

1 jigger Absolut Citron vodka
1¾ jiggers cranberry juice

- Place lime juice, Cointreau, vodka, and cranberry juice in shaker and shake with ice, or store in freezer.
- Strain into frosted martini glass.

BOURBON SLUSHES

If you have pewter or silver julep cups, here's your chance to show them off!

Yield: 16 servings

4 tea bags
2 cups boiling water
1 cup sugar
1 (6-ounce) can orange juice
   concentrate, thawed

1 (6-ounce) can lemonade
   concentrate, thawed
5 cups crushed ice
2 cups ice water
2 cups premium-quality bourbon
1 (1-liter) bottle ginger ale, chilled

- At least 6 hours before serving time, steep tea bags in freshly-boiled water for 10 minutes. Remove tea bags.
- Combine sugar and hot tea in 1-gallon plastic or glass container, stirring until sugar is dissolved.
- Add orange juice and lemonade concentrates, stirring until thawed and mixed.
- In batches in blender, blend ice with enough ice water to make slush. Add slush to tea mixture.
- Add bourbon and any remaining ice water. Pour mixture into plastic pitcher and place in freezer until serving time, stirring about every 2 hours to break up slush and freeze evenly.
- To serve, pour slush into frosted glasses or julep cups, top with cold ginger ale, and garnish with mint sprigs.

SWAMP WATER

Be sure you don't confuse this recipe with Creek Water Tea — only the names are similar!

2 (12-ounce) cans frozen limeade
   concentrate
1 (6-ounce) can frozen lemonade
   concentrate

2 big handfuls mint leaves
1 (12-ounce) can water
   Rum, bourbon, or gin
   Club soda

- Blend limeade and lemonade concentrates, mint leaves, and water in blender until puréed. Keep in refrigerator or freezer.
- To serve, use ratio of ⅓ swamp mix, ⅓ liquor of your choice, and ⅓ club soda for each drink or batch.

PEACH FUZZIES

A great summer drink when fresh peaches are at their best.
Don't peel the peaches — that's the fuzzy!

Yield: 4 drinks

1 (6-ounce) can frozen lemonade
   concentrate, unthawed
6 ounces white rum (use lemonade
   can for measuring)

3 ounces (½ can) water
1 peach, pitted but unpeeled, cut
   into large chunks
   Ice

- Place lemonade concentrate, rum, water, and peach chunks in blender and blend until mixed.
- Add ice and blend until slushy. Serve immediately.

CHOCOLATE MARTINI

Chocolate with a grown-up kick!

Yield: 10-12 servings

2-2½ cups vodka, chilled
1¼ cups chocolate liqueur
¼ cup raspberry liqueur

¼ cup half-and-half (optional)
Chocolate liqueur or syrup
Sweetened cocoa

- Stir together vodka, liqueurs, and half-and-half (if using) in large pitcher. Refrigerate for at least 1 hour.
- Fill martini glasses with ice: Let stand 5 minutes. Discard ice.
- Dip rims of chilled glasses in chocolate liqueur. Dip in cocoa, coating rims.
- Pour vodka mixture into glasses and serve immediately.

For individual martini:

¼ cup vodka
2 tablespoons chocolate liqueur
1½ teaspoons raspberry liqueur

6 ice cubes
Dash of half-and-half (optional)

- Combine all ingredients in martini shaker. Cover with lid and shake until thoroughly chilled. Remove lid and strain into chilled martini glass. Serve immediately.

HOMEMADE IRISH CREAM LIQUEUR

Yield: about 5 cups

1¾ cups Irish whiskey
1 (14-ounce) can sweetened condensed milk
1 cup heavy or light cream

2 tablespoons chocolate syrup
2 teaspoons instant coffee
1 teaspoon vanilla extract
½ teaspoon almond extract

- Combine whiskey, milk, cream, chocolate syrup, coffee, vanilla, and almond extract in blender. Blend well and refrigerate in covered container.
- Stir well before serving.

Will keep up to a month in the refrigerator.

Pre-Requisites

SOUPS
AND
SALADS

SOUPS & STEWS

Vegetable Beef Soup 45

Taco Soup 45

Football Stew 46

Sausage Tortellini Soup 47

New Year's Day
   Black-Eyed Pea Stew 48

Crock Pot Chicken
   Brunswick Stew 49

Chicken Chili 50

Chicken & Artichoke Soup 51

Creamy Chicken & Pasta Soup 52

Tuscan White Bean Soup
   with Prosciutto 53

Brown Rice & Red Lentil Soup 54

Creamy Tomato Basil Soup 55

Frogmore Stew 56

Potato Soup Plus 56

Broccoli Chowder 57

Seafood Chowder 58

Rob's Manhattan Clam Chowder 59

Chilled Summer Squash Soup
   with Curry 60

Gazpacho 61

SALADS

Sunflower Spinach Salad 62

Strawberry Spinach Salad 63

Winter Spinach Salad 64

Salad with Spiced Pecans
   & Balsamic Vinaigrette 65

Sautéed Apple Salad with
   Roquefort & Walnuts 66

Emeril's Wedgie Salad 67

Hicks Family Reunion
   Marinated Slaw 68

Broccoli Slaw Salad 69

Broccoli & Cranberry Slaw 70

Crunchy Romaine Toss 71

Oriental Slaw 72

Peas & Peanuts Salad 73

Greek Marinated Vegetable Salad 73

Miss Virginia's Blue Cheese Dressing . . . 74

Light Caesar Salad 74

Grape Tomatoes & Capers 75

Double Tomato Salad 75

Warm Goat Cheese Salad 76

Ensalada Nochebuena
   (Winter Fruit Salad) 77

Summer Fruit Salad 78

Fresh Fruit with Lime Sauce 79

Apple Lime Salad 80

Strawberry Cheesecake Salad 81

Roasted Potatoes & Green Beans
   with Rosemary Vinaigrette 82

Potato Salad with
   Blue Cheese & Walnuts 83

Red Onion Potato Salad 84

Hermione's Couscous Salad 84

Wild Rice Salad 85

Tortellini & Shells Salad 86

Chicago Pasta Salad 87

Almond Chicken Salad 88

Chicken Pecan Salad
   with Cranberries 89

Chicken & Cranberry Mold 90

VEGETABLE BEEF SOUP

*A good basic soup that's easy to tailor to your family's tastes —
add green beans, okra, carrots, or whatever you like.*

Yield: 6 quarts

1½ pounds stew beef (cut into bite-
size pieces, if desired)
Salt and black pepper to taste
1 (16-ounce) package frozen butter
beans
1 (16-ounce) package frozen corn

5-6 small potatoes, diced
1 large onion, chopped
4 (14½-ounce) cans diced
tomatoes, undrained
1 tablespoon sugar

- Cover beef with water in Dutch oven or 6-quart pot. Add salt and pepper.
Bring to boil, reduce heat, and simmer gently for 1½ hours.
- Add butter beans, corn, potatoes, and onion. Boil for 5 to 10 minutes.
- Reduce heat, add tomatoes and sugar, and simmer for 1 to 2 hours over low
heat. Add water if necessary.

TACO SOUP

Yield: 6 servings

1 pound ground beef or turkey
1 cup chopped onion
½ cup prepared taco sauce
1 (16-ounce) can stewed tomatoes
1 (16-ounce) can kidney beans,
undrained
1 (16-ounce) can whole kernel corn,
undrained

1 (16-ounce) can black beans
(optional)
2-3 teaspoons chili powder
⅓ teaspoon garlic powder
¾ cup shredded Cheddar cheese
⅓ cup sour cream
Tortilla chips

- In a large saucepan, brown ground meat and onion; drain if needed.
- Add taco sauce, tomatoes, kidney beans, corn, black beans, if using, chili
powder, and garlic powder. Bring to boil, reduce heat, and simmer 15 to 20
minutes.
- Served hot, garnished with cheese, sour cream, and tortilla chips.

45

FOOTBALL STEW

Great if you need to fill up hungry athletes of any variety.
Try this with corn muffins for an easy supper.

Yield: serves 4 football players or 6 regular people!

2 pounds beef tips or stew beef, cut into 1-inch chunks
1 (14½-ounce) can Mexican tomatoes, undrained
1 (10½-ounce) can condensed beef broth, undiluted
1 (8-ounce) jar picante sauce, mild or medium

1 (10-ounce) box frozen corn
3 carrots, cut into ½-inch slices
2 cloves garlic, minced
½ teaspoon ground cumin
½ teaspoon salt
⅓ cup water
¼ cup all-purpose flour

- Combine beef, tomatoes, broth, picante sauce, corn, carrots, garlic, cumin, and salt in 3- or 4-quart electric slow cooker. Cook on high for 3 to 4 hours or on low for 6 to 8 hours.
- Combine water and flour, whisking until smooth. Stir into stew.
- Cook on high 15 minutes, stirring often.

Wine corks contain tannin. Drop one into a pot of stew to tenderize the meat, but don't forget to remove it before you serve!

SAUSAGE TORTELLINI SOUP

This soup is very hearty made with sausage, but can also be made with ground beef or turkey, chunks of chicken, or even shrimp.

Yield: 4-6 servings

1 pound bulk Italian sausage
1 medium onion, chopped
1 (14½-ounce) can diced tomatoes, undrained
1 (8-ounce) can tomato sauce
3 (14-ounce) cans beef broth
2½ cups water
½ cup red wine
½ teaspoon dried basil
½ teaspoon dried oregano
1 zucchini, diced
3 carrots, shredded
1 green bell pepper, diced
½ (8-ounce) package dried tortellini, uncooked

- In large stockpot, cook sausage with onion until well done. Drain very well and return to pot.
- Add tomatoes, tomato sauce, beef broth, water, wine, basil, oregano, zucchini, carrots, and bell pepper to pot and simmer 30 minutes.
- Stir in tortellini and simmer another 30 minutes.
- Before serving, skim off any fat that has risen to top of soup.

Fresh herbs lose their distinctive flavor when cooked a long time. Add extra herbs just before serving.

NEW YEAR'S DAY
BLACK-EYED PEA STEW

Kids and husbands love this hearty meal — you may want to double the recipe!

Yield: 4 generous servings

½ small package dried black-eyed
  peas, soaked overnight and
  drained
½ bell pepper, chopped
½ onion, chopped
2 cloves garlic, finely chopped
2 stalks celery, chopped

1 tablespoon oil
1 pound sausage, browned and
  drained (hot or mild to taste)
1 tablespoon sugar
2 (11½-ounce) cans tomato juice
1 (10-ounce) can Rotel tomatoes and
  chiles, undrained

- On day before making soup, place dried black-eyed peas in saucepan and cover with cold water. Soak overnight.
- Sauté bell pepper, onion, garlic, and celery in oil in large stockpot until tender.
- Add drained black-eyed peas, cooked sausage, sugar, tomato juice, and tomatoes.
- Cover pot and cook for 2 to 3 hours or until peas are tender, stirring occasionally to prevent sticking.
- If stew becomes too thick, add water, a small amount at a time, until desired consistency. If too thin, cook uncovered until it thickens.
- Spoon off excess fat from top if necessary after cooking.

Put dried beans in a bowl of cold water before cooking and discard any that float to the surface, as this indicates mold or insect damage.

CROCK POT CHICKEN BRUNSWICK STEW

Takes the mystery out of Brunswick stew.

Yield: 6-8 servings

2 large onions, chopped
6 skinless, boneless chicken breast halves
2 (15-ounce) cans cream-style corn
1 (28-ounce) can crushed tomatoes
1 (12-ounce) bottle chili sauce
1 (14-ounce) can chicken broth

¼ cup Worcestershire sauce
½ stick (¼ cup) butter, cut into pieces
2 tablespoons cider vinegar
2 teaspoons dry mustard
½ teaspoon salt
½ teaspoon black pepper
½ teaspoon Tabasco sauce

- Place onion in 4-quart electric slow cooker.
- Place chicken over onion. Add corn, tomatoes, chili sauce, chicken broth, Worcestershire, butter, vinegar, dry mustard, salt, pepper, and Tabasco sauce.
- Cover and cook on high for 4 hours.
- Remove chicken, shred, and return to stew. Stir well.
- Delicious served by itself or over rice.

To shred chicken or other meats, hold a fork in each hand with the prongs down and facing each other. Insert prongs into meat and gently pull the forks away from each other, breaking the meat apart into long, thin strands.

CHICKEN CHILI
Yield: 10 servings

2-3 (14-ounce) cans fat-free chicken
broth, divided
2 pounds boneless, skinless
chicken breasts
2 medium onions, chopped
2 medium green bell peppers,
chopped
6 celery stalks, trimmed, chopped
1 (4½-ounce) can chopped green
chiles, drained
3 (14½-ounce) cans stewed
tomatoes, undrained

3 (14½-ounce) cans great Northern
beans, drained
1 (14-ounce) bag frozen Cope's
Silver Queen corn (or other
frozen white corn)
2 teaspoons cumin, or to taste
Salt and black pepper to taste
1 bunch fresh cilantro, stems
removed and leaves chopped
Oyster crackers, shredded
Monterey Jack cheese, sour
cream, Tabasco sauce

- In large stockpot, bring 1 can chicken broth to boil. Add chicken breasts, reduce heat, and simmer, covered, until tender.
- Remove chicken from broth and add onions, bell peppers, and celery to broth in pot. Simmer until vegetables are tender.
- While vegetables are cooking, chop chicken into bite-size pieces.
- Add another can chicken broth, chopped chicken, chiles, tomatoes, beans, and corn to onion mixture. Stir well.
- Add cumin, salt, and pepper and simmer for 1 hour. Add third can chicken broth if needed as soup simmers.
- Sprinkle individual servings with cilantro and top with oyster crackers, grated Monterey Jack cheese, sour cream, and Tabasco.

CHICKEN & ARTICHOKE SOUP

Creamy and flavorful, and elegant enough for company.

Yield: 8-10 servings

4 cups chicken stock or
   2 (14-ounce) cans chicken broth
1 cup dry white wine
4 teaspoons butter
1 medium onion, diced
1 medium carrot, peeled and diced
1 stalk celery, diced
⅓ cup all-purpose flour
¼ cup uncooked rice

1½ cups half-and-half
1 (14-ounce) can artichoke hearts
   (not marinated), drained and
   quartered
¼ cup black olives, sliced (optional)
4 boneless chicken breast halves,
   broiled or grilled and cut into
   bite-size pieces
Salt and black pepper to taste

- In saucepan, heat chicken stock and wine until simmering. Let simmer while cooking vegetables.
- In large skillet, melt butter and sauté onion until translucent.
- Add carrot and celery and sauté 5 to 6 minutes.
- Sprinkle vegetables with flour and cook 2 to 3 minutes, stirring.
- Gradually stir hot stock mixture into vegetable mixture, stirring constantly to avoid lumps.
- Stir in uncooked rice and simmer very gently for 20 to 30 minutes.
- Just before serving, stir in half-and-half, artichoke hearts, olives, and chicken. Heat through and adjust seasonings if necessary. Serve immediately.

To thicken a stew or soup, add one slice of crustless bread and let simmer for 10 minutes. Stir.

CREAMY CHICKEN & PASTA SOUP

A rich, comforting soup with the surprise crunch of sugar snap peas.

3 tablespoons butter
1 cup sliced button mushrooms
1 cup sliced celery
1 cup shredded carrots
1 medium onion, chopped
3 tablespoons all-purpose flour
3 (14-ounce) cans low-fat chicken
     broth
1½ cups half-and-half

2 tablespoons chopped fresh
     parsley
1½ pounds chicken tenders, cut into
     ½-inch pieces
1 cup dry penne pasta
¼ pound sugar snap peas, cut in
     half diagonally
3 tablespoons fresh lemon juice
     Salt and black pepper to taste

- Melt butter in large, heavy stockpot over medium heat. Add mushrooms, celery, carrots, and onion; sauté 5 minutes or until onions are tender.
- Add flour and cook 3 minutes, stirring frequently.
- Gradually stir in chicken broth. Bring to boil and reduce heat to simmer, stirring frequently.
- Add half-and-half and parsley; simmer 5 minutes.
- Add chicken and simmer until cooked through, about 5 minutes. Soup can be prepared 1 day ahead up to this point. Cool, then cover and refrigerate.
- Before serving, cook penne in boiling salted water until just tender. Drain penne.
- Bring soup to simmer. Mix in penne and sugar snaps; simmer 3 minutes.
- Add lemon juice and season to taste with salt and pepper. Serve immediately.

TUSCAN WHITE BEAN SOUP WITH PROSCIUTTO

*When you want a hearty soup without cooking
all afternoon, this recipe fits the bill.*

Yield: 4 servings

2 teaspoons olive oil
½ cup chopped prosciutto or ham
   (about 2 ounces)
1 cup chopped onion
¾ cup chopped celery
¾ cup chopped carrot
1 clove garlic, minced
1 cup water

2 (19-ounce) cans cannellini beans
   or other white beans, undrained
2 bay leaves
1 (15¾-ounce) can fat-free,
   low-sodium chicken broth
2 tablespoons minced fresh parsley
2 tablespoons sherry (optional)
¼ teaspoon black pepper

- Heat oil in large stockpot over medium heat. Add prosciutto and sauté for 2 minutes.
- Add onion, celery, carrot, and garlic; sauté for 2 minutes or until soft.
- Add water, beans, bay leaves, and broth. Bring soup to a boil. Partially cover, reduce heat, and simmer for 20 minutes.
- Add parsley, sherry, and pepper; cook for 1 minute. Discard bay leaves before serving.

Prosciutto, Italian for "ham," is a term broadly used to describe a ham that has been seasoned, salt-cured, and air-dried. The meat is pressed, producing a firm, dense texture.

BROWN RICE & RED LENTIL SOUP

Once your chopping is done, this is an effortless soup. Makes a great meatless meal, but ½ to 1 pound of smoked sausage or kielbasa may be added during last 15 minutes of cooking, if desired.

Yield: 10 servings

6 cups chicken broth (homemade, or use 3 14-ounce cans)

4 cups water

1 cup uncooked brown rice (not quick-cooking type)

1 (35-ounce) can diced tomatoes, undrained

3 carrots, sliced

1 large onion, chopped

1 large stalk celery, chopped

3 cloves garlic, minced

½ teaspoon dried basil

½ teaspoon dried oregano

½ teaspoon dried thyme

1 bay leaf

1½ cups red lentils, picked over and rinsed

½ cup chopped fresh parsley

1-2 tablespoons cider vinegar

Salt and black pepper to taste

- In large stockpot, combine chicken broth, water, rice, tomatoes, carrots, onion, celery, garlic, basil, oregano, thyme, bay leaf, and lentils.
- Bring to boil, then simmer, covered, for 45 to 55 minutes. Stir occasionally while simmering.
- Before serving, remove bay leaf and stir in parsley, vinegar, salt, and pepper.

Lentils are richer in protein than any other legumes except soybeans. Most lentils do not need soaking before cooking. Red or split orange lentils are quick-cooking, making them useful for thickening curries, stews, or casseroles.

CREAMY TOMATO BASIL SOUP

The cookbook committee met for lunch to test this soup, and it was a big hit! Rich and delicious enough for even the fanciest luncheon.

Yield: 8 servings

1 (28-ounce) can diced tomatoes, drained, 12 fresh Roma tomatoes, or 1 box Pomi tomatoes (see note below)
3 cups tomato juice
2 cups chicken stock
15 fresh basil leaves

1½ cups heavy cream
1½ sticks (¾ cup) butter
½ teaspoon salt
½ teaspoon freshly ground black pepper
  Freshly grated Parmesan cheese (optional)

- If using Roma tomatoes, peel and chop.
- Combine tomatoes, tomato juice, and chicken stock in large saucepan. Bring to boil, reduce heat, and simmer for 30 minutes over medium-low heat.
- Add basil, cool slightly, and transfer, in batches, to food processor or blender. Process until smooth.
- Return soup to saucepan over low heat.
- Whisk in cream, butter, salt, and pepper. Whisk until butter is melted and soup is thoroughly heated.
- Garnish with freshly grated Parmesan.

Note: Pomi tomatoes are shelf-stable fresh tomatoes. They taste great in soups and sauces, and one 26.5-ounce package works well for this soup. Look for them in a box with the canned tomatoes at the supermarket.

POTATO SOUP PLUS

Yield: 4-6 servings

2 tablespoons butter
1 onion, sliced
2 (14-ounce) cans chicken broth
4 large Yukon Gold potatoes, sliced
2 bay leaves
1 slice ham hock or bacon
1 cup half-and-half

1 cup chopped ham
1 cup steamed broccoli florets
   and/or sliced carrots (tester
   recommends using both)
Salt and black pepper to taste
Sour cream or plain yogurt
   (optional)

- In large stockpot, melt butter over very low heat. Add onion and brown very slowly — may take 15 minutes or longer, but worth it for the rich taste.
- Add chicken broth, potatoes, bay leaves, and ham hock or bacon. Bring to boil, reduce heat to low, cover, and simmer about an hour. Add water if needed to keep soup from getting too thick or sticky (may need up to 1 cup water).
- When potatoes are very tender, use potato masher to break potatoes into small pieces.
- Gently stir in half-and-half, ham, broccoli, and carrots. Heat carefully (if it boils, it may curdle), and season well with salt and pepper.
- May be served with a dollop of sour cream or yogurt on each bowl of soup.

FROGMORE STEW

Great fun for a crowd!

Yield: 8 servings

¼ cup Old Bay seasoning
12 links Smithfield sausage or
   kielbasa

8 ears yellow corn, broken in half
4 pounds medium shrimp, raw and
   unshelled

- Bring Old Bay and 6 quarts of water to boil. Add sausage and boil 5 minutes.
- Add corn and boil 5 more minutes.
- Add shrimp and cook until pink, about 2 minutes.
- Drain immediately. Dump on newspapers spread on table.
- Serve with French bread, dirty rice, and tossed salad.

BROCCOLI CHOWDER
Yield: 8-10 servings

1 tablespoon vegetable oil
1 medium onion, chopped
3 (10¾-ounce) cans condensed
   cream of potato soup
3 (12-ounce) cans evaporated milk
3 large potatoes, peeled and
   chopped, steamed until tender

1 (14-ounce) bag frozen corn
   (Cope's Silver Queen corn
   preferred)
3 cups chopped fresh broccoli,
   steamed until tender
   Shredded Cheddar cheese

- In large stockpot, heat oil and add onion. Sauté until tender.
- Add soup, milk, potatoes, and corn. Cook over low heat for 30 minutes. Do not boil.
- Add broccoli and heat until hot. Sprinkle with Cheddar cheese before serving.

Serve hot soup in bread bowls for an attractive presentation. Cut the top quarter off of individual round loaves of country bread and hollow them out, being careful not to cut through the bottom. Brush the insides of the loaves with olive oil and toast, along with the lids, at 350° for about 10 minutes. Ladle hot soup into bread bowls and serve immediately with lids on top or alongside.

SEAFOOD CHOWDER

Yield: 8-10 servings

4 slices bacon
1 small onion, diced
1 red bell pepper, chopped
5 medium potatoes, diced
¾ pound raw peeled shrimp

¾ pound raw scallops
2 cups half-and-half
1 cup water
2 cups frozen corn
Salt and black pepper to taste

- Fry bacon in large stockpot. Remove from pan with slotted spoon, crumble, and reserve.
- In same pot, sauté onion, bell pepper, and potato in bacon drippings until tender but not mushy.
- In separate saucepan, boil shrimp and scallops for 1 minute (no longer). Drain and reserve.
- Add half-and-half, water, and corn to potato mixture. Simmer for 10 minutes.
- Add shrimp and scallops to pot; continue simmering another 10 minutes.
- Add salt and pepper to taste. Garnish with crumbled bacon.

ROB'S MANHATTAN CLAM CHOWDER

The non-creamy tomato version of clam chowder.

Yield: 6-8 servings

6 slices bacon
2 tablespoons unsalted butter
1 cup chopped onions
½ cup chopped celery
½ cup chopped green bell pepper
½ cup chopped carrots
½ cup chopped leeks
2 (6-ounce) cans chopped clams

1 (15-ounce) can diced tomatoes, undrained
1 cup chicken broth
1½ cups diced, peeled potatoes
½ teaspoon dried thyme
½ teaspoon dried parsley
Salt and freshly ground black pepper to taste

- Fry bacon until crisp; drain and chop. Set aside.
- Melt butter in large stockpot. Add onions, celery, bell pepper, carrots, and leeks. Cook over low heat until tender, about 10 minutes.
- Drain clams, reserving liquid. Coarsely chop clams and set aside.
- Add bacon, clam liquid, tomatoes, chicken broth, and potatoes to pot. Bring to boil, reduce heat, cover, and simmer for 15 minutes.
- Add clams, thyme, parsley, salt, and pepper. Cook, uncovered, for 10 to 15 more minutes.

To prevent staining, spray plastic storage dishes with nonstick spray before filling with tomato-based sauces or other foods.

CHILLED SUMMER SQUASH SOUP WITH CURRY

This is very refreshing, but may also be served hot if your family objects to cold soup.

Yield: 4 servings

2 tablespoons unsalted butter
2 large shallots, minced
1 clove garlic, minced
1½ teaspoons curry powder
1¼ pounds yellow squash, diced

2 cups (or more) chicken stock or canned broth
Salt to taste
Plain yogurt
Fresh mint leaves, minced

- Melt butter in large saucepan over medium-low heat.
- Add shallots, garlic, and curry; sauté 3 minutes.
- Add squash, cover, and cook until squash is tender, stirring occasionally, about 10 minutes.
- Add chicken stock, cover, and simmer 10 minutes.
- Purée in batches in blender or processor. Thin with additional stock, if necessary. Season with salt to taste.
- Cover and refrigerate until serving.
- To serve, top with dollop of yogurt and garnish with mint.

Ever wonder, when a recipe calls for one shallot, whether it means an entire shallot or one clove from a shallot? A shallot may consist of one to four irregularly sized cloves. Most shallots, whether they have one clove or four, are about the same size. For this reason, it's more accurate to consider an entire shallot, not an individual clove, the equivalent of "one shallot." Generally, a shallot yields about 3 tablespoons minced.

GAZPACHO

*Must be made ahead, makes a lot, and doesn't need
heating — perfect for summer entertaining!*

Yield: 12 servings

1 (46-ounce) can V-8 Juice
½ cup vegetable oil
½ cup red wine vinegar
    Dash of Tabasco sauce
¼ cup lemon juice
1 teaspoon Worcestershire sauce
1 clove garlic, crushed
1 teaspoon celery seed
1½ teaspoons salt
⅛ teaspoon black pepper

⅛ teaspoon paprika
1 large cucumber, peeled and seeded
    (cut in half lengthwise and
    scrape out seeds with teaspoon)
1 green bell pepper, cored
2 stalks celery, trimmed
6 sprigs fresh parsley
2 tomatoes, peeled and cored
5 green onions, trimmed

- Combine V-8 juice, oil, vinegar, Tabasco, lemon juice, Worcestershire, garlic, celery seed, salt, pepper, and paprika; mix well with electric mixer.
- Using food processor or blender, finely chop cucumber, bell pepper, celery, parsley, tomatoes, and green onions.
- Add vegetables (along with any liquid from processing) to soup base. Stir well to blend.
- Refrigerate for at least 24 hours before serving.

SUNFLOWER SPINACH SALAD
Yield: 4-6 servings

For salad:

1 pound baby spinach leaves, washed, dried, and trimmed

8 ounces fresh mushrooms, sliced

6 slices bacon, fried crisp and crumbled

½ cup dry roasted sunflower seeds

1½ cups alfalfa sprouts (optional)

1 large avocado

For dressing:

3 tablespoons sugar

⅛ teaspoon salt

¼ teaspoon dry mustard

2 teaspoons minced onion

3 tablespoons cider vinegar

3 tablespoons oil

½ teaspoon ginger

- Toss together spinach, mushrooms, bacon, sunflower seeds, and sprouts, if using. Cover and refrigerate.
- Place sugar, salt, mustard, onion, vinegar, oil, and ginger in large jar and shake well to make dressing. Store in refrigerator.
- Just before serving, slice avocado and add to salad. Shake dressing thoroughly, pour over salad, and toss lightly.

Look for washed baby spinach leaves with the bagged salads at the supermarket. Much less work – better texture and flavor!

STRAWBERRY SPINACH SALAD

This dressing was a favorite among our testers — easy, different, and so tasty.

Yield: 6-8 servings

For salad:

8 cups baby spinach leaves, washed, dried, and trimmed

3 kiwi fruits, peeled and sliced

1 cup sliced fresh strawberries

¾ cup chopped pecans

For dressing:

2 tablespoons strawberry jam

2 tablespoons balsamic vinegar

⅓ cup vegetable oil

- Toss together spinach, kiwi, strawberries, and pecans in large bowl, reserving several kiwi and strawberry slices for garnish.
- For dressing, combine jam and vinegar in blender. Process until smooth.
- With blender running, add oil in a steady stream until blended.
- Pour dressing over spinach mixture and toss gently.
- Garnish with reserved fruit.

Balsamic vinegar is made from the Italian White Trebbiano grape. It is aged in barrels, giving it a dark color and pungent sweetness.

WINTER SPINACH SALAD
Yield: 6 servings

For dressing: (make the day before serving)

2 teaspoons garlic powder

6 tablespoons sugar

1 tablespoon salt

¾ cup apple cider vinegar

1 cup vegetable oil

For salad:

6 cups spinach, washed and torn

⅓ cup dried sour cherries

3 scallions, thinly sliced

1 Granny Smith apple, thinly sliced

2 cups seedless red grapes

¼ cup walnuts, coarsely chopped

- Whisk together garlic powder, sugar, salt, vinegar, and oil. Let sit overnight.
- For salad, toss together spinach, cherries, scallions, apple, grapes, and walnuts.
- Pour dressing over salad and toss well to mix.

When washing spinach, add salt to the first rinse water and let it soak a minute to remove the grit.

SALAD WITH SPICED PECANS & BALSAMIC VINAIGRETTE

Another great combination of ingredients — the dressing and pecan recipes make enough for several salads.

Yield: 6 servings

For Balsamic Vinaigrette dressing:

½ cup balsamic vinegar
3 tablespoons Dijon mustard
3 tablespoons honey
2 cloves garlic, minced

2 small shallots, minced
¼ teaspoon salt
¼ teaspoon black pepper
1 cup olive oil

For Spiced Pecans:

1 egg white
1 teaspoon water
1 pound pecan halves
½ cup sugar

1 teaspoon salt
½ teaspoon cinnamon
½ teaspoon cayenne pepper

For salad:

¾ pound mixed salad greens
4 ounces blue cheese, crumbled
2 oranges, peeled and thinly sliced

1 pint fresh strawberries or red grapes, quartered or halved

- Combine vinegar, mustard, honey, garlic, shallots, salt, pepper, and oil in blender or large jar. Blend or shake well.
- Store in refrigerator (makes enough for several salads). Keeps well.
- For pecans, preheat oven to 225°. Line 10x15-inch rimmed baking sheet with foil and grease generously.
- Beat egg white and water together until frothy.
- Stir in pecans until well coated.
- In large bowl, mix together sugar, salt, cinnamon, and cayenne pepper. Add coated pecans and mix well. Spread pecans on prepared baking sheet.
- Bake nuts for 1 hour, turning every 15 minutes.
- Store in airtight container (makes enough for several salads).
- For salad, toss greens, blue cheese, oranges, and strawberries or grapes together gently.
- Drizzle with about ½ to ¾ cup dressing and toss.
- Sprinkle with about 1½ cups pecans.

65

SAUTÉED APPLE SALAD WITH ROQUEFORT & WALNUTS

A sophisticated salad for autumn dinner parties.

Yield: 6-8 servings

For dressing:

¼ cup sherry or red wine vinegar

1 tablespoon chopped fresh thyme
   (or 1 teaspoon dried)

½ cup olive oil or walnut oil

Salt and freshly ground black
   pepper

For salad:

1 tablespoon olive oil

1½ pounds Golden Delicious apples,
   peeled and cut in thin wedges

1 tablespoon sugar

6 cups mixed salad greens

3 cups watercress, trimmed

1 Belgian endive, sliced

4 ounces Roquefort cheese,
   crumbled (1 cup)

½ cup toasted walnuts, chopped
   (to toast, see sidebar on page 33)

- For dressing, whisk together vinegar and thyme in small bowl. Gradually whisk in oil. Season with salt and pepper to taste.

- For salad, heat olive oil in nonstick skillet over medium-high heat. Add apples and sugar. Sauté until apples are almost tender, about 8 minutes. Increase heat and sauté until golden brown, about 5 minutes.

- Toss together salad greens, watercress, and endive in large salad bowl. Toss in apples. Sprinkle with Roquefort and walnuts. Toss with enough dressing to coat.

You can toast walnuts ahead and cook apples until almost done, then finish cooking just before tossing salad. If you can't find endive and watercress, just increase salad greens or add baby spinach.

EMERIL'S WEDGIE SALAD

One man we know calls this "the only true salad."

Yield: 8 servings

½ pound blue cheese, crumbled
¼ cup fresh lemon juice
1 teaspoon Worcestershire sauce
½ teaspoon Tabasco sauce
½ teaspoon salt
¾ teaspoon freshly ground black
   pepper

1 cup olive oil
¼ cup buttermilk
2 large heads iceberg lettuce,
   outside leaves removed, cored,
   washed and patted dry (do not
   separate leaves)

- In medium bowl, combine blue cheese, lemon juice, Worcestershire, Tabasco, salt, and pepper. With back of a fork, mash mixture into a thick paste.
- Drizzle in olive oil, stirring continuously with fork until creamy.
- Stir in buttermilk, mix well, cover, and refrigerate for 1 hour.
- Cut heads of lettuce into 4 wedges each and spoon about ¼ cup of dressing over each wedge.
- Serve immediately.

May sprinkle chopped tomato or red bell pepper on top for color, if desired.

HICKS FAMILY REUNION MARINATED SLAW

Yield: 24 servings

For slaw:

2 large heads cabbage, shredded

2 large onions, thinly sliced

2 large green bell peppers, thinly
    sliced into rings

4 stalks celery, finely chopped

2 cups sugar

For dressing:

2   cups white vinegar

1½ cups salad oil

2   tablespoons salt

4 teaspoons sugar

2 teaspoons dry mustard

2 teaspoons celery seed

- Place half of shredded cabbage in very large bowl.
- Top with sliced onion, bell pepper, and chopped celery.
- Place rest of cabbage on top of onion and peppers. Sprinkle with 2 cups sugar.
- Heat vinegar, oil, salt, 4 teaspoons sugar, dry mustard, and celery seed to boiling.
- Pour over cabbage and cover at once. Do not mix.
- Refrigerate for at least 4 hours. Slaw improves with age.

BROCCOLI SLAW SALAD

For salad:

¼ cup sesame seeds or ½ cup
    sunflower seeds, or both
1 cup slivered almonds
1 (16-ounce) package shredded
    broccoli (found with bagged
    salads)

3 green onions, chopped
1 package Ramen noodles, uncooked
    (discard flavor packet)

For dressing:

4 cloves fresh garlic (may use
    minced garlic in jar)
3 tablespoons sugar
½ cup vegetable oil

3 tablespoons red wine vinegar
½ teaspoon salt
½ teaspoon black pepper

- Preheat oven to 325°.
- Toast sesame seeds and/or sunflower seeds and almonds in oven until golden brown; cool.
- Toss together broccoli and green onions.
- Crumble dry Ramen noodles and stir into seeds and almonds.
- Add noodle mixture to shredded broccoli just before adding dressing to salad.
- To make dressing, whisk together garlic, sugar, oil, vinegar, salt, and pepper. Toss with broccoli mixture just before serving.

For variety, the following dressing is also recommended (use same method):

¼ cup sugar
6 tablespoons rice vinegar or white
    vinegar

⅔ cup vegetable oil
1 teaspoon salt
1 teaspoon black pepper

BROCCOLI & CRANBERRY SLAW

Not your average slaw — great color and flavor!

Yield: 8 servings

2 cups broccoli florets, blanched
  (see instructions below)
1¼ cups fresh or dried cranberries
4 cups shredded cabbage
1 small onion, minced
8 slices bacon, cooked until crisp
  and crumbled

1 cup raisins
1 cup coarsely chopped walnuts
  (may also use pine nuts or
  cashews)
⅓ cup sugar
2 tablespoons cider vinegar
1 cup mayonnaise

- Toss together broccoli, cranberries, cabbage, onion, bacon, raisins, and walnuts in salad bowl.
- Blend sugar, vinegar, and mayonnaise in small bowl. Add to salad and toss gently. Cover and refrigerate 20 minutes to blend flavors.

To blanch broccoli or other vegetables, bring water to a boil in saucepan, add broccoli, and cook briefly just until it turns bright green, about 2 minutes. Drain and immediately plunge into ice water to stop cooking and set color.

CRUNCHY ROMAINE TOSS
Yield: 10-12 servings

For dressing:

1 cup vegetable oil
¼ cup sugar
½ cup balsamic vinegar or red wine
    vinegar

2 teaspoons soy sauce
    Salt and black pepper to taste
    Oriental flavor packet from
        noodles, if desired

For topping:

½ stick (¼ cup) unsalted butter
1 cup chopped pecans

1 package Oriental flavor Ramen
    noodles, uncooked and broken
    up (discard flavor packet or use
    in dressing)

For salad:

1 bunch broccoli, washed, trimmed,
    and coarsely chopped
1 head Romaine lettuce (or 1 bag
    Romaine hearts), torn

4 green onions, chopped (white part
    only)
1 carton raspberries
1 (11-ounce) can Mandarin oranges,
    drained

- Whisk together oil, sugar, vinegar, soy sauce, salt, pepper, and contents of flavor packet, if using. Makes 2½ cups dressing - use 1 cup for salad.
- For topping, melt butter in small skillet and add pecans and noodles. Brown carefully. Remove from skillet and cool on paper towels.
- To assemble salad, toss together broccoli, Romaine, and green onions. Add 1 cup dressing and toss to mix.
- Add raspberries and oranges; toss gently. Cover and refrigerate until serving time.
- Just before serving, sprinkle with topping and toss.

All-Vegetable Variation: You may substitute 1 fresh tomato, peeled, seeded, and diced, for raspberries and oranges, if desired.

ORIENTAL SLAW

For variations on this recipe, see Crunchy Romaine Toss and Broccoli Slaw recipes. We think we've covered the bases on this popular salad!

Yield: 8 servings

For salad:
1 large head Napa cabbage, chopped

1 bunch green onions, sliced

For topping:
1 (3.75-ounce) package sunflower kernels
½ cup sliced almonds

1 (3-ounce) package beef flavor Ramen noodles (reserve flavor packet for dressing)
1 tablespoon butter

For dressing:
½ cup oil
¼ cup white vinegar
⅓ cup sugar

1 teaspoon soy sauce
Flavor packet from noodles

- Toss together cabbage and onions in large bowl.
- For topping, sauté sunflower kernels, almonds, and noodles in butter in small skillet over medium-low heat until browned.
- To make dressing, mix oil, vinegar, sugar, soy sauce, and contents of flavor packet; blend or shake well.
- Just before serving, toss salad with dressing and top with nut mixture.

Napa cabbage has an elongated shape, celadon-tipped cream-colored leaves, and a wonderful mild flavor.

GREEK MARINATED VEGETABLE SALAD

Yield: 4-6 servings

1 (6-ounce) jar marinated artichoke hearts
2 tomatoes, cut into wedges
1 medium zucchini, cut in julienne strips
1 medium cucumber, sliced
1 cup black olives, sliced
1 medium purple onion, sliced
¾ cup crumbled feta cheese
¼ cup balsamic vinegar
1 teaspoon dried oregano
¼ teaspoon black pepper
½ teaspoon salt

- Drain artichoke hearts, reserving marinade.
- Toss together drained artichoke hearts, tomatoes, zucchini, cucumber, olives, onion, and feta cheese in large serving bowl.
- Whisk together reserved artichoke marinade, vinegar, oregano, pepper, and salt.
- Pour over vegetable mixture and refrigerate for 2 to 8 hours, stirring occasionally.

PEAS & PEANUTS SALAD

So easy, so green, and so crunchy! Try substituting cashews or adding crisp crumbled bacon next time.

Yield: 6 servings

1 (10-ounce) package frozen green peas
½ cup chopped celery
¼ cup chopped onion
½ cup mayonnaise
⅓ cup sour cream
1 teaspoon Worcestershire sauce
⅛ teaspoon black pepper
Salt to taste
1 cup cocktail peanuts

- Thaw peas in colander under cold running water. Pat dry with paper towels.
- Combine peas with celery, onion, mayonnaise, sour cream, Worcestershire, pepper, and salt. Mix well.
- Cover and refrigerate until serving time. Stir in peanuts just before serving.

LIGHT CAESAR SALAD

Yield: four 2-cup servings

4 slices French bread, cut into ¾-inch cubes

2 cloves garlic, crushed

8 cups loosely packed, torn Romaine lettuce

½ cup freshly shaved Parmesan cheese (1 ounce)

3 tablespoons water

3 tablespoons fresh lemon juice

2½ teaspoons olive oil

1 teaspoon low-sodium Worcestershire sauce

1 teaspoon anchovy paste

½ teaspoon sugar

3 cloves garlic

- Preheat oven to 350°.
- Combine bread cubes and crushed garlic in large Ziploc bag. Seal and shake to coat bread cubes.
- Pour bread cubes onto rimmed baking sheet and arrange in single layer. Bake at 350° for 15 minutes or until toasted.
- Toss together cooled bread cubes, lettuce, and cheese in large bowl; set aside.
- Combine water, lemon juice, olive oil, Worcestershire, anchovy paste, sugar, and garlic cloves in blender. Cover and process until smooth.
- Pour over lettuce mixture, toss well, and serve.

MISS VIRGINIA'S BLUE CHEESE DRESSING

You might want to try Maytag Blue in this dressing.
A smooth, pleasant tasting blue cheese with heavy mold throughout,
it is considered one of the best domestic blues and is perfect in salad.

Yield: 1 quart

1 (8-ounce) carton sour cream

1 (8-ounce) package cream cheese, softened

2 tablespoons lemon juice

2 (4-ounce) packages blue cheese

2 cups mayonnaise

1 clove garlic, minced

½-1 cup chopped green onion

- Mix sour cream, cream cheese, lemon juice, blue cheese, mayonnaise, garlic, and green onion in electric mixer. Refrigerate overnight before serving for best flavor.

DOUBLE TOMATO SALAD

Use only the reddest, ripest fresh summer tomatoes for this colorful salad.

Yield: 6-8 servings

4 large fresh tomatoes, unpeeled and sliced

4 ounces mozzarella cheese, thinly sliced

2 tablespoons oil from sun-dried tomatoes (see below)

1 tablespoon olive oil

1 tablespoon red wine vinegar

Salt and black pepper to taste

¼ cup drained, chopped oil-pack sun-dried tomatoes, oil reserved

2 tablespoons capers, rinsed and drained

2 tablespoons chopped fresh basil

- Arrange tomatoes and mozzarella cheese in alternating slices on serving platter.
- Whisk sun-dried tomato oil, olive oil, and vinegar in small bowl. Drizzle over tomatoes and cheese.
- Season with salt and pepper. Sprinkle with sun-dried tomatoes, capers, and basil.

If desired, crumbled feta cheese may be substituted for mozzarella.

GRAPE TOMATOES & CAPERS

Yield: 6 servings

3 tablespoons small capers, drained

3 tablespoons balsamic vinegar

2 tablespoons olive oil

½ teaspoon salt

½ teaspoon black pepper

2 pints grape tomatoes, halved

6 large fresh basil leaves, shredded

3 tablespoons grated Parmesan cheese

Bibb lettuce leaves (optional)

- Stir together capers, vinegar, oil, salt, and pepper. Drizzle over tomatoes, tossing to coat. Cover with plastic wrap and let stand at room temperature at least 15 minutes or up to 1 hour.
- At serving time, sprinkle with basil and cheese. Serve over Bibb lettuce leaves, if desired.

WARM GOAT CHEESE SALAD

You no longer have to go to a restaurant for this delicacy!

Yield: 6 servings

For dressing:
½ cup olive oil
⅓ cup lemon juice

1 tablespoon diced green onions
1½ teaspoons Dijon mustard

For goat cheese:
½ cup Italian-seasoned dry
   breadcrumbs
1½ tablespoons grated Parmesan
   cheese

1½ tablespoons sesame seeds
3 (4-ounce) logs goat cheese
1 large egg, lightly beaten
3 tablespoons butter or margarine

For salad:
6 cups torn mixed salad greens

12 ripe olives, sliced (optional)

- Combine oil, lemon juice, green onions, and mustard. Set aside.
- To prepare goat cheese, stir together breadcrumbs, Parmesan cheese, and sesame seeds.
- Cut each goat cheese log into 4 slices. Dip each slice into beaten egg and dredge in breadcrumb mixture. Cover and refrigerate 2 hours.
- Melt butter in large skillet over medium-high heat. Add goat cheese slices and fry 1 to 2 minutes on each side or until browned. Drain on paper towels.
- Toss mixed greens and olives, if using, with dressing. Top with warm goat cheese.

Found in specialty produce markets and many supermarkets, mesclun (also called salad mix or gourmet salad mix) is simply a potpourri of young, small salad greens. The mix varies, but often includes arugula, dandelion, frisée, oak leaf, radicchio, and sorrel. Choose mesclun with crisp leaves and no sign of wilting. Refrigerate in a plastic bag for up to 5 days, washing and blotting dry just before using.

ENSALADA NOCHEBUENA (WINTER FRUIT SALAD)

Yield: 12-14 servings

4 oranges, peeled with white
   membrane removed
4 red apples, cored and unpeeled
4 bananas, peeled
1 fresh pineapple, peeled and cored
   (or 1 30-ounce can pineapple
   chunks in juice, drained)

3 limes, peeled with white
   membrane removed
2 cups seedless red grapes
1 head iceberg lettuce, shredded
¼ cup sugar
1 cup peanuts, chopped
1 cup orange juice or French
   dressing

- Thinly slice oranges, apples, bananas, pineapple, and limes. Remove grapes from stems. Toss all fruits together gently.
- Line large, shallow serving bowl or platter with lettuce and top with fruit. (Pineapple and citrus will keep apples and bananas from browning.)
- Sprinkle with sugar, cover with plastic wrap, and refrigerate.
- Just before serving, top with peanuts and juice or dressing and toss gently to combine.

> ⟡ *Coring Fruit* ⟡
>
> *A good trick for coring and seeding halved apples or pears is to use a small melon baller – or try a metal 1/2-teaspoon measuring spoon if you don't have a melon baller.*

SUMMER FRUIT SALAD
Another wonderful dressing!

Yield: 10 servings

For salad:

1 fresh pineapple, peeled, cored and
     cubed
1 quart fresh hulled strawberries
½ cup fresh blueberries

½ cup fresh raspberries
1 (11-ounce) can Mandarin oranges,
     drained

For dressing:

2 cups orange juice
½ cup sugar
¼ cup cream sherry

½ teaspoon almond extract
½ teaspoon vanilla extract

- Gently toss together pineapple, strawberries, blueberries, raspberries, and oranges in large serving bowl.
- For dressing, whisk together orange juice, sugar, sherry, almond extract, and vanilla, stirring until sugar dissolves.
- Pour dressing over fruit, tossing lightly. Cover and refrigerate 2 to 3 hours.
- Drain before serving or serve with a slotted spoon.

FRESH FRUIT WITH LIME SAUCE

This dish makes a refreshing salad or a healthy dessert.

Yield: 10 servings

For dressing:

1 cup water
1 tablespoon cornstarch
1 cup sugar

1 teaspoon lime zest
¼ cup fresh lime juice

For salad:

1 pineapple, peeled and cored, cut into 1-inch pieces
2 cups red seedless grapes
1 large pink grapefruit, peeled and sectioned (or pink grapefruit sections from refrigerated section of supermarket, drained)

2 kiwi fruits, peeled and thickly sliced
2 oranges, peeled and sectioned

- In small saucepan, whisk together water and cornstarch over low heat until combined. Add sugar, zest, and juice.
- Cook over low heat, whisking constantly, about 10 minutes or until thickened. Cool slightly and refrigerate for 2 hours.
- At serving time, toss together pineapple, grapes, grapefruit, kiwi, and oranges in large serving bowl. Drizzle with dressing, tossing to coat. Serve immediately.

APPLE LIME SALAD
Yield: 8-10 servings

1 (3-ounce) package lime Jello
  powder
1½ cups boiling water
1 (15-ounce) can pineapple tidbits,
  undrained
1 (8-ounce) can crushed pineapple,
  drained

1 (5-ounce) can less 3 tablespoons
  evaporated milk
1 (8-ounce) package cream cheese,
  softened
1 cup mayonnaise
1 small apple, peeled and finely
  chopped
½ cup chopped pecans

- Spray 2-quart mold or casserole dish with nonstick spray.
- Dissolve Jello in boiling water. Let cool. Add both cans of pineapple and refrigerate until slightly thickened.
- With electric mixer, beat together milk, cream cheese, and mayonnaise. Stir in apples and nuts. Blend into Jello mixture.
- Pour into prepared mold and chill until firm.
- Invert molded salad onto a lettuce-lined plate to serve.

To keep cut apples and other fruits from turning brown, drop them into 4 cups of cold water combined with 4 tablespoons lemon or pineapple juice, 2 teaspoons white vinegar, or ½ cup white wine.

STRAWBERRY CHEESECAKE SALAD

May also be served as a dessert!

Yield: 15 servings

2 (3-ounce) packages strawberry
  Jello powder
1 cup boiling water
2 (10-ounce) packages frozen
  strawberries, thawed

1 (20-ounce) can crushed pineapple,
  drained
3 medium bananas, mashed
½ cup chopped pecans
1 (10-ounce) package cheesecake
  mix (filling only)

- Spray a 9x13-inch glass dish with nonstick spray.
- Dissolve Jello in boiling water. Cool. Stir in strawberries, pineapple, bananas, and pecans.
- Pour half of Jello mixture into prepared dish. Cover remaining Jello and reserve.
- Prepare cheesecake filling according to package directions. Discard crumbs or save for another use.
- Spoon cheesecake filling over Jello layer in dish. Top with reserved Jello.
- Refrigerate until firm.

ROASTED POTATOES & GREEN BEANS WITH ROSEMARY VINAIGRETTE
Yield: 8-10 servings

⅔ cup olive oil, divided
3 pounds red potatoes, unpeeled, halved, and cut into 1-inch wedges
1 clove garlic
¼ cup red wine vinegar
1 tablespoon fresh rosemary leaves (or 1 teaspoon dried, crumbled)
Salt to taste

1 red onion, halved lengthwise and sliced thin
Ice and cold water for soaking onion
2 pounds green beans, trimmed and cut into 1-inch pieces
24 Kalamata or Niçoise olives, pitted and halved
Fresh rosemary sprigs for garnish

- Preheat oven to 425°.
- In large roasting pan, heat ⅓ cup of oil in middle of oven for 5 minutes. Add potatoes to pan, tossing to coat with oil. Roast at 425°, stirring every 10 minutes, for 30 minutes or until tender. Let potatoes cool in pan.
- In blender, purée garlic, vinegar, rosemary, and salt. With motor running, add remaining ⅓ cup oil in a stream and blend dressing until emulsified.
- Soak onion for 5 minutes in small bowl of ice and cold water. Drain well and pat dry.
- Boil green beans in salted water for 5 minutes or until bright green and crisp tender. Drain, refresh under cold water, and pat dry.
- In very large bowl, toss together potatoes, onion, green beans, and olives. Add dressing and toss gently.
- Serve at room temperature, garnished with rosemary sprigs.

POTATO SALAD WITH BLUE CHEESE & WALNUTS

Potato salad for grown-ups!

Yield: 6 servings

2-3 pounds red potatoes
Salt to taste
1 (4-ounce) package blue cheese, crumbled (about ¾ cup)
¼ cup olive oil
¼ cup fresh lemon juice

4 green onions with tops, chopped
¾ cup chopped celery
½ cup coarsely chopped walnuts, toasted (see sidebar instructions on page 33)

- Cook potatoes in simmering water until tender. Drain well.
- Cut potatoes into chunks and place in large serving bowl. Add salt to taste.
- Whisk together cheese, olive oil, and lemon juice in small bowl.
- Pour mixture over warm potatoes and toss gently to mix.
- Add onions, celery, and walnuts; toss gently.
- Serve at room temperature or slightly warm.

Roquefort, a variety of blue cheese, is made of sheep's milk. This cheese looks white when first cut, the characteristic blue-green veining appearing only after exposure to the air. It is delicious with crusty bread, walnuts, and raisins.

RED ONION POTATO SALAD

Light sour cream and light mayonnaise may be used in this salad.

Yield: 10-12 servings

4 pounds small red potatoes
1 medium red onion, sliced thin
½ cup sour cream
¼ cup milk
½ cup mayonnaise

2 teaspoons Dijon mustard
1½ teaspoons fresh dill
1 teaspoon sugar
1 teaspoon salt
½ teaspoon black pepper

- Cook potatoes 20 to 30 minutes until tender. Drain, cool, and chop into bite-size pieces.
- Place potatoes and onion in large serving bowl.
- In small bowl, whisk together sour cream, milk, mayonnaise, mustard, dill, sugar, salt, and pepper.
- Pour dressing over potatoes and toss gently to mix.
- Cover and refrigerate for 2 to 3 hours before serving.

HERMIONE'S COUSCOUS SALAD

1 cup chicken broth
¾ cup uncooked couscous
½ cup Italian dressing
12 cherry tomatoes, halved

1 (8-ounce) can water chestnuts,
   drained and coarsely chopped
2 cups fresh baby spinach leaves,
   trimmed and sliced into strips

- Bring broth to boil. Add couscous, stir, and cover. Remove from heat and set aside for 5 minutes.
- Stir in Italian dressing, cover, and refrigerate 2 hours or overnight.
- Before serving, fluff couscous with fork to break up lumps. Add tomatoes, water chestnuts, and spinach; toss well to mix.

WILD RICE SALAD

Can be a main-dish salad with or without added chunks of chicken breast. A great nutty taste, perfect for tailgating or beach trips.

Yield: 8-12 servings

For salad:

2 packages Uncle Ben's Wild & White Rice mix

1 package dried fruit bits or dried cranberries

1 (14½-ounce) can shoe peg corn, drained

1 (6-ounce) package chopped almonds

½ cup chopped celery (or more to taste)

½ cup chopped onion

For dressing:

2 tablespoons red wine vinegar

1 tablespoon lemon juice

1 clove garlic

1 teaspoon Dijon mustard

1 teaspoon sugar

1 teaspoon salt

Black pepper to taste

¼ cup vegetable oil

2 tablespoons olive oil

- Cook rice according to package directions.
- While rice is cooking, prepare dressing. Blend vinegar, lemon juice, garlic, mustard, sugar, salt, pepper, vegetable oil, and olive oil in food processor.
- Toss cooked rice with dried fruit bits, corn, almonds, celery, and onion.
- Pour dressing over salad. Cover and refrigerate until serving time.

TORTELLINI & SHELLS SALAD

Packaged or homemade grilled chicken may be added for a hearty main-dish salad.
This looks as good as it tastes!

Yield: 18-20 servings

For salad:

1 (8-ounce) package shell pasta
1 (8-ounce) package dried cheese
    tortellini
1 bunch broccoli, cut into florets
    and blanched (see sidebar
    instructions on page 70)

1 (10-ounce) package frozen green
    peas, thawed to room
    temperature
1 yellow bell pepper, chopped
1 red bell pepper, chopped
2 cups fresh mushrooms, sliced

For dressing:

1 (16-ounce) bottle Paul Newman's
    oil and vinegar dressing
2 teaspoons red wine vinegar
1 teaspoon Dijon mustard

2 teaspoons chopped fresh dill
1 teaspoon chopped fresh basil
2 teaspoons chopped fresh parsley
2 teaspoons sugar

1 box grape tomatoes and Parmesan
    cheese for garnish

- Cook shell pasta and tortellini according to package directions, drain, and let cool.
- Add broccoli, peas, yellow and red bell peppers, and mushrooms. Toss gently to mix.
- Whisk together all dressing ingredients. Toss half of dressing with pasta salad.
- Cover and refrigerate overnight. Add more dressing before serving if needed.
- Garnish with grape tomatoes and Parmesan.

CHICAGO PASTA SALAD

Perfect for potlucks.

Yield: 8-10 servings

3 (9-ounce) packages refrigerated tortellini (2 cheese, 1 spinach and cheese)

3 small heads broccoli, cut into florets

¼ pound hard salami, chopped

1 (14-ounce) can hearts of palm, drained and sliced

1 box cherry tomatoes

½ cup grated Parmesan cheese

1 bottle Seven Seas Italian dressing (or your favorite Italian)

- Cook pasta according to package directions. Drain and cool.
- Blanch broccoli and cool in ice water (see sidebar instructions on page 70).
- Toss together tortellini, broccoli, salami, hearts of palm, and tomatoes in large serving bowl. Top with Parmesan cheese.
- Pour dressing over all and toss well.

ALMOND CHICKEN SALAD

Yield: 6-8 servings

4 cups cubed cooked chicken breasts
1½ cups halved seedless green grapes
1 cup chopped celery
¾ cup sliced green onions
3 hard-cooked eggs, chopped
½ cup mayonnaise
¼ cup sour cream
1 tablespoon prepared mustard (Dijon or your choice)

1 teaspoon salt
½ teaspoon black pepper
¼ teaspoon onion powder
¼ teaspoon celery salt
⅛ teaspoon dry mustard
⅛ teaspoon paprika
½ cup slivered almonds
1 kiwi fruit, peeled and sliced, for garnish (optional)

- In large bowl, toss together chicken, grapes, celery, green onions, and eggs.
- In small bowl, whisk together mayonnaise, sour cream, prepared mustard, salt, pepper, onion powder, celery salt, dry mustard, and paprika until smooth.
- Pour dressing over chicken mixture and toss gently. Cover and refrigerate until serving time.
- To serve, stir in almonds and garnish with kiwi fruit, if desired.

CHICKEN PECAN SALAD
WITH CRANBERRIES

A delicious homemade mayonnaise dressing enhances this salad.

Yield: 4 servings

For dressing:

2 large eggs yolks
2 tablespoons apple cider vinegar
2 tablespoons sugar

1 teaspoon Dijon mustard
¼ teaspoon salt
¾ cup vegetable oil

For salad:

4 whole boneless, skinless chicken
    breast halves, cooked and diced
¾ cup fresh or dried cranberries

3 stalks celery, diced
1 cup pecans, coarsely chopped
1 head red leaf lettuce, torn

- Blend egg yolks, vinegar, sugar, mustard, and salt in food processor. With machine running, add oil slowly in a thin stream. Cover and refrigerate.
- To prepare salad, toss together chicken, cranberries, and celery in serving bowl.
- Add dressing to salad and toss to coat. Cover and refrigerate for 8 to 10 hours.
- Just before serving, add pecans and toss gently. Serve over lettuce.

Fresh cranberries can be hard to find except at Thanksgiving and Christmas. Buy them when they're available and freeze in the original bags for up to a year.

CHICKEN & CRANBERRY MOLD

May also be made in a 9x13-inch baking dish and served in squares.

Yield: 8-10 servings

2 tablespoons unflavored gelatin, divided
¾ cup cold water
2 tablespoons soy sauce
1 cup light mayonnaise
1½ cups diced, cooked chicken breast

½ cup diced celery
¼ cup chopped pecans
1 (8-ounce) can crushed pineapple, undrained
1 (16-ounce) can whole cranberry sauce
2 tablespoons lemon juice

- In saucepan, soften 1 tablespoon gelatin in cold water. Place over low heat and whisk constantly until dissolved. Remove from heat, whisk in soy sauce, and set aside to cool.
- Stir mayonnaise, chicken, celery, and pecans into cooled gelatin mixture. Blend well.
- Pour into 6-cup mold sprayed with nonstick spray. Refrigerate until top is sticky and slightly firm.
- While chicken layer is chilling, drain pineapple, reserving juice. Add water to juice to measure ½ cup.
- Soften remaining 1 tablespoon gelatin in juice mixture. Cook over low heat, whisking constantly until dissolved. Set aside.
- Break up cranberry sauce with fork, then stir in drained pineapple and lemon juice. Add warm gelatin mixture.
- Refrigerate cranberry mixture until syrupy, then pour over chicken layer. Return to refrigerator until set.
- To serve, dip bottom of mold into hot water to loosen and unmold onto lettuce-lined serving plate.

Required
Courses

MEAT

Eye of the Round Roast 91
Julie Taylor's
    Marinated Beef Tenderloin 91
Julia's Easy Pot Roast 92
Filets with Mushroom Sauce 93
Company Beef Stroganoff 94
French Dip Sandwiches 95
Grandmommy's Mazetti 96
Casserole à la Nini 97
Enticing Enchiladas 98
Cornbread Casserole 99
Taco Cheesecake 100
Beef & Pork Barbecue 101
Slow Cooker Barbecue 102
Crock Pot Pork Tenderloin 103
Baby Back Ribs with Peach Sauce 104
Black Beans & Pork over Rice 105
Provençal Pork Roast 106
Grilled Spice-Rubbed
    Pork Tenderloin 107
Pork Tenderloin
    with Mustard Sauce 108
Pork Chops in
    Honey Mustard Sauce 109
Grilled Pork Tenderloin
    with Chili Maple Glaze 109
Marinade for Grilled
    Pork or Chicken 110
Marinade for Pork Tenderloin 111
Grilled Lamb 111
Spring Lamb with
    Fresh Mint Vinaigrette 112
Lamb Chops with Mint Butter 113
Vermouthy Veal 114

POULTRY

Bourbon Chicken with Peaches 115
Raspberry-Balsamic
    Glazed Chicken 116
Lemon Garlic Chicken 117
Orange-Basil Chicken 118
Parmesan Chicken with
    Balsamic Butter Sauce 119
Chicken Breasts Stuffed with
    Mozzarella & Canadian Bacon . . . 120
Mahogany Glazed Chicken 121
Sautéed Chicken with
    Grape Tomatoes & Basil 122
Grace's Chicken 122
Quick & Colorful Cutlets 123
Creamy Almond Chicken 124
Sweet & Spicy Grilled Chicken 125
Chicken-Chutney Croissants 125
Uncle Charlie's
    Grilled Barbecue Chicken 126

Chicken Spectacular 127
Three-Cheese Chicken Pasta 128
Creole Chicken Pasta 129
Poppy Seed Chicken 130
Incredulada Enchiladas 131
Stovetop Cooked Chicken
    for Recipes 131
Gourmet Quesadillas 132
Tortilla Torta 133
Chicken Lo Mein 134
Ainslie's Chicken Pot Pie 135
Mexican Chicken & Rice 136
Citrus Marinated Turkey Breast 136
How to Cook a
    Frozen Turkey Breast 137
Raisin Bread-Cranberry Stuffing 138
Teriyaki Turkey Burgers 139
Turkey Meat Loaf 140
Tipsy Cornish Hens 141

FISH & SEAFOOD

Crook's Corner Shrimp & Grits 142
Shrimp Frederic 143
Shrimp, Artichoke,
    & Grits Casserole 144
Greek Shrimp over Pasta 145
Barbecued Shrimp 146
Crab Casserole 147
Meg's Crabcakes 148
Soft Shelled Crabs in Brown Butter . . . 149
Crawfish Étouffée 150
Rémoulade Sauce 151
Stuffed Lobster Tails 152
Oysters Mosca 153
Rush's Oyster Special 153
Salmon Fillets with
    Sautéed Corn & Spinach 154
Salmon Topped with Fresh Veggies . . . 155
Salmon with Lemon Mayonnaise 156
Dressed Baked Flounder 157
Salmon in Ginger Soy Sauce 158
Grilled Grouper 158
Stuffed Sole or Flounder Fillets
    with Lemon Sauce 159
Orange Roughy with
    Tomato Cilantro Salsa 160
Red Snapper Joliet Rouge 161
Sautéed Red Snapper
    with Tomato Olive Sauce 162
Sea Bass Roasted with Capers 163
Pan-Seared Tuna with Ginger-Shiitake
    Cream Sauce 164
Grilled Maple-Mustard Salmon 165
Summertime Fresh Peach Salsa 166

EYE OF THE ROUND ROAST

Yield: depends on size of roast

Eye of round roast (any size)
Adolph's meat tenderizer

⅔ cup red wine vinegar
⅓ cup olive oil

- Rinse roast and sprinkle all over with tenderizer.
- Place in Ziploc bag with vinegar and oil.
- Seal bag and marinate in refrigerator for 8 hours or overnight.
- Preheat oven to 400°. Remove roast from marinade and place in baking pan.
- Bake, uncovered, at 400° for 20 minutes per pound.

JULIE TAYLOR'S
MARINATED BEEF TENDERLOIN

Yield: 12-16 servings

2 envelopes Italian dressing mix
1 cup water
1 cup ketchup

2 teaspoons Dijon mustard
½ teaspoon Worcestershire sauce
1 (4-5 pound) beef tenderloin

- Whisk together dressing mix, water, ketchup, mustard, and Worcestershire.
- Place beef in large Ziploc bag. Pour in marinade and seal. Marinate in refrigerator for 24 hours.
- To cook, preheat oven to 425°. Bake, uncovered, at 425° for 38 to 40 minutes or to desired doneness.

JULIA'S EASY POT ROAST

A pot roast that is easy to prepare and clean up after! Doesn't sound like it would make enough sauce, but that's the best part — delicious over the meat and accompanying rice or noodles.

Yield: 4-6 servings

1 (about 2½ pound) London broil cut of beef
1 teaspoon salt
⅛ teaspoon black pepper
1 slice bacon, cooked and crumbled
1 (8-ounce) can tomato sauce with onions

1 teaspoon prepared mustard (yellow or your choice)
1 teaspoon brown sugar
½ teaspoon horseradish
1 tablespoon cornstarch
¼ cup cold water

- Preheat oven to 300°.
- Place meat on large sheet of heavy duty aluminum foil in roasting pan. Sprinkle with salt and pepper.
- Mix crumbled bacon, tomato sauce, mustard, brown sugar, and horseradish. Pour over meat.
- Seal loosely and bake at 300° for about 2 hours.
- Remove meat from foil with fork or tongs, place on serving platter, and cover, reserving drippings in foil.
- To make sauce, whisk cornstarch and cold water in small saucepan until cornstarch dissolves. Add drippings from meat and cook over medium heat, whisking frequently, until sauce thickens and becomes somewhat clear.
- Slice meat on diagonal and pour sauce over to serve.

FILETS WITH MUSHROOM SAUCE

This one was rated "by far the best thing I have tested"
by its tester! A rich dish for your favorite guests.

Yield: 10 servings

For marinade:

1	(16-ounce) container sour cream	1	teaspoon black pepper
1	cup finely chopped chives	½	teaspoon onion powder
2	cups mayonnaise	1	teaspoon white vinegar
¼	cup red wine	½	teaspoon celery salt
¾	cup buttermilk	½	teaspoon garlic salt
4-8	ounces blue cheese, crumbled	½-1	cup minced onion
1	tablespoon Worcestershire sauce		Tabasco sauce to taste

10 (8-ounce) beef filets

For mushroom sauce:

1	stick (½ cup) butter	3	cloves garlic, minced
1	pound mushrooms, thickly sliced	¼	cup chopped fresh parsley
½	cup chopped green onions		

- Whisk together sour cream, chives, mayonnaise, wine, buttermilk, blue cheese, Worcestershire, pepper, onion powder, vinegar, celery salt, garlic salt, onion, and Tabasco in large bowl.
- Place beef filets in single layer in two 9x13-inch pans and pour marinade over meat. Cover and marinate in refrigerator up to 72 hours.
- When ready to serve, prepare mushroom sauce. Melt butter in large skillet and sauté mushrooms, green onions, garlic, and parsley until tender.
- Remove filets from pans, keeping as much marinade on meat as possible. Place meat on grill over hot coals. Cook to desired doneness. Serve with mushroom sauce.

COMPANY BEEF STROGANOFF

Delicious and tender — an excellent company entrée.
Serve with peas and fresh orange salad.

Yield: 6 servings

2 tablespoons all-purpose flour
1 teaspoon salt
   Dash of black pepper
2 pounds round steak, cut into thin
   strips
½ stick (¼ cup) butter
2 onions, finely chopped
½ pound fresh button mushrooms,
   sliced

1 clove garlic
1 (14-ounce) can beef broth
1 tablespoon Worcestershire sauce
1 teaspoon paprika
   Salt and black pepper to taste
1 (8-ounce) package wide egg
   noodles
1 (16-ounce) container sour cream

- Combine flour, salt, and pepper in large Ziploc bag. Add meat and shake to coat.
- Melt butter in medium saucepan and sauté onions, mushrooms, and garlic until tender.
- Add meat and brown lightly. Add broth and cover. Simmer meat until tender (about 2 hours).
- Add Worcestershire and paprika. Season with salt and pepper. Add a little water during cooking, if needed, to keep meat tender.
- Just before serving, cook noodles according to package directions.
- While noodles are cooking, add sour cream to meat mixture. Blend well and cook over low heat (do not boil) another 5 minutes, stirring occasionally. Serve immediately or reheat in double boiler. Serve over hot noodles.

FRENCH DIP SANDWICHES

Teenage boys especially love these!

Yield: 12 sandwiches

1 (3½-4 pound) boneless chuck
   roast, trimmed
½ cup soy sauce
1 beef bouillon cube
1 bay leaf
3-4 peppercorns

1 teaspoon dried rosemary,
   crushed
1 teaspoon dried thyme
1 teaspoon garlic powder
12 French rolls, split

- Place trimmed roast in 5-quart electric slow cooker.
- Stir together soy sauce, bouillon cube, bay leaf, peppercorns, rosemary, thyme, and garlic powder; pour over roast.
- Add water to pot until roast is almost covered.
- Cover and cook on low heat for 7 hours or until tender.
- Remove roast, reserving broth. Shred roast with fork and serve in French rolls with hot broth for dipping.

GRANDMOMMY'S MAZETTI

*This was a family favorite growing up — and
now the grandchildren love it! Doubles easily.*

Yield: 8-10 servings

1   (8-ounce) package wide egg
    noodles
1¼ pounds ground beef
¼   pound ground pork
1   stalk celery, chopped
1   medium bell pepper, seeded and
    chopped

1   medium onion, chopped
1   (10¾-ounce) can condensed
    tomato soup
1   (10¾-ounce) can condensed cream
    of mushroom soup
1   can mushrooms, drained
4   ounces Cheddar cheese, shredded

- Preheat oven to 350°. Spray 9x13-inch baking dish with nonstick spray.
- Cook noodles according to package directions.
- While noodles are cooking, brown ground beef, ground pork, celery, bell pepper, and onion in large skillet.
- Drain noodles and return to cooking pot. Add meat mixture, tomato soup, mushroom soup, and mushrooms. Mix well.
- Pour into prepared dish and top with shredded cheese. Bake, uncovered, at 350° for 30 minutes.

CASSEROLE À LA NINI

Perfect when you need to take a casserole to someone and feed
your own family, too. And it only dirties up one big pot!

Yield: 12-16 servings

2 pounds ground beef
2 onions, chopped
1 (15-ounce) can kidney beans, undrained
1 (14¾-ounce) can creamed corn, undrained
1 (14½-ounce) can diced tomatoes, undrained

½ cup uncooked rice
1½ teaspoons salt
½ teaspoon chili powder
¼ teaspoon garlic powder
½ teaspoon oregano
1 teaspoon sugar

- Preheat oven to 325°. Spray one large or two smaller casserole dishes with nonstick spray.
- In large saucepan or stockpot, cook ground beef and onions until meat is grainy and onions are tender. Drain well and return to pot.
- Add kidney beans, creamed corn, and tomatoes, along with all liquids.
- Add uncooked rice, salt, chili powder, garlic powder, oregano, and sugar. Mix very well. Adjust seasonings if necessary.
- Pour into prepared dishes, cover, and bake at 325° for 2 hours. If all liquid is not absorbed after baking, stir well and return to oven uncovered for about 10 minutes.

ENTICING ENCHILADAS

Serve these with a dollop of sour cream or guacamole, if desired.

Yield: 4-6 servings

1 pound ground chuck
1 small onion, chopped
1 cup cream-style cottage cheese
1 (10-ounce) can Rotel tomatoes and green chiles
1 (8-ounce) can tomato sauce
1 (4½-ounce) can chopped green chiles (optional)
10 (6-inch) flour tortillas
2 cups shredded Mexican cheese blend
Chopped fresh parsley for garnish

- Preheat oven to 350°. Spray 9x13-inch baking dish with nonstick spray.
- Cook ground chuck and onion in large skillet over high heat, stirring, until meat crumbles and is no longer pink. Drain well.
- Return meat to skillet, stir in cottage cheese, and set aside.
- Process tomatoes and tomato sauce in food processor until smooth, stopping to scrape down sides. Stir in chopped chiles, if using.
- Spoon 2 to 3 tablespoons ground beef mixture down the center of each tortilla. Top with 2 tablespoons tomato mixture and 1½ tablespoons cheese.
- Roll up tortillas and place, seam side down, in prepared dish. Pour remaining tomato mixture over top and sprinkle with remaining cheese.
- Bake at 350° for 20 minutes or until bubbly. Garnish with fresh parsley, if desired.

CORNBREAD CASSEROLE

Yield: 4 servings

1 pound ground beef
¾ teaspoon salt
1 teaspoon chili powder
1 tablespoon Worcestershire sauce
1 (14½-ounce) can diced tomatoes, drained

1 (16-ounce) can black beans, drained and rinsed
¾ cup shredded sharp Cheddar cheese
1 (8½-ounce) package cornbread mix plus ingredients to prepare cornbread

- Preheat oven to 400°. Spray 9x9-inch baking dish with nonstick spray.
- Brown beef in large skillet, drain, and return to skillet.
- Add salt, chili powder, Worcestershire, and tomatoes. Cover and simmer for 10 minutes.
- Stir in beans and cheese. Pour into prepared dish.
- Prepare cornbread according to package directions. Spread cornbread batter over beef mixture in dish.
- Bake at 400° for 20 minutes.

TACO CHEESECAKE

Yield: 8 servings

1 cup crushed tortilla chips
1 tablespoon butter or margarine, melted
1 pound ground round
1 packet taco seasoning, divided
2 tablespoons water
2 (8-ounce) packages cream cheese, softened
2 large eggs

2 cups (8 ounces) shredded sharp Cheddar cheese
1 (8-ounce) container sour cream
2 tablespoons all-purpose flour
Shredded lettuce
Chopped tomatoes
1 (3.8-ounce) can sliced black olives, drained

- Preheat oven to 325°. Spray 9-inch springform pan with nonstick spray.
- Combine crushed tortilla chips and melted butter. Press mixture into bottom of pan. Bake at 325° for 10 minutes, then cool on wire rack.
- While crust is baking, cook beef in skillet over medium heat until it crumbles and is no longer pink. Drain and return to skillet.
- Reserve 1 teaspoon taco seasoning. Stir remaining taco seasoning and 2 tablespoons water into beef. Cook over medium heat for 5 minutes or until liquid evaporates.
- With electric mixer, beat cream cheese at medium speed until fluffy.
- Add eggs and reserved teaspoon taco seasoning; beat until blended.
- Add Cheddar cheese and mix well.
- Spread cream cheese mixture evenly over cooled crust and up sides of pan.
- Spoon beef mixture over cream cheese mixture.
- Combine sour cream and flour. Spread over beef mixture.
- Bake at 325° for 25 minutes.
- Cool pan on wire rack for 10 minutes, then run knife around edges and release sides. Sprinkle with lettuce, tomatoes, and olives. Slice and serve.

BEEF & PORK BARBECUE

*This recipe also makes great "All-Pork Barbecue"
using 4 to 6 pork tenderloins and no beef.*

Yield: 16 servings

1 (3-pound) beef rump roast
2 pork tenderloins
1 envelope dry onion soup mix

2 cups water
2 (12-ounce) bottles barbecue sauce
Dash of salt

- Preheat oven to 425°.
- Trim away all visible fat from meat and place in large stockpot.
- Pour soup mix over meat and add water.
- Cover and bake at 425° for 30 minutes, then lower oven temperature to 325°. Cook for 4 hours, turning occasionally.
- When meat is tender, remove from pot and cool, discarding liquid.
- Chop or shred meat (see sidebar on page 49 for shredding instructions) and place back in pot. Pour 1 bottle of sauce over meat and sprinkle with salt. Return to oven to heat.
- Heat remaining bottle of sauce to add to sandwiches if needed. Serve on buns or dinner rolls.

SLOW COOKER BARBECUE

Tastes like the real thing, with almost no effort!

Yield: 12 servings

1 (3-pound) boneless pork loin
   roast, trimmed
1 cup water
1 (18-ounce) bottle barbecue sauce
¼ cup brown sugar

2 tablespoons Worcestershire sauce
½-1 teaspoon Tabasco sauce
1 teaspoon salt
½-1 teaspoon black pepper
   Hamburger buns

- Place roast in 4-quart electric slow cooker and add water.
- Cover and cook on high for 7 hours.
- Drain water and shred meat with fork. Return meat to cooker.
- Add barbecue sauce, brown sugar, Worcestershire, Tabasco, salt, and pepper.
- Stir well, cover, and cook on low for 1 hour.
- Serve on hamburger buns with coleslaw on the side.

Leave that lid on while the electric slow cooker cooks! After each peek, it takes 15 to 20 minutes for the cooker to regain lost steam and return to the right temperature.

BLACK BEANS & PORK OVER RICE

*Great recipe for leftover pork, but also makes a tasty
(and healthy) vegetarian meal if you leave out the meat.*

Yield: 4 servings

1 teaspoon ground cumin
½ teaspoon ground coriander
¼ teaspoon chili powder
½ pound diced cooked pork roast
⅓ cup orange juice
2 tablespoons vegetable oil
1 medium onion, chopped
1 cup chopped red bell pepper
2 cloves garlic, minced

1 (16-ounce) can black beans, rinsed
  and drained
1 medium tomato, peeled, seeded,
  and chopped
2 tablespoons chopped green chiles
¼ teaspoon salt
⅛ teaspoon black pepper
3 cups cooked rice
  Cilantro sprigs for garnish
  (optional)

- Combine cumin, coriander, and chili powder. Toss pork in spice mixture to coat.
- Heat large skillet over medium-high heat until hot; add pork. Cook, stirring constantly, 2 minutes or until thoroughly heated.
- Remove pork from skillet and place in medium bowl. Add orange juice, stirring well. Set aside.
- Heat oil in same skillet and sauté onion, bell pepper, and garlic until vegetables are tender. Stir in reserved pork mixture, beans, tomato, chiles, salt, and pepper.
- Cook, stirring occasionally, until thoroughly heated.
- Serve over rice. Garnish with cilantro, if desired.

PROVENÇAL PORK ROAST

Yield: 10-12 servings

6 cloves garlic, divided	2 teaspoons herbes de Provence
3-4 pounds boneless double pork loin roast, rolled and tied	½ teaspoon salt
	½ teaspoon black pepper
2 teaspoons olive oil	1 cup chicken broth
2 teaspoons tomato paste	1 tablespoon all-purpose flour

- Preheat oven to 400°.
- Cut 4 garlic cloves in half lengthwise. Cut 8 small slits in pork and insert garlic.
- Mince remaining garlic and combine with olive oil, tomato paste, herbes de Provence, salt, and pepper.
- Rub mixture over pork and place on rack in roasting pan. Roast at 400° for 30 minutes, then reduce heat to 350° and cook 30 minutes more.
- Add broth; cook another 30 minutes or until internal temperature reaches 155°. Remove pork from rack and let rest 15 minutes before slicing, reserving juices.
- Pour pan juices into saucepan. Set pan over medium heat and whisk in flour. Bring to boil, reduce heat, and simmer, whisking for 5 minutes or until gravy is thickened. Serve over sliced pork.

Herbes de Provence is a blend of dried herbs commonly used in southern France. The blend can be found packed in tiny clay crocks in the spice sections of large supermarkets. It generally contains basil, fennel seed, lavender, marjoram, rosemary, sage, summer savory, and thyme. Herbes de Provence may be used to season meat, poultry, or vegetables.

PORK CHOPS IN
HONEY MUSTARD SAUCE
Yield: 4 servings

4 (6-ounce) bone-in, center cut pork
    chops, trimmed, about ¾-inch
    thick
¼ teaspoon salt
⅛ teaspoon black pepper

2   teaspoons olive oil
1½ cups dry white wine
⅓   cup honey
¼   cup Dijon mustard

- Sprinkle both sides of pork chops with salt and pepper.
- Heat oil in large nonstick skillet over medium-high heat.
- Add chops and cook for 5 minutes on each side until browned. Remove pork from pan.
- Add wine, honey, and mustard to skillet, bring to boil, and cook 3 minutes.
- Add chops, reduce heat, and simmer for 12 minutes, turning chops after 6 minutes.
- Serve immediately.

GRILLED PORK TENDERLOIN
WITH CHILI MAPLE GLAZE
Yield: 4 servings

1½ tablespoons sea salt
2   cups water
2   pork tenderloins
    (about 1½ pounds total)

1½ tablespoons pure maple syrup
1   tablespoon chili powder

- Dissolve sea salt in water. Pour over pork tenderloins, cover, and marinate pork in brine for 24 hours in refrigerator.
- When ready to cook, preheat grill on high.
- Stir together syrup and chili powder until blended.
- Remove pork from brine, discarding brine. Brush chili maple glaze on all sides of meat.
- Grill pork about 15 to 25 minutes or until internal temperature reaches 160°.

MARINADE FOR GRILLED PORK OR CHICKEN

One tester called this her family's new favorite marinade.

Yield: enough for 3 pounds of meat

6 green onions, finely chopped
5 large cloves garlic, crushed
½ cup dark soy sauce
2 tablespoons vegetable oil
2 tablespoons brown sugar

2 tablespoons Mount Gay rum or
   dry sherry
2 tablespoons sesame seeds, toasted
   Freshly ground black pepper
3 pounds pork tenderloins or
   chicken breasts

- Whisk together green onions, garlic, soy sauce, oil, brown sugar, rum or sherry, sesame seeds, and pepper.
- Place meat in large Ziploc bag and pour marinade over meat. Seal bag and shake gently.
- Marinate in refrigerator at least 1 hour (preferably 3 or 4 hours). Turn bag over several times during marinating.
- Remove meat from marinade and grill or cook as desired.

Soak garlic cloves in cold water for a few minutes and the skins will slip off more easily.

MARINADE FOR PORK TENDERLOIN

One more great marinade!

Yield: enough for 2 pork tenderloins

¼ cup bourbon
¼ cup soy sauce
¼ cup brown sugar
3 cloves garlic, minced
¼ cup Dijon mustard

½ teaspoon salt
1 teaspoon Worcestershire sauce
¼ cup vegetable oil
2 pork tenderloins

- Whisk together bourbon, soy sauce, brown sugar, garlic, mustard, salt, Worcestershire, and oil.
- Pour marinade over pork tenderloins in large Ziploc bag, seal, and marinate in refrigerator 6 to 8 hours or overnight.
- Grill marinated pork to desired doneness (15 to 30 minutes depending on thickness of meat).

GRILLED LAMB

Yield: 6-8 servings

1 cup dry red wine
¾ cup soy sauce
4 large cloves garlic, minced
1 tablespoon dried mint leaves

1 tablespoon dried rosemary
1 tablespoon black pepper
1 (4-5 pound) butterflied leg of lamb

- Whisk together wine, soy sauce, garlic, mint, rosemary, and pepper.
- Pour marinade over lamb, cover, and refrigerate for 24 hours, turning once.
- Grill 30 minutes for rare meat or until meat registers desired temperature (140° for rare, 160° for medium, and 170° to 180° for well done).

SPRING LAMB WITH FRESH MINT VINAIGRETTE
Yield: 6-8 servings

¼ cup chopped fresh mint leaves
¼ cup chopped fresh basil leaves
¼ cup chopped green onions
2 tablespoons balsamic vinegar
1 tablespoon olive oil
1 teaspoon salt

Freshly ground black pepper, to taste
1 leg of lamb (about 7 pounds), trimmed of excess fat
1 cup Fresh Mint Vinaigrette (recipe follows)

- In small bowl, whisk together mint, basil, green onions, vinegar, oil, salt, and pepper.
- Rub mixture over lamb. Cover lamb and refrigerate overnight.
- When ready to cook, preheat oven to 450°.
- Place lamb on rack in roasting pan and roast at 450° for 20 minutes.
- Reduce heat to 350° and roast another 1¼ hours for medium-rare.
- Transfer lamb to serving platter, cover loosely with aluminum foil, and let rest for 15 minutes. Slice lamb thinly and serve with Fresh Mint Vinaigrette.

Fresh Mint Vinaigrette
⅔ cup olive oil
¼ cup white wine vinegar
2 teaspoons whole-grain mustard
1 teaspoon salt

Freshly ground black pepper to taste
½ teaspoon sugar
⅓ cup chopped fresh mint leaves
2 ripe plum tomatoes, finely diced

- Whisk together oil, vinegar, mustard, salt, pepper, and sugar in small bowl until smooth.
- Stir in mint and tomatoes.
- Serve immediately, or cover and refrigerate for up to 1 hour.

LAMB CHOPS WITH MINT BUTTER
Yield: 4 servings

2 tablespoons chopped fresh mint leaves (or 1 tablespoon dried)

5 tablespoons unsalted butter, softened

¼ teaspoon salt

Freshly ground black pepper to taste

1 teaspoon lemon juice

4-6 lamb chops

- In food processor or blender, process mint, butter, salt, pepper, and lemon juice until smooth.
- With sharp knife, score lamb chops on both sides. Coat chops with half of mint butter and let stand for 30 to 40 minutes at room temperature. Refrigerate remaining mint butter.
- Preheat broiler.
- Broil chops for 8 to 10 minutes, turning at least twice. (Cooking time depends on thickness of chops; time given is for chops about 1 inch thick and done to medium rare.)
- Spread remaining mint butter on top of chops and serve directly from broiler pan.

Cover the broiler pan with foil (punch holes through foil) for easier clean-up.

VERMOUTHY VEAL

Great company dish served with barley, noodles, or rice.

Yield: 6 servings

3-4 tablespoons all-purpose flour
2 pounds very thin veal slices or cutlets
5 tablespoons butter
1 clove garlic, minced

1 small onion, chopped
1 small red bell pepper, chopped
½ pound mushrooms, chopped
1 tablespoon lemon juice
½ cup dry vermouth

- Lightly flour veal. Melt butter in large skillet and brown veal.
- Add garlic, onions, bell peppers, and mushrooms to veal in skillet. Sprinkle with lemon juice. Add vermouth. Can be made in advance to this point and refrigerated.
- Cover and simmer over low heat for 25 minutes or until veal is tender.

May substitute turkey or chicken cutlets for veal.

When buying veal, look for a creamy-white to pale pink color. This indicates a younger calf and therefore a more tender cut of meat.

BOURBON CHICKEN WITH PEACHES

You'll have to call it something else, but this dish is also delicious without the peaches!

Yield: 4 servings

4 bone-in chicken breast halves
½ teaspoon salt
¼ teaspoon black pepper
2 tablespoons butter
1 large onion, diced
1 teaspoon paprika

1½ cups chopped green onions, divided
½ cup orange juice
2 tablespoons bourbon
1 cup sliced fresh peaches
Dash of ground nutmeg

- Preheat oven to 400°. Spray 9x13-inch baking dish with nonstick spray.
- Sprinkle chicken with salt and pepper and arrange in prepared dish.
- Melt butter in skillet over medium heat. Add onion and sauté for 5 minutes or until tender. Stir in paprika.
- Add green onions, reserving 1 tablespoon. Cook, stirring occasionally, for 4 minutes.
- Spread onion mixture evenly over chicken. Drizzle with orange juice and bourbon.
- Bake, uncovered, for 50 minutes, turning occasionally and basting with pan drippings.
- Top with sliced peaches and sprinkle with nutmeg. Bake 15 more minutes or until chicken is done.
- Transfer to serving platter, drizzle with pan drippings, and sprinkle with reserved green onions.

RASPBERRY-BALSAMIC GLAZED CHICKEN

Yield: 4 servings

1 teaspoon vegetable oil	½ teaspoon salt, divided
½ cup chopped red onion	⅓ cup seedless raspberry preserves
4 boneless, skinless chicken breast halves	2 tablespoons balsamic vinegar
1½ teaspoons minced fresh thyme (or ½ teaspoon dried)	¼ teaspoon black pepper

- Heat oil in large nonstick skillet coated with cooking spray over medium-high heat. Add onion and sauté 5 minutes.
- Rinse chicken breasts and pat dry. If thick, pound between sheets of plastic wrap to even thinness. Sprinkle chicken with thyme and ¼ teaspoon salt. Add to skillet and sauté 6 minutes on each side or until cooked through. Remove chicken from skillet and keep warm.
- Reduce heat to medium-low. Add preserves, vinegar, remaining ¼ teaspoon salt, and pepper. Whisk constantly until preserves melt.
- Place chicken on serving platter and spoon raspberry sauce over chicken.

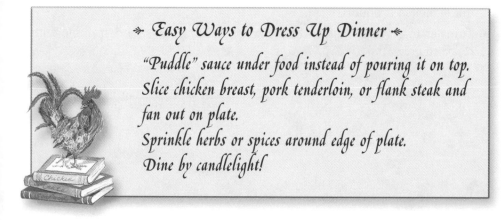

❖ Easy Ways to Dress Up Dinner ❖

"Puddle" sauce under food instead of pouring it on top.
Slice chicken breast, pork tenderloin, or flank steak and fan out on plate.
Sprinkle herbs or spices around edge of plate.
Dine by candlelight!

116

LEMON GARLIC CHICKEN

An easy dinner with angel hair pasta or couscous and a green salad.

Yield: 10 servings

4 cloves garlic, minced
2 tablespoons olive oil
3-4 pounds boneless, skinless
    chicken breast halves
3 eggs, beaten
1½ cups Italian-seasoned dry
    breadcrumbs

Juice of 1 lemon
1 cup chicken broth
½ cup white wine
1 lemon, thinly sliced
¼ cup (or slightly more) grated
    Parmesan cheese
Salt and black pepper to taste

- Preheat oven to 350°. Spray 9x13-inch baking dish with nonstick spray.
- Sauté garlic in olive oil just until tender. Remove garlic from oil in skillet and reserve.
- Dip chicken in egg and dredge in breadcrumbs. If you have time, follow the sidebar instructions below!
- Brown chicken on both sides in same skillet, adding more olive oil if necessary. Drain on paper towels.
- Place chicken and reserved garlic in prepared dish and sprinkle with lemon juice.
- Add chicken broth and wine, top with lemon slices, and sprinkle with Parmesan cheese. Season with salt and pepper.
- Cover and bake at 350° for 50 to 60 minutes, uncovering for last 10 minutes to brown.

Keep the crumbs: After coating chicken with any breadcrumb mixture, chill it for an hour before cooking. The coating will adhere better.

ORANGE-BASIL CHICKEN
Yield: 4 servings

1 teaspoon olive oil
4 (4-ounce) skinless, boneless
   chicken breast halves
1 cup unsweetened orange juice
1 tablespoon chopped fresh basil
¼ teaspoon salt

¼ teaspoon freshly ground black
   pepper
1 clove garlic, minced
2 teaspoons cornstarch
1 tablespoon water

- Coat large nonstick skillet with nonstick spray; add oil. Place over medium heat until hot. Add chicken; cook 2 minutes on each side or until browned.
- Add orange juice, basil, salt, pepper, and garlic; bring to boil. Reduce heat, cover, and simmer 15 minutes or until chicken is cooked through and tender.
- Remove chicken from skillet using slotted spoon. Set aside and keep warm.
- Bring orange juice mixture in skillet to boil. Reduce heat and simmer, uncovered, 10 minutes or until mixture reduces to about ¾ cup. In small cup, combine cornstarch and water, stirring well. Add to juice mixture and cook over medium heat, stirring constantly, until mixture thickens.
- Place warm chicken on serving platter and spoon sauce over chicken.

PARMESAN CHICKEN WITH BALSAMIC BUTTER SAUCE

This dish rated a "Fabulous!" from our tester.

Yield: 4 servings

1 chicken, cut up, or 4 large
  boneless, skinless chicken breast
  halves
¼ cup extra-virgin olive oil
¼ cup freshly grated Parmesan
  cheese
2 tablespoons minced fresh oregano

2 cloves garlic, minced
  Salt and freshly ground black
  pepper to taste
1 cup chicken stock or canned low-
  sodium broth
½ cup balsamic vinegar
2 tablespoons cold unsalted butter

- Preheat oven to 400°. Spray large rimmed baking sheet with nonstick spray.
- In large bowl, toss chicken with olive oil, Parmesan, oregano, and garlic.
- Arrange chicken on prepared pan and season with salt and pepper. Bake at 400° for about 45 minutes or until lightly browned and cooked through.
- While chicken is baking, stir together chicken stock and vinegar in small saucepan. Boil over high heat until reduced to ⅓ cup, about 10 minutes. Remove from heat and whisk in butter, 1 tablespoon at a time, until smooth. Season with salt and pepper.
- Transfer chicken to serving plates and spoon sauce on top to serve.

CHICKEN BREASTS STUFFED WITH MOZZARELLA & CANADIAN BACON

Quick and easy with wonderful flavor.

Yield: 4 servings

1 ounce whole-milk mozzarella cheese, diced
1 ounce Canadian bacon, diced
½ teaspoon dried basil, crumbled
4 large skinless, boneless chicken breast halves
  Flour seasoned with salt and black pepper for dredging
1 large egg, lightly beaten

1 cup fine fresh bread crumbs
½ tablespoon olive oil
1½ tablespoons unsalted butter
1 tablespoon green onion, thinly sliced (use green part)
1 tablespoon chopped fresh parsley
1 teaspoon fresh lemon juice
  Salt and black pepper to taste

- Toss together mozzarella, bacon, and basil in small bowl.
- Place chicken breasts between sheets of dampened wax paper or plastic wrap and pound to ⅜ inch thick.
- Spoon cheese mixture onto one side of each chicken breast and fold breast over filling. Press edges together and secure with toothpicks.
- Dredge chicken in seasoned flour, shaking off excess.
- Dip floured chicken breasts in beaten egg, coating well, then roll in bread crumbs, patting crumbs to adhere.
- In heavy skillet, heat oil over moderate heat until hot but not smoking. Add chicken and cook for 10 to 12 minutes, turning once, until juices run clear when chicken is pierced with fork. Add more oil if necessary. Remove chicken to heated platter and keep warm.
- Wipe skillet with paper towel, then melt butter and add green onions to skillet. Cook, stirring, for about 1 minute.
- Add parsley, lemon juice, salt, and pepper to skillet and stir to make sauce. Pour sauce over chicken and serve.

QUICK & COLORFUL CUTLETS

Yield: 4 servings

¼ cup chicken broth

3 tablespoons balsamic vinegar

2 teaspoons honey

2 teaspoons olive oil

2 cloves garlic, minced

1 pound thin chicken or turkey cutlets

Salt and black pepper to taste

1 red bell pepper, seeded and cut into strips

1 green bell pepper, seeded and cut into strips

4 cups hot cooked rice

- Combine broth, vinegar, and honey; set aside.
- Heat oil in large nonstick skillet over high heat. Add garlic, reduce heat slightly, and sauté 30 seconds.
- Add cutlets and sauté on both sides until done, about 3 to 4 minutes per side.
- Sprinkle with salt and pepper and remove cutlets to warm platter.
- Reduce heat to medium, add bell peppers to skillet, and sauté 2 minutes.
- Add chicken broth mixture and cook 30 seconds, stirring constantly.
- Return cutlets to skillet to reheat and blend briefly. Serve over rice.

When keeping cooked rice warm, place a double layer of paper towels under the lid so that steam will be absorbed by the towels and not condense, which would make the rice sticky.

CREAMY ALMOND CHICKEN

For all those lucky folks with low cholesterol, here's your chance to indulge!

Yield: 6 servings

⅔ cup sliced almonds
3 tablespoons butter, divided
6 skinless, boneless chicken breast
    halves
⅛ teaspoon salt

⅛ teaspoon black pepper
1½ cups heavy cream
1 tablespoon Dijon mustard
2 tablespoons orange marmalade
    Hot cooked rice

- Sauté almonds in 1 tablespoon butter. Set aside.
- Flatten chicken breasts to ¼-inch thickness. Sprinkle with salt and pepper.
- Melt 1 tablespoon butter in large skillet over medium-high heat. Add half of chicken and cook about 1 minute on each side or until golden brown. Remove from skillet, add remaining butter, and brown remaining chicken. Remove chicken from skillet and keep warm.
- Reduce heat to medium and stir in ½ cup almonds (reserving remainder for garnish), cream, mustard, and marmalade, mixing well.
- Cook about 15 minutes or until sauce thickens, stirring frequently.
- Sprinkle with remaining almonds. Serve chicken over rice with sauce.

SWEET & SPICY GRILLED CHICKEN

Yield: 4-6 servings

½ cup brown sugar
⅓ cup olive oil
¼ cup cider vinegar
3 cloves garlic, crushed
3 tablespoons coarse mustard
1½ tablespoons lemon juice

1½ tablespoons lime juice
1½ teaspoons salt
¼ teaspoon black pepper
6 boneless, skinless chicken breast
    halves

- Whisk together brown sugar, oil, vinegar, garlic, mustard, lemon juice, lime juice, salt, and pepper.
- Place chicken in large Ziploc bag and pour marinade over chicken. Marinate chicken in refrigerator for at least 8 hours (longer is even better), turning bag to coat chicken thoroughly.
- Remove from refrigerator and let stand at room temperature for 1 hour.
- Grill chicken until done.

CHICKEN-CHUTNEY CROISSANTS

A nice luncheon dish.

Yield: 6 servings

1 (8-ounce) container whipped
    cream cheese
3 tablespoons commercial chutney,
    chopped
1½ teaspoons curry powder

3 cups chopped, cooked chicken
    breasts
    Green leaf lettuce
6 large croissants, split
    Chopped peanuts, grated coconut,
    and/or raisins (optional)

- Combine cream cheese, chutney, and curry powder, stirring until blended.
- Add chicken and mix well.
- Place lettuce on bottom half of each croissant, spread with chicken mixture, and replace top half of croissant.
- May add chopped peanuts, grated coconut, and/or raisins to chicken mixture, or sprinkle over chicken before replacing croissant top.

UNCLE CHARLIE'S
GRILLED BARBECUE CHICKEN

When you taste this, you'll wish you had an Uncle Charlie!

Yield: 4 servings

1 cup white vinegar	2 tablespoons prepared mustard
¼ cup olive oil	2 tablespoons lemon zest
2 teaspoons chili powder	Juice of 2 lemons
1 teaspoon Tabasco sauce	2 tablespoons salt
1 teaspoon black pepper	2 tablespoons sugar
2 tablespoons Worcestershire sauce	1 chicken, cut up
2 cloves garlic, minced	

- Stir together vinegar, olive oil, chili powder, Tabasco, pepper, Worcestershire, garlic, mustard, lemon zest, lemon juice, salt, and sugar in saucepan. Bring to boil, reduce heat, and simmer for 15 minutes. Cool.
- Reserve 1 cup of sauce. Marinate chicken in remaining sauce for 4 to 6 hours.
- Grill chicken over medium-high heat, using reserved sauce for basting.

To extract the most juice from lemons and limes, make sure they are at room temperature (may warm slightly in microwave or boiling water if they are cold) and roll them under your palm on a countertop, pressing firmly, before squeezing.

CHICKEN SPECTACULAR

*The original and still the best. Freezes well before
baking, and doubles easily for entertaining.*

Yield: 12 servings

3 cups cooked chicken
1 package Uncle Ben's Wild and
   White Rice, cooked
1 medium onion, chopped
1 (10-ounce) box frozen French-
   style green beans, cooked and
   drained

1 (8-ounce) can water chestnuts,
   drained and diced
1 (2-ounce) jar sliced pimentos
1 (10¾-ounce) can condensed cream
   of celery soup
1 cup mayonnaise
   Salt and black pepper to taste
   Paprika

- Preheat oven to 350°. Spray 9x13-inch baking dish with nonstick spray.
- In large bowl, toss together chicken, cooked rice, onion, beans, water chestnuts, and pimentos.
- In small bowl, whisk together soup, mayonnaise, salt, and pepper.
- Pour soup mixture over chicken mixture and mix thoroughly.
- Pour into prepared dish, sprinkle with paprika, and bake, uncovered, at 350° for 30 minutes.

There are more chickens in the world than people!

THREE-CHEESE CHICKEN PASTA
Yield: 8 servings

6 boneless chicken breast halves
1 carrot, cut into chunks
1 stalk celery, cut into chunks
1 onion, cut into chunks
4 cups chicken broth (reserved from cooking chicken)
1 (8-ounce) package wide egg noodles
1 stick (½ cup) butter
½ cup all-purpose flour
1¼ teaspoons salt

½ teaspoon black pepper
1 (24-ounce) container low-fat small curd cottage cheese
1 large egg
1 tablespoon chopped fresh basil (or 1 teaspoon dried)
2 cups shredded mozzarella cheese
¾ cup grated Parmesan cheese
1 teaspoon paprika
½ cup chopped fresh parsley

- Simmer chicken breasts in water to cover for 30 minutes with carrot, celery, and onion. Remove chicken, reserving broth. Cool chicken and cut into bite-size pieces. Strain broth and return to pot.
- Cook noodles in boiling chicken broth. Drain noodles, reserving broth. Set aside.
- Melt butter in another saucepan. Whisk in flour, salt, pepper, and 4 cups reserved chicken broth. Bring to boil. Reduce heat and simmer 5 minutes.
- Stir chicken into broth mixture.
- In bowl, mix cottage cheese, egg, and basil.
- Preheat oven to 350°. Spray 9x13-inch baking dish with nonstick spray.
- Spread half of noodles in bottom of dish. Top with half of cottage cheese mixture, half of mozzarella, and half of chicken mixture.
- Repeat layers and sprinkle top with Parmesan cheese, paprika, and parsley.
- Bake, uncovered, at 350° for 30 minutes or until bubbly.

CREOLE CHICKEN PASTA

Yield: 4-6 servings

1 pound skinless, boneless chicken breasts, cut into ½-inch strips
1 tablespoon Creole seasoning
1 cup chopped red bell pepper
1 cup chopped green bell pepper
1 cup sliced mushrooms
¼ cup sliced green onions
4 cups hot, cooked linguine (8 ounces uncooked)
2 cups fat-free evaporated milk
¼ cup (1 ounce) freshly grated Parmesan cheese
½ teaspoon dried basil
¼ teaspoon salt

- Place chicken and Creole seasoning in large Ziploc bag, seal, and shake to coat.
- Heat large nonstick skillet coated with nonstick spray over medium heat. Add chicken and sauté about 7 minutes or until lightly browned.
- Add red and green bell peppers, mushrooms, and onions; cook 3 minutes.
- Stir in pasta, milk, Parmesan, basil, and salt; bring to boil. Cook 1 minute, stirring constantly.
- Serve immediately.

For easier cutting of raw chicken or other meat, put the meat in the freezer for about 20 minutes. The meat will firm up but not freeze, making it easier to slice, cube, or trim. If using frozen meat, cut it before it has thawed completely.

POPPY SEED CHICKEN

Every once in a while, you just need some comfort food.

Yield: 4 servings

1 cup uncooked rice

½ stick (¼ cup) margarine

4 boneless, skinless chicken breast halves, cooked and shredded

1 small yellow onion, chopped

1 stalk celery, sliced

½ cup chicken broth

1 (10¾-ounce) can condensed cream of chicken soup

1 (10¾-ounce) can condensed cream of celery soup

1 (8-ounce) container sour cream

⅓ cup slivered almonds (optional)

2 tablespoons poppy seeds

Ritz crackers

- Preheat oven to 350°. Spray 9x13-inch baking dish with nonstick spray.
- Cook rice according to package directions.
- While rice is cooking, melt margarine in skillet and sauté chicken with chopped onion and celery. When vegetables are tender, add broth and continue cooking over low heat.
- In bowl, stir together both soups, sour cream, almonds if using, and poppy seeds.
- Mix soup mixture and chicken mixture together.
- Pour into prepared dish and sprinkle crumbled Ritz crackers over top.
- Bake, uncovered, at 350° for 15 to 20 minutes or until bubbly.

INCREDULADA ENCHILADAS

Sounds like a lot of onions, but they cook down and add great flavor. Use Vidalias or your family's favorite.

Yield: 6 servings

3   tablespoons butter
3   medium onions, thinly sliced
2½ cups shredded, cooked chicken
¾   cup canned diced green chiles, drained
2   (3-ounce) packages cream cheese, diced

12 (6-inch) tortillas
1   cup heavy cream
3   cups shredded Monterey Jack cheese
Salsa

- Preheat oven to 350°. Spray 9x13-inch glass baking dish with nonstick spray.
- Melt butter in large skillet and sauté onions for 15 minutes or until transparent.
- Remove from heat and stir in chicken, chiles, and cream cheese.
- Spoon mixture into tortillas. Roll and place seam side down in prepared dish.
- Pour cream over enchiladas. Cover with cheese and bake, uncovered, at 350° for 35 minutes or until cream thickens and cheese bubbles.
- Serve with salsa. Spoon some salsa over enchiladas before serving for a more colorful presentation.

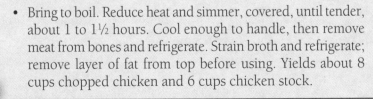

Stovetop Cooked Chicken for Recipes

Place the following ingredients in a large stockpot:

2 roasting chickens (about 4½ pounds each)
6 cups hot water

1 tablespoon salt
2 teaspoons onion salt
1 teaspoon celery salt

- Bring to boil. Reduce heat and simmer, covered, until tender, about 1 to 1½ hours. Cool enough to handle, then remove meat from bones and refrigerate. Strain broth and refrigerate; remove layer of fat from top before using. Yields about 8 cups chopped chicken and 6 cups chicken stock.

GOURMET QUESADILLAS

May be assembled ahead of time and then baked when you're ready to serve, so this makes a good "company" meal — but kids love it too!

Yield: 6-8 servings

6 small boneless, skinless chicken breast halves
3 tablespoons olive oil, divided
1 packet taco seasoning, divided
1 red bell pepper, sliced into julienne strips
1 yellow bell pepper, sliced into julienne strips
1 red onion, thinly sliced
1 teaspoon minced garlic (or more to taste)

2 tablespoons capers
1 (8-ounce) package cream cheese, softened
1 (8-ounce) package shredded cheese (Mexican mix, Cheddar, or your favorite)
12 flour tortillas
Fresh cilantro
Salsa
Sour cream

- Brush chicken breasts with 1 to 2 tablespoons olive oil and sprinkle with some of taco seasoning. Grill until cooked through and reserve.
- Preheat oven to 400°.
- Heat remaining oil in large skillet and sauté red and yellow bell peppers and onion for 8 to 10 minutes or until tender.
- Add garlic and capers; set aside.
- Stir together cream cheese, shredded cheese, and 1 tablespoon taco seasoning. Set aside.
- Cut chicken into thin strips.
- Place 6 tortillas on large rimmed baking sheet. Spread cream cheese mixture on each tortilla. Top with strips of chicken, then peppers and onions.
- Sprinkle with remaining taco seasoning and cilantro, and cover with remaining tortillas.
- Cover with foil and bake 10 to 15 minutes or until heated through.
- Serve with salsa and sour cream.

TORTILLA TORTA

Yield: 6 servings

1 (3½-4 pound) cooked chicken
   (a rotisserie chicken from the
   deli works great)
1 (16-ounce) container plain yogurt
1 cup heavy cream
1 (9-ounce) package corn tortillas

1 (16-ounce) jar tomatillo salsa
2 (4½-ounce) cans chopped chiles,
   drained
1 (8-ounce) package shredded
   Monterey Jack cheese

- Preheat oven to 375°. Spray 9-inch square or 10x7-inch baking dish with nonstick spray.
- Remove chicken meat from bones and chop coarsely.
- Whisk together yogurt and cream in bowl.
- Arrange one-third of tortillas in prepared dish and top with half of salsa, half of chicken, half of yogurt mixture, half of chiles, and one-third of cheese.
- Cover with another third of tortillas, remaining salsa, chicken, yogurt mixture, and chiles, and another third of cheese.
- Cover with remaining tortillas and sprinkle with remaining cheese.
- Cover with foil and bake at 375° for 15 minutes. Remove foil and bake 10 to 20 minutes more or until bubbly. Let stand 10 minutes before serving.

CHICKEN LO MEIN

Other lightly steamed or sautéed vegetables may be added to this dish — try diagonally sliced carrots, snow peas, or water chestnuts.

Yield: 4 servings

4 skinless, boneless chicken breast halves, sliced into thin strips
5 teaspoons sugar, divided
3 tablespoons rice wine vinegar, divided
½ cup soy sauce, divided
2 cups chicken broth
1 tablespoon sesame oil
½ teaspoon black pepper
2 tablespoons cornstarch

2 tablespoons vegetable oil, divided
2 tablespoons minced fresh ginger
1 tablespoon minced garlic
½ pound shiitake mushrooms, whole, or white mushrooms, quartered
½ bunch green onions, sliced fine
8 ounces linguine, cooked according to package directions

- Toss chicken strips with half each of sugar, vinegar, and soy sauce in medium bowl. Set aside to marinate.
- Whisk together broth, sesame oil, pepper, and remaining sugar, vinegar, and soy sauce in another bowl.
- In small bowl, dissolve cornstarch in small amount of sauce. Whisk back into bowl of sauce. Reserve.
- Heat 1 tablespoon vegetable oil in wok or skillet. Remove chicken from marinade and stir-fry chicken until lightly browned.
- Transfer chicken and juices to warm plate and reserve.
- Heat remaining oil until hot. Add ginger, garlic, mushrooms, and green onions; stir-fry 30 seconds.
- Add sauce mixture and then chicken. Simmer 2 minutes to thicken.
- Add pasta and toss gently to combine. Let sit 15 minutes over low heat for pasta to absorb sauce before serving.

AINSLIE'S CHICKEN POT PIE

This pie may be made ahead and refrigerated or frozen before baking. It looks beautiful and is great comfort food to take to a friend in need!

Yield: 6 servings

3   tablespoons butter
1⅔ cups frozen peas and carrots or mixed vegetables
1-2 medium potatoes, peeled and cubed
¼   cup all-purpose flour
1¼ cups chicken broth
1   cup half-and-half

3   cups chopped, cooked chicken breasts
1½ teaspoons salt
¼   teaspoon poultry seasoning
⅛   teaspoon black pepper
1   refrigerated pie crust (from package of 2 folded crusts)

- Preheat oven to 350°. Lightly spray deep-dish pie pan with nonstick spray.
- Melt butter in large skillet. Add peas and carrots and potatoes. Cook for 10 minutes or until carrots are tender and potatoes begin to soften.
- Add flour, stirring until smooth. Gradually stir in chicken broth and half-and-half. Cook until thickened, stirring frequently.
- Remove from heat and stir in chicken, salt, poultry seasoning, and pepper.
- Pour into prepared pie pan.
- Unfold refrigerated pie crust, press out fold lines, and place over filling. Fold edges under and crimp. Cut slits in top.
- Place pie pan on baking sheet and bake at 350° for 45 minutes or until golden brown. May need to cover edges with foil at end of baking to prevent burning.

A rotisserie chicken from the supermarket yields a fast, nearly effortless 3 cups of chopped chicken.

MEXICAN CHICKEN & RICE

If you prefer a spicier dish, use a hotter flavor of Rotel tomatoes.

Yield: 6-8 servings

1 box Rice-a-Roni Spanish Rice mix
1 (10-ounce) can Rotel diced tomatoes and chiles, mild flavor, drained
2 (15-ounce) cans black beans, drained

1 (8-ounce) carton sour cream
3 cups chopped, cooked chicken breast
2 cups shredded Cheddar cheese, divided
1½ cups crushed tortilla chips

- Preheat oven to 350°. Spray 9x13-inch baking dish with nonstick spray.
- Prepare Rice-a-Roni according to package directions, stirring in Rotel tomatoes while cooking.
- Add beans, sour cream, chicken, and 1½ cups cheese to hot rice and mix well.
- Spoon mixture into prepared dish and top with remaining cheese and crushed tortilla chips.
- Bake at 350° for 20 to 30 minutes.

CITRUS MARINATED TURKEY BREAST

Yield: 1 turkey breast

1 cup orange juice
¼ cup lime juice
¼ cup olive oil
2 teaspoons dried oregano

2 teaspoons salt
1 teaspoon black pepper
1 (6-7 pound) turkey breast (thawed if frozen)

- Whisk together orange juice, lime juice, olive oil, oregano, salt, and pepper.
- Place turkey in large Ziploc bag and pour in marinade.
- Refrigerate for 8 hours, turning bag occasionally.
- Preheat oven to 325°.
- Place turkey in foil-lined roasting pan and bake at 325° for 2½ hours until done.

HOW TO COOK A
FROZEN TURKEY BREAST

An easy way to serve moist, tasty turkey — or have it for sandwiches and casseroles — any time of year.

Yield: 1 turkey breast

1 frozen turkey breast, unthawed
Salt
Onion salt
Celery salt

Accent seasoning
1 tablespoon sugar
1 stick (½ cup) butter, melted

- Preheat oven to 450°.
- Rinse and dry frozen turkey breast. Place on length of heavy duty aluminum foil long enough to fold around turkey, and seal.
- Generously shake salt, onion salt, celery salt, and Accent over turkey, and sprinkle with sugar. Rub in seasonings with fingers.
- Pour melted butter over turkey. Fold foil around turkey as though wrapping a box, sealing top and ends tightly.
- Place turkey "package" in small roasting pan.
- Roast at 450° for 2 hours, then open foil and cook another 20 minutes to brown. If using meat thermometer, temperature should read 190° when fully cooked.

RAISIN BREAD-CRANBERRY STUFFING

This stuffing may be roasted in the turkey or baked separately, and it's delicious either way. Try it with dried cranberries when fresh ones are out of season.

Yield: 8-10 servings

12 slices raisin bread

2 cups finely chopped onion

1 stick (½ cup) butter, plus additional 2 tablespoons if baking separately

2 cups fresh cranberries, washed and chopped (or 1½ cups dried cranberries)

2 tablespoons brown sugar, firmly packed

2 teaspoons crumbled dried rosemary

½ teaspoon crumbled dried sage

Salt and black pepper to taste

½ cup fresh orange juice

½ cup chicken broth, if baking separately

- If baking separately, preheat oven to 325° and grease 3- or 4-quart baking dish.

- Cut raisin bread into ½-inch cubes (you should have about 7½ cups) and carefully toast cubes until golden brown. Cool and reserve.

- In large skillet over medium-low heat, sauté onion in 1 stick butter until softened.

- Add cranberries, brown sugar, rosemary, sage, salt, and pepper to onions. Stir over medium-low heat about 3 minutes.

- Transfer mixture to large bowl and add bread cubes and orange juice, plus additional salt and pepper if desired. Mix gently until thoroughly combined. If stuffing turkey, let cool completely before using to stuff a 12 to 14 pound turkey.

- To bake separately, spoon stuffing into prepared pan and drizzle with chicken broth. Dot with 2 tablespoons butter, cut into small chunks. Bake, covered, at 325° for 30 minutes. Uncover and bake an additional 30 minutes.

TERIYAKI TURKEY BURGERS

*These are made with ground turkey breast, so
they are low in fat — but still moist and tasty.*

Yield: 4 burgers

1 pound ground turkey breast
1 teaspoon garlic salt
1 teaspoon Creole seasoning
¼ teaspoon black pepper
3 tablespoons teriyaki sauce

1 tablespoon water
1 large onion, thinly sliced
Olive oil
4 hamburger buns
Lettuce and tomato, if desired

- Mix together turkey, garlic salt, Creole seasoning, and pepper in large bowl, using hands if necessary. Shape into four patties, about ½-inch thick.
- Stir together teriyaki sauce and water in small bowl.
- Spray large nonstick skillet with nonstick spray and heat over medium heat. Add onion slices, cover, and cook about 10 minutes or until onion is golden brown, stirring frequently. Stir in 1 tablespoon teriyaki mixture. Remove onion from skillet and keep warm.
- Add olive oil to skillet and heat. Place patties in skillet and cook 5 minutes over medium heat. Add remaining teriyaki mixture to skillet, turn patties over, and continue cooking 3 to 5 minutes until golden.
- Place one burger in each bun and top with ¼ cup onions, lettuce, and tomato, if desired.

Wet your hands in cold water before mixing or shaping ground meat. Meat will not stick to them.

TURKEY MEAT LOAF

Children love this easy, healthy meat loaf. Bake in muffin cups instead of a loaf pan for "Meat Loaf Muffins" — a fun presentation for kids. Reduce baking time by about 10 minutes for muffins.

For meat loaf:

¼ cup old-fashioned oats
¼ cup wheat germ
⅓ cup milk
½ cup chopped onion
1 tablespoon butter

1 package ground turkey (not turkey breast)
1 egg, beaten
2 tablespoons ketchup
½ teaspoon salt
Black pepper to taste

For glaze:

3 tablespoons brown sugar
¼ cup ketchup

¼ teaspoon nutmeg
1 teaspoon dry mustard

- Preheat oven to 350°. Spray 8-inch loaf pan with nonstick spray.
- In large bowl, stir together oats, wheat germ, and milk; set aside.
- Sauté chopped onion in butter until tender.
- Add sautéed onion, turkey, egg, ketchup, salt, and pepper to oatmeal mixture. Mix well (works best to mix with hands) and pat into prepared pan.
- Bake at 350° for 40 minutes.
- While meat loaf is baking, prepare glaze. Whisk together brown sugar, ketchup, nutmeg, and dry mustard until smooth. Spread over meat loaf, return to oven, and bake at 350° an additional 20 minutes.

TIPSY CORNISH HENS

*Looks and tastes exotic, but easy to make with everyday
ingredients. Doubles or triples easily for entertaining.*

Yield: 8 servings

4 whole Cornish game hens
½ cup soy sauce
¾ cup olive oil
½ cup gin or rum
2 small onions, minced
2 cloves garlic, minced

¼ teaspoon black pepper
⅛ teaspoon red pepper flakes,
   crushed
1 teaspoon ginger
1 tablespoon sugar
1 tablespoon Worcestershire sauce

- Rinse hens and cut in half with large kitchen shears.
- Whisk together soy sauce, olive oil, gin or rum, onion, garlic, black pepper, pepper flakes, ginger, sugar, and Worcestershire.
- Put hens in large (2-gallon) Ziploc bags with marinade and refrigerate up to 24 hours, turning occasionally. (May be frozen at this point.)
- When ready to cook, preheat oven to 350°. Place hens and marinade in large pan and bake at 350° for 1 hour. May finish on grill, basting with marinade, if desired. Discard remaining marinade.

CROOK'S CORNER SHRIMP & GRITS

Many give credit for the Shrimp & Grits craze to Crook's Corner restaurant in Chapel Hill. When you make these, you'll see why they caught on!

Yield: 4-6 servings

4 cups water
1 cup grits (buy the Crook's Corner brand if you can find them)
½ teaspoon salt
½ stick (¼ cup) butter
1 cup shredded sharp Cheddar cheese
½ cup grated Parmesan cheese
  Pinch of white pepper
  Pinch of cayenne pepper
  Pinch of nutmeg
6 slices bacon

1 tablespoon peanut oil
  (may need slightly more)
2 cups sliced fresh mushrooms
1½ pounds fresh shrimp, peeled and cleaned
1 cup sliced green onions
  (use some green)
1 large clove garlic, put through press
4 teaspoons lemon juice
½ cup fresh parsley
  Tabasco sauce, salt, and black pepper to taste

- For grits, bring water to boil. Stir in grits slowly to prevent lumps.
- Reduce heat and simmer, stirring frequently, for about 20 minutes or until grits are thick and tender.
- Stir in ½ teaspoon salt, butter, Cheddar cheese, Parmesan cheese, white pepper, cayenne pepper, and nutmeg.
- While grits are cooking, dice bacon and cook until just crisp in very large skillet. Remove bacon with slotted spoon and add peanut oil to drippings.
- When oil is hot, add mushrooms and stir until mushrooms start to become tender.
- Add shrimp and cook just until shrimp start to turn pink.
- Add green onions and garlic. Continue cooking until shrimp are pink and mushrooms are tender but not browned.
- Stir in lemon juice and parsley, Season to taste with Tabasco, salt, and pepper.
- Divide grits among warm plates. Top with shrimp and serve immediately.

SHRIMP FREDERIC

Yield: 4 servings

1 stick (½ cup) unsalted butter
1 tablespoon fresh lemon juice
1 teaspoon dried parsley
1 teaspoon dried chives
½ teaspoon dried tarragon
½ teaspoon dry mustard

¾ teaspoon seasoned salt
⅛ teaspoon cayenne pepper
⅛ teaspoon garlic powder
1 pound medium shrimp, uncooked, peeled
2 cups hot cooked rice

- Melt butter in skillet. Whisk in lemon juice, parsley, chives, tarragon, mustard, seasoned salt, cayenne, and garlic powder until blended.
- Add shrimp and cook, uncovered, over medium heat, turning once, for 5 minutes or until shrimp are uniformly pink.
- Serve over hot cooked rice.

Shrimp are easier to peel while partially frozen.

SHRIMP, ARTICHOKE, & GRITS CASSEROLE

*A different take on shrimp & grits! This is a rich, elegant
casserole that can be made ahead and doubles (even triples) easily.
It's perfect for entertaining — either brunch or a dinner party.*

Yield: 8 servings

For grits:

4 cups salted water
1 cup grits
¼ teaspoon white pepper

2 tablespoons butter
1 cup shredded Cheddar cheese
Salt to taste

For white sauce:

3 tablespoons butter
3 tablespoons all-purpose flour
½ teaspoon salt

2 cups whole milk
Dash of Tabasco sauce
Dash of white pepper

For casserole:

3 tablespoons butter
1 small onion, chopped
1¼ cups sliced fresh mushrooms
1 (14-ounce) can artichoke hearts,
   drained and quartered
2 tablespoons white wine

1½ pounds medium shrimp, cooked
   just until pink and peeled
½ cup fine dry bread crumbs
¼ cup grated Parmesan cheese
2 tablespoons butter, melted

- In saucepan, bring salted water to boil and slowly pour in grits. Cook according to package instructions. When fully cooked, add pepper, butter, cheese, and salt. Cover and reserve.
- To make white sauce, melt butter in a saucepan. Slowly whisk in flour and salt until smooth.
- Whisk in milk and bring to boil, stirring constantly.
- Add Tabasco and pepper and continue whisking until thickened.
- Remove from heat and cool slightly, then press plastic wrap onto surface to prevent "skin" from forming. Reserve.
- Preheat oven to 350°. Spray 9x13-inch baking dish with nonstick spray.

SHRIMP, ARTICHOKE, & GRITS CASSEROLE *(continued)*

- For casserole, melt butter in medium skillet. Add onions and mushrooms; sauté until onions are translucent. Add artichoke hearts and wine. Cook until wine evaporates and mixture is heated through.
- Mix grits, vegetable mixture, and shrimp together. Place in prepared dish and spread white sauce over top.
- Mix bread crumbs and Parmesan; sprinkle over casserole. Drizzle with melted butter.
- Bake, uncovered, at 350° for about 20 minutes until bubbly and golden brown on top. Do not overbake or shrimp will toughen.

May be prepared one day in advance of serving and refrigerated before baking. Be sure to remove from refrigerator at least 1 hour before putting in oven.

GREEK SHRIMP OVER PASTA
Yield: 4-6 servings

2 cloves garlic, chopped
4 tablespoons olive oil, divided
2 (14-ounce) cans diced tomatoes, undrained
2 teaspoons dried basil
2 teaspoons dried oregano
   Salt and black pepper to taste

½ cup white wine
1 pound raw shrimp, peeled and cleaned
   Crushed red pepper flakes to taste
½ pound crumbled feta cheese
1 pound uncooked linguini or other pasta

- Preheat oven to 350°. Spray 8x8-inch baking dish with nonstick spray.
- In skillet, sauté chopped garlic in 2 tablespoons olive oil (do not brown). Add tomatoes, basil, oregano, salt, pepper, and wine. Cook about 20 minutes.
- In another skillet, sauté shrimp in remaining 2 tablespoons olive oil. Add pepper flakes to taste.
- Place shrimp with juices in prepared dish. Cover with crumbled feta and sauce.
- Bake, uncovered, at 350° for about 20 minutes. Cook pasta while shrimp dish is baking and serve shrimp over pasta.

BARBECUED SHRIMP

*Go to the beach (or just pretend you're there), buy good
fresh shrimp, cover the table with newspapers, and enjoy!*

Yield: 8 servings

4   pounds raw shrimp, unshelled
4   sticks (2 cups) unsalted butter
½   cup extra-virgin olive oil
10 cloves garlic, minced
3   bay leaves
¼   cup Worcestershire sauce
1   tablespoon "Essence" (see recipe below)
½   teaspoon cayenne pepper

2   teaspoons chopped fresh rosemary
2   teaspoons chopped fresh oregano
1   teaspoon crushed whole peppercorns
1   teaspoon salt
1   teaspoon ground black pepper
    Juice of 2 lemons
1   large loaf crusty French bread

- Preheat oven to 350°.
- Rinse shrimp under cold running water and drain. Spread in single layer in large roasting pans or baking dishes.
- Melt butter in large saucepan.
- Add olive oil, garlic, bay leaves, Worcestershire, Essence, cayenne, rosemary, oregano, peppercorns, salt, pepper, and lemon juice. Stir to blend well.
- Remove mixture from heat and pour over shrimp.
- Bake, uncovered, at 350° for 30 to 40 minutes or until shrimp are pink and cooked through. Stir occasionally to keep shrimp from drying out.
- Remove from oven and pour into large serving bowl or individual bowls.

Peel and eat at the table with hot French bread for dunking in the sauce.

"Essence"
2 tablespoons salt
2 tablespoons garlic powder
1 tablespoon black pepper
1 tablespoon onion powder

1 tablespoon cayenne pepper
1 tablespoon dried oregano
1 tablespoon dried thyme

- Combine all ingredients thoroughly and store in an airtight container.

CRAB CASSEROLE

Yield: 8 servings

¼ cup sherry
1 pound backfin lump crabmeat
¼ pound fresh mushrooms, sliced
1 stick plus 2 tablespoons butter, divided

1 (8-ounce) package Velveeta cheese, shredded
1 cup half-and-half
8 ounces linguine, cooked and drained
¾ cup sliced almonds, toasted

- Preheat oven to 325°. Grease 9x13-inch baking dish.
- Pour sherry over crabmeat and allow to marinate while preparing recipe.
- In small skillet, sauté mushrooms in 1 tablespoon butter until tender.
- In top of double boiler, combine cheese, half-and-half, 1 stick butter, and sautéed mushrooms. Cook until cheese and butter are melted and mixture is blended.
- Place cooked linguini in bottom of prepared dish.
- Place marinated crabmeat on top of linguini and top with cheese mixture.
- Sprinkle with almonds and dot with remaining tablespoon of butter.
- Bake at 325° for 20 to 30 minutes or until bubbly.

When buying crabmeat, ask what grade it is. The best is jumbo, lump, or backfin and is composed of large chunks of meat from the body. "Flake" indicates smaller bits of body meat. The lowest grade of crabmeat comes from the claw.

MEG'S CRABCAKES
Yield: 4 servings

¼ cup olive oil

3 tablespoons balsamic vinegar

½ onion, diced

6 sun-dried tomatoes, cut into strips

1 sleeve Ritz crackers

¾ pound crabmeat

2 tablespoons mayonnaise

1 tablespoon sherry

1 tablespoon Italian seasoning

2 eggs

1 stick butter, divided

- Heat olive oil and balsamic vinegar in small skillet. Add onion and sun-dried tomatoes and sauté until onions are translucent.
- In large mixing bowl, crumble Ritz crackers over crabmeat.
- Add onion-tomato mixture, mayonnaise, sherry, Italian seasoning, and eggs to crabmeat. Mix very gently with hands and form into small patties.
- Preheat skillet to medium-high setting. Reduce heat to medium and add ½ stick butter to skillet for cooking.
- Place half of patties in hot skillet and cook, waiting about 2 minutes to flip. Cook crabcakes until light brown.
- Use remaining butter for second batch of crabcakes.

Uncooked crabcakes may be prepared ahead and refrigerated or frozen. Be sure your pan is hot before cooking crabcakes. If the mixture looks too watery, add more cracker crumbs.

SOFT SHELLED CRABS IN BROWN BUTTER

This recipe has a spicy "kick." Measurements for
Tabasco and cayenne may be adjusted for milder flavor.

Yield: 4 servings

2 cups milk
2 teaspoons Tabasco sauce
2 cups all-purpose flour
1 teaspoon dry mustard
1 teaspoon cayenne pepper
1 teaspoon black pepper
½ teaspoon salt

6 tablespoons unsalted butter, divided
8 soft-shelled crabs, cleaned and dried
⅔ cup fresh lemon juice, divided
⅓ cup minced fresh parsley

- Stir together milk and Tabasco sauce in shallow bowl.
- Whisk together flour, mustard, cayenne, black pepper, and salt in another bowl.
- Heat 2 tablespoons butter until foamy in large skillet over medium heat.
- Dip each crab in milk mixture and dredge in flour mixture. Shake off excess flour.
- Place crabs in skillet and sauté until done, about 3 minutes on each side. Drain on paper towels, then place on platter and keep warm.
- Add ½ cup lemon juice to skillet and boil over high heat until mixture is reduced to syrupy glaze. Whisk in remaining 4 tablespoons butter and cook until brown.
- Whisk in remaining lemon juice and season with salt and pepper to taste.
- Bring sauce to boil and spoon over crab. Sprinkle with parsley and serve.

CRAWFISH ÉTOUFFÉE

You might as well double this recipe, because it tastes even better after being refrigerated or frozen and reheated. Once you try it, you'll be glad there's more for another night! The list of ingredients and instructions is long, but there's nothing complicated about it.

Yield: 6-8 servings

2 sticks (1 cup) butter, divided
¼ cup all-purpose flour
1 cup chopped green onions
1 cup chopped yellow onions
2 cloves garlic, minced
½ cup chopped green bell pepper
½ cup chopped celery
1 bay leaf
¼ teaspoon dried thyme
½ teaspoon dried basil
1 (8-ounce) can tomato sauce
½ teaspoon white pepper
2 teaspoons salt

1 tablespoon Worcestershire sauce
Tabasco to taste
1 cup water
1 cup white wine
2 pounds frozen, cooked crawfish tails, unthawed (4 8-ounce packages)
1 tablespoon lemon juice
1 tablespoon lemon zest
¼ cup minced parsley
2 tablespoons cognac (optional)
Hot cooked rice

- As they say in New Orleans, "First you make a roux." In large, heavy saucepan, melt 1 stick of butter. Whisk in flour and cook over medium-low heat, whisking constantly, until walnut-colored.

- Add remaining stick of butter, green onions, yellow onions, garlic, bell pepper, celery, bay leaf, thyme, and basil. Sauté over medium-low heat for 30 minutes.

- Add tomato sauce, pepper, salt, Worcestershire, Tabasco, water, and wine. Bring to boil, reduce heat, and simmer, uncovered, over medium-low heat for 1 hour, stirring occasionally.

- Take saucepan off heat and add crawfish, lemon juice, lemon zest, parsley, and cognac. Stir gently until crawfish is thawed and separated.

- Pour étouffée into refrigerator container, cover, and refrigerate (best if made the day before serving and refrigerated overnight).

CRAWFISH ÉTOUFFÉE *(continued)*

- One hour before serving, remove étouffée from refrigerator. Heat quickly on stove, without boiling. Serve immediately over hot cooked rice.

Crawfish are freshwater crustaceans that resemble tiny lobsters, complete with tails. Also known as crayfish or crawdads, the majority of the United States harvest comes from the waters of the Mississippi River basin.

RÉMOULADE SAUCE

For a very elegant first course, try Shrimp Rémoulade — mix boiled, peeled shrimp with this sauce and serve over lettuce in large scallop shells or on salad plates. The sauce is also a wonderful dip for seafood at a cocktail party.

Yield: about 2½ cups

2 cups mayonnaise
2 hard-boiled eggs, finely mashed
3 stalks celery, finely minced
1 small onion, finely minced
1 tablespoon Worcestershire sauce
3 tablespoons prepared yellow
    mustard

3 tablespoons Creole mustard (with
    horseradish)
1 teaspoon salt
1 teaspoon sugar
½ teaspoon cayenne pepper

- Combine mayonnaise, eggs, celery, onion, Worcestershire, yellow and Creole mustards, salt, sugar, and cayenne. Mix well and keep tightly covered in refrigerator. Keeps indefinitely!

Serve with cold boiled shrimp, crabmeat, or other seafood.

151

STUFFED LOBSTER TAILS

See instructions for cooking lobsters below. The cooked lobster meat may be refrigerated for up to three days — just don't label the container or it may be gobbled up!

Yield: 4 servings

4 (1¼-pound) lobsters, cooked
2 cups Ritz cracker crumbs
¼ cup chopped fresh parsley
3 tablespoons grated Parmesan cheese

2½ tablespoons butter, melted
2 tablespoons fresh lemon juice
2 tablespoons Worcestershire sauce
Lemon wedges for garnish

- Preheat broiler.
- Remove meat from cooked lobster tails and claws. Set tail shells aside and chop meat.
- Toss together chopped lobster meat, cracker crumbs, parsley, Parmesan, butter, lemon juice, and Worcestershire. Divide equally among tail shells and stuff shells with mixture.
- Broil for about 8 minutes or until golden brown.
- Serve hot with lemon wedges.

Buy only live lobsters – the more active, the better! Cook lobsters as soon as you get them home by putting them in a large pot of boiling water. If it bothers you to do this to live lobsters, try to remember that they have a simple nervous system and they feel no pain (we have no idea whether this is true, of course, but it makes us feel better to believe it). The taste is worth the moral dilemma!

OYSTERS MOSCA

2 cups seasoned dry bread crumbs
1 cup freshly grated Parmesan
   cheese
2 cloves garlic, finely chopped
2 tablespoons finely chopped fresh
   parsley

1 tablespoon Tony Chachere's
   seasoning or other Creole
   seasoning
3 dozen oysters, drained
⅓ cup olive oil
   Cayenne pepper to taste

- Preheat oven to 300°. Spray 15x10-inch jelly roll pan with nonstick spray.
- Mix bread crumbs, cheese, garlic, parsley, and seasoning in plate or bowl.
- Roll oysters in mixture and place in prepared pan. Drizzle with olive oil and sprinkle with cayenne pepper to taste.
- Bake at 300° for 20 minutes.

RUSH'S OYSTER SPECIAL

Yield: 4-6 servings

2 eggs
2 cups buttermilk
1 teaspoon baking soda
1 teaspoon salt
½ cup corn meal

1 heaping teaspoon sugar
   Thin-sliced country ham
1 pint oysters, undrained
1 tablespoon butter
½ teaspoon Worcestershire sauce

- To make corn cakes, beat eggs in medium bowl. Add buttermilk, baking soda, salt, corn meal, and sugar. Batter should be thin.
- Using about ¼ cup of batter for each, cook in hot greased skillet to make thin, lacy cakes.
- Stack 3 to 4 cakes on each hot serving plate with slices of country ham between cakes.
- While corn cakes are cooking, simmer oysters in their own juice until edges curl. Add butter and Worcestershire sauce to oysters and continue heating until butter melts. Stir sauce well.
- Place 5 to 6 oysters on top of each corn cake stack. Pour sauce over stacks or serve sauce on the side.

SALMON FILLETS WITH SAUTÉED CORN & SPINACH

A wonderful summer dish with fresh corn. Makes a beautiful presentation and tastes as good as it looks!

Yield: 4 servings

4   salmon fillets
1   tablespoon olive oil
    Salt and black pepper to taste
½   stick (¼ cup) butter
4-6 ears corn, cut off cob and scraped
1   medium red onion, chopped
1   cup coarsely chopped shiitake or button mushrooms

2   medium tomatoes, peeled, seeded, and diced
½   cup balsamic vinegar
1   bag baby leaf spinach
1   tablespoon olive oil
1   teaspoon fresh dill for garnish

- Preheat oven to broil.
- Brush salmon with olive oil and sprinkle with salt and pepper.
- Broil salmon under high heat for 18 minutes, turning once, until golden and cooked through. Salmon may also be grilled over hot coals for about 12 minutes.
- While salmon is cooking, melt butter in skillet. Add corn and onion; sauté for 5 minutes.
- Add mushrooms and tomatoes to skillet; stir for 2 to 3 minutes.
- Add vinegar and simmer 5 minutes or until mixture is creamy.
- In separate skillet, sauté spinach in olive oil for about 3 minutes.
- Spoon corn mixture into center of platter. Top with spinach and then salmon. Sprinkle with dill and serve.

SALMON TOPPED
WITH FRESH VEGGIES

Perfect for a rainy or winter day when you don't want to grill salmon outside.

Yield: 4 servings

4 salmon fillets
6 tablespoons fresh lemon juice
1 cup finely grated carrot
1 cup finely chopped tomato
6 tablespoons chopped green onion

6 tablespoons mayonnaise
½ (8-ounce) package cream cheese, softened
¼ cup chopped fresh parsley
¼ teaspoon black pepper

- Preheat oven to 400°. Line 9x13-inch baking dish or jelly-roll pan with foil and spray with nonstick spray.
- Arrange salmon fillets in dish and drizzle with lemon juice.
- Combine carrot, tomato, green onion, mayonnaise, cream cheese, parsley, and pepper in bowl. Mix well.
- Mound vegetable mixture on each fillet, covering salmon completely.
- Bake at 400° for 20 minutes or until salmon flakes easily.

A little chopped fresh parsley enhances the flavor and appearance of almost any savory dish — yet recipes usually call for only a small amount, and parsley comes only in a large bunch. Chop the whole bunch, divide it into smaller amounts if desired, and freeze it in Ziploc bags until needed.

SALMON WITH LEMON MAYONNAISE

Yield: 4 servings

1 (1½-pound) boneless, skinless fresh or frozen salmon fillet

½ cup mayonnaise

2 tablespoons snipped fresh chives

1 teaspoon finely shredded lemon zest

3 tablespoons lemon juice, divided

1 tablespoon snipped fresh parsley

¼ teaspoon coarsely cracked black pepper

1½ teaspoons olive or cooking oil

½ teaspoon Worcestershire sauce

1 teaspoon snipped fresh rosemary (or ¼ teaspoon dried and crushed)

• Thaw salmon if frozen.

• Stir together mayonnaise, chives, lemon zest, 1 tablespoon lemon juice, parsley, and pepper in small bowl. Cover and refrigerate.

• In another small bowl, combine remaining 2 tablespoons lemon juice, olive oil, Worcestershire, and rosemary. Set aside to use for basting.

• Place salmon in greased grill basket or cut several slits in heavy foil and place on foil. Turn under thin ends of fish for even thickness. Measure fillet thickness. Close basket.

• Preheat gas grill to hot and adjust for direct cooking.

• Place fillet on grill, cover, and grill 4 to 6 minutes per ½-inch thickness, brushing often with oil mixture. Turn halfway through cooking time.

• Serve hot with dollops of chilled lemon mayonnaise.

DRESSED BAKED FLOUNDER

This easy recipe works equally well with other mild white fish such as grouper, orange roughy, or Asian bassa. Cooking time may be longer for thicker cuts of fish; simply bake until fish is opaque and beginning to flake with a fork. With a food processor to make breadcrumbs and chop the onion, this takes just minutes to prepare!

Yield: 4-6 servings

6 slices whole wheat bread
½ medium onion, chopped
1 tablespoon lemon juice
½ teaspoon marjoram
¼ teaspoon salt, or more to taste
¼ teaspoon black pepper

2 tablespoons butter or margarine, melted
1½ pounds flounder fillets
1 medium tomato, coarsely chopped
½ cup grated Parmesan cheese

- Preheat oven to 400°. Cover shallow baking dish or jelly roll pan with foil and spray with nonstick spray.
- Shred bread into crumbs, by hand or in food processor.
- In medium bowl, stir together bread crumbs, onion, lemon juice, marjoram, salt, pepper, and melted butter.
- Arrange fish in single layer in prepared pan.
- Spread breadcrumb mixture over fish, then sprinkle with chopped tomato and top with Parmesan cheese.
- Bake, uncovered, at 400° for about 15 minutes or until fish is opaque.

SALMON IN GINGER SOY SAUCE

Yield: 4 servings

1 tablespoon cornstarch
2 tablespoons all-purpose flour
4 (8-ounce) fresh salmon fillets
4 tablespoons butter (olive oil may
  be substituted)
2 tablespoons honey

2 tablespoons diced fresh ginger
3 tablespoons soy sauce
½ teaspoon garlic powder
1 tablespoon rice wine vinegar
⅓ cup dry sherry
2 green onions, chopped, divided

- Combine cornstarch and flour. Sprinkle on both sides of salmon.
- In skillet, melt butter and sauté salmon over medium heat for 15 minutes, turning once. Transfer to serving dish and keep warm.
- Add honey, ginger, soy sauce, garlic powder, vinegar, sherry, and half of green onions to skillet. Mix well, bring to boil, and pour over salmon.
- Garnish with remaining green onions.

GRILLED GROUPER

This grilling sauce also works with swordfish steaks or mahi mahi.

Yield: 2-4 servings

¼ cup sour cream
1 tablespoon Dijon mustard
2 teaspoons lemon juice
1 clove garlic, minced

¼ teaspoon dried dill
1 pound grouper fillets
2 tablespoons butter, melted
Salt and black pepper to taste

- Whisk together sour cream, Dijon mustard, lemon juice, garlic, and dill in small bowl. Mix well.
- Brush fillets with melted butter and sprinkle with salt and pepper.
- Grill grouper over hot coals until fish flakes easily, basting frequently with sour cream mixture.

STUFFED SOLE OR FLOUNDER FILLETS WITH LEMON SAUCE

Yield: 8 servings

For fillets:

8 fresh or frozen fillets of sole or flounder

½ stick (¼ cup) margarine or butter

1 stalk celery, finely chopped

1 cup chopped fresh mushrooms

⅔ cup herb-seasoned stuffing mix

1 teaspoon grated Parmesan cheese

Dash of garlic powder

1 tablespoon dry sherry

½ teaspoon lemon juice

1 egg, beaten

For lemon sauce:

½ stick (¼ cup) margarine or butter

½ cup sliced fresh mushrooms

2-3 teaspoons lemon juice

Dash of garlic powder

⅛ teaspoon salt

Dash of black pepper

Snipped parsley

- Thaw fish in refrigerator if frozen. Preheat oven to 450°. Spray 2-quart rectangular baking dish with nonstick spray.
- Melt margarine in medium skillet over medium heat. Add celery and mushrooms and sauté until tender. Remove from heat.
- Stir in stuffing mix, Parmesan, garlic powder, sherry, lemon juice, and beaten egg.
- Divide stuffing among fillets. Wrap ends of fillets around stuffing and place in prepared baking dish.
- Bake, uncovered, at 450° for 12 to 15 minutes or until stuffing is hot and fish flakes with a fork.
- To make lemon sauce, melt margarine in small saucepan over medium heat. Reduce heat to medium-low, add mushrooms, and sauté for 2 minutes. Remove from heat and stir in lemon juice, garlic powder, salt, and pepper.
- Spoon sauce over each fillet before serving and garnish with parsley.

ORANGE ROUGHY WITH TOMATO CILANTRO SALSA

Yield: 6 servings

For salsa:

8 plum tomatoes, seeded and diced

1 red onion, diced

1 bunch fresh cilantro, chopped (about ½ cup)

¼ cup fresh lime juice

2 tablespoons olive oil

2 teaspoons minced canned chipotle chiles

½ teaspoon ground cumin

For fish:

3 tablespoons olive oil

6 (6-ounce) orange roughy fillets (each about ¾ inch thick)

Salt and black pepper to taste

½ cup all-purpose flour

1 pound haricots verts or other slender green beans, trimmed

Fresh lemon juice

Additional olive oil

- To prepare salsa, toss together tomatoes, onion, cilantro, lime juice, olive oil, chiles, and cumin in large bowl. Cover and refrigerate. Salsa may be made 4 hours ahead and kept in refrigerator.
- Preheat oven to 400°. Spray large rimmed baking sheet with nonstick spray.
- To prepare fish, heat oil in large skillet over medium-high heat.
- Sprinkle fish with salt and pepper. Place flour in shallow baking dish and coat fish with flour.
- Working in batches, sauté fish in skillet until golden brown, about 3 minutes per side.
- Transfer fish to baking sheet. Bake at 400° for 5 minutes or until opaque in center.
- Meanwhile, cook haricots verts in large pot of boiling salted water for 3 minutes or until crisp-tender. Drain. Transfer to ice water to cool and drain again.
- Divide haricots verts equally among plates. Top with fish fillets and salsa.

RED SNAPPER JOLIET ROUGE

Yield: 8 servings

4 sticks (2 cups) butter
3 jumbo yellow onions, finely
   chopped
¾ pound fresh small whole
   mushrooms
1 clove garlic, minced

1 tablespoon salt
2 teaspoons white pepper
2 pounds fresh lump white crabmeat
1 bunch green onions, thinly sliced
8 red snapper fillets, trimmed

- Preheat broiler to 450°. Spray broiling pan with nonstick spray.
- In large skillet, melt butter and sauté onion, mushrooms, and garlic until tender.
- Add salt, white pepper, crabmeat, and green onions, stirring gently so you don't break up lumps of crabmeat.
- Place fillets on prepared broiling pan.
- Broil at 450° until fillets turn opaque.
- Spread crabmeat topping over fillets and continue broiling until crabmeat begins to brown on top. Serve immediately.

To cook a flat fillet evenly, fold the thin tail end under. The thickness of the fillet will be more uniform and it will cook more consistently.

SAUTÉED RED SNAPPER WITH TOMATO OLIVE SAUCE

Yield: 4 servings

8 ounces dry fusilli pasta	2 tablespoons honey
4 (5-ounce) red snapper fillets	10 pitted Kalamata olives
Salt and freshly ground black	2 bay leaves
pepper to taste	1 teaspoon dried oregano
4 teaspoons olive oil, divided	Grated Parmesan cheese
1 (14-ounce) can diced tomatoes	

- Cook pasta in large pot of rapidly boiling water for 9 minutes or until just tender.
- While pasta is cooking, season both sides of red snapper fillets with salt and pepper.
- Heat 2 teaspoons olive oil in large skillet over medium-high heat. Add fillets and cook 2 minutes on each side or until golden. Remove fillets from pan and set aside.
- In same skillet, cook tomatoes, honey, olives, bay leaves, and oregano over medium-high heat. Bring to boil, reduce heat to low, and simmer 5 minutes.
- Return fillets to skillet and cook 2 minutes or until fish is fork tender. Remove bay leaves.
- Drain pasta and toss with remaining 2 teaspoons olive oil.
- Spoon pasta onto serving plates and sprinkle with Parmesan. Arrange red snapper fillets beside pasta and spoon tomato sauce on top.

SEA BASS ROASTED WITH CAPERS

Yield: 2-4 servings

1 tablespoon olive oil	1 sea bass fillet, about 1½ pounds
2 tablespoons lemon juice	1 tablespoon chopped fresh basil
2 tablespoons capers	Dry breadcrumbs
¼ teaspoon salt	¼ cup pine nuts
¼ teaspoon black pepper	

- Preheat oven to 400°.
- Combine olive oil, lemon juice, capers, salt, and pepper in shallow bowl.
- Dip sea bass in mixture, turning to coat both sides. Reserve remaining olive oil mixture.
- Sprinkle fish with basil, breadcrumbs, and pine nuts.
- Place fish in roasting pan and pour reserved olive oil mixture over fish.
- Roast at 400° for 20 minutes.

⇒ Fish Facts ⇐

Whole fish should look bright and shiny, with clear eyes, red gills, and a tail that is not dry.

Fish fillets and steaks should be firm and not bruised or slimy.

One pound of whole fish will serve one person.

One (7-ounce) fillet or steak equals one serving.

PAN-SEARED TUNA WITH GINGER-SHIITAKE CREAM SAUCE

Yield: 6 servings

6 (6-ounce) tuna steaks, about
   1 inch thick
Freshly ground black pepper
2 tablespoons peanut oil
3 tablespoons butter
⅓ cup thinly sliced green onions
¼ cup chopped cilantro
2 tablespoons finely chopped fresh
   ginger

4 cloves garlic, finely chopped
8 ounces fresh shiitake
   mushrooms, stems removed
   and caps sliced
6 tablespoons soy sauce
1½ cups heavy cream
3 tablespoons fresh lime juice
Lime wedges and fresh cilantro
   sprigs for garnish

- Preheat oven to 200°.
- Sprinkle 1 side of tuna steaks with pepper.
- Heat oil in large, heavy skillet over high heat. Place tuna steaks, pepper-side down, in skillet, and sear for 2 minutes. Turn tuna over and continue cooking to desired doneness, about 2 more minutes for rare. Transfer tuna to rimmed baking sheet and place in oven to keep warm.
- To same skillet, add butter, onions, cilantro, ginger, and garlic. Sauté about 30 seconds.
- Add mushrooms and soy sauce; simmer another 30 seconds.
- Add cream and simmer about 3 minutes or until sauce lightly coats back of spoon. Stir in lime juice.
- Spoon sauce onto serving plates and arrange tuna on sauce. Garnish with lime wedges and cilantro sprigs, if desired.

Fresh shiitake mushrooms should be firm and dry. The stems are always tough and should be removed before using. (Incidentally, shiitake mushrooms were used as models for the dancing and singing mushrooms in the movie Fantasia.)

GRILLED MAPLE-MUSTARD SALMON

Children love this!

Yield: about 4 servings

3 tablespoons Dijon mustard
3 tablespoons pure maple syrup
1 tablespoon balsamic vinegar

¼ teaspoon salt
⅛ teaspoon black pepper
4 (6-ounce) salmon fillets

- Combine mustard, syrup, vinegar, salt, and pepper in large Ziploc bag.
- Add salmon to bag and seal. Refrigerate about 20 minutes.
- Heat grill to hot and grill salmon 12 to 15 minutes or until it flakes easily.

To grill salmon, sear the skin side first over high heat, then flip fish over. The skin will peel right off as you continue to cook.

SUMMERTIME FRESH PEACH SALSA

Wonderful served over grilled tuna medallions as well as baked or grilled chicken.

1 cup diced peaches, peeled
1 cup diced plums, unpeeled
¼ cup minced onion or shallots
3 tablespoons orange juice
2 tablespoons chopped fresh parsley
1 teaspoon lime zest
2 tablespoons fresh lime juice

1½ tablespoons minced, seeded jalapeño pepper
1 tablespoon minced fresh mint
1 tablespoon honey
1 tablespoon minced, peeled fresh ginger

Mix all ingredients in bowl. Cover and chill.

To seed jalapeño peppers, halve lengthwise. Hold pepper by its stem and use a serrated grapefruit spoon or melon baller to scrape out the seeds and veins.

Electives

VEGETABLES

Asparagus with
   Maple Vinaigrette 167

Marinated Asparagus 168

Roasted Asparagus 169

Green Bean Bundles 169

Green Beans Y'all Won't Believe 170

Roasted Green Beans 171

Glazed Carrots 171

Regal Mushrooms 172

Vidalia Onion Casserole 173

Oregano Peas 174

Roasted Roquefort Potatoes 174

Savory Roasted New Potatoes 175

Overnight Company Potatoes 175

Creamy Scalloped Potatoes 176

California Sweet Potato Bake 177

Purefoy Hotel
   Sweet Potato Pudding 178

Sweet Potato Carrot Purée 179

Spinach Spoon Bread 180

Spinach Orzo 181

Zucchini Casserole 181

Greek-Style Squash 182

Southern Squash Casserole 183

Favorite Squash Casserole 184

Southern Okra & Tomatoes 185

Tomato Pie 186

Carson's Tomato Pie 187

Ratatouille Tart 188

Tomatoes Rockefeller 189

Roasted Summer Vegetables 190

Summer Vegetable Skillet 191

Easy Vegetable Casserole 191

FRUITS

Baked Apricots 192

Pineapple Casserole 192

Cranberry Apple Bake 193

Cold Spiced Fruit 194

ASPARAGUS WITH MAPLE VINAIGRETTE

May be served as an appetizer or a vegetable.

Yield: 4-6 servings

2	tablespoons red wine vinegar	3	tablespoons maple syrup
1	tablespoon Dijon mustard	2	teaspoons dried tarragon
½	teaspoon salt	3-4	pounds fresh asparagus
¼	cup olive oil	2	hard boiled eggs, chopped
⅓	cup vegetable oil	½	cup pine nuts, lightly toasted

- Whisk together vinegar, mustard, salt, olive oil, vegetable oil, syrup, and tarragon. Cover and refrigerate.
- Steam asparagus just until bright green. Rinse in cold water and refrigerate.
- Prior to serving, arrange asparagus on platter and pour vinaigrette over the top. Sprinkle with eggs and pine nuts.

To store asparagus, snap or trim off the tough end of the spear and store covered in the refrigerator with the spears standing upright in about an inch of water. A quart-size canning jar is ideal for this. Or, wrap the cut ends in a wet paper towel and store in a sealed plastic bag. Stored properly, asparagus will keep for 4 to 6 days.

MARINATED ASPARAGUS

A few tablespoons of chopped fresh tomato or red bell pepper makes a nice garnish.

Yield: 10-12 servings

1 cup vegetable oil
½ cup white wine vinegar
½ cup lemon juice
½ cup chopped green onion
¼ cup minced parsley
1 teaspoon sugar

1 teaspoon dry mustard
¼ teaspoon black pepper
½ teaspoon salt
4 pounds fresh asparagus spears, trimmed

- Whisk together oil, vinegar, lemon juice, onion, parsley, sugar, dry mustard, pepper, and salt until blended.
- Steam asparagus until bright green and crisp tender. Arrange in large baking dish.
- Pour marinade over asparagus, cover, and refrigerate 6 hours or overnight.
- Drain and serve chilled.

When choosing asparagus, look for bright green spears with tightly closed, compact tips. Size doesn't indicate a woody texture or diminished flavor. Thicker spears are just as tender as thinner ones; tenderness relates to color, so the greener the better.

ROASTED ASPARAGUS

Easy and good, served warm or at room temperature.
This method may also be used to roast baby carrots.

Yield: 8 servings

2 pounds thick asparagus stalks
(thin stalks do NOT roast well)
¼ cup olive oil

Jane's Krazy Salt
Black pepper
¼ cup grated Parmesan cheese

- Preheat oven to 450°. Spray large jelly roll pan with nonstick spray.
- Rinse asparagus and snap or trim off tough ends. Pat dry and arrange on prepared pan.
- Drizzle with olive oil and season with Krazy Salt and pepper. Toss gently to mix.
- Roast at 450° for 10 minutes, turning asparagus after 5 minutes.
- When slightly cooled, sprinkle with Parmesan cheese.

GREEN BEAN BUNDLES

Even if you wouldn't dream of serving canned green beans, try
these — they'll change your mind. Must be made the day before serving.

Yield: 12-14 servings

15-16 strips bacon, cut in half
3 (16-ounce) cans Blue Lake
whole green beans, drained
Toothpicks

2 sticks (1 cup) butter
1 cup brown sugar
½ teaspoon garlic salt
Dash of soy sauce

- Wrap half-strips of bacon around bundles of about 10 green beans, using toothpicks to secure.
- Place bundles in 9x13-inch baking dish sprayed with nonstick spray.
- Melt butter in saucepan and whisk in brown sugar, garlic salt, and soy sauce.
- Pour sauce over bundles, cover, and marinate overnight in refrigerator.
- When ready to cook, preheat oven to 350°. Uncover and bake at 350° for 30 minutes.

GREEN BEANS Y'ALL WON'T BELIEVE

Green beans with sugar and bacon drippings?? What can we say — it's a Southern thing. And these are delicious!

Yield: 6-8 servings

2 (16-ounce) cans French-style green beans, or 1½ pounds fresh

10 strips bacon

6 tablespoons sugar

6-8 tablespoons apple cider vinegar

¼ cup slivered almonds

- If using fresh green beans, rinse beans and remove ends and strings. Leave whole or cut into 1-inch pieces. In 2-quart saucepan, cook beans in small amount of salted boiling water, covered, for 20 to 25 minutes or until crisp-tender. Drain well. For canned beans, rinse and drain. Set aside.
- In 10-inch skillet, cook bacon until crisp. Remove bacon and crumble, reserving drippings in skillet. Whisk sugar and vinegar into drippings.
- Preheat oven to 350° and spray 1½-quart baking dish with nonstick spray.
- Layer half of beans, half of bacon and half of almonds in prepared dish. Repeat layers. Pour drippings mixture over all.
- Bake at 350° for 30 to 45 minutes or until heated through.

ROASTED GREEN BEANS

Yield: 4 servings

1 teaspoon olive oil
1 teaspoon balsamic vinegar
½ teaspoon dried tarragon

½ teaspoon salt
1 pound green beans, rinsed and
    trimmed

- Preheat oven to 500°.
- Combine olive oil, vinegar, tarragon, and salt in large bowl.
- Add green beans. Toss to coat.
- Pour beans into 9x13-inch baking dish.
- Roast at 500° for 10 minutes or until crisp tender, stirring halfway through.

When buying green beans, break one. If it doesn't snap, it isn't fresh. Buy about ¼ pound per serving. Refrigerate unwashed fresh beans in open or perforated plastic bags for up to 3 days.

GLAZED CARROTS

Yield: 8 servings

6 cups sliced carrots
3 tablespoons butter, melted
3 tablespoons Dijon mustard
    (or your favorite mustard)

½ cup brown sugar
1½ tablespoons chopped fresh
    parsley

- Steam carrots until crisp-tender.
- While carrots are steaming, whisk together melted butter, mustard, brown sugar, and parsley.
- Toss mixture with drained carrots, reheating if carrots have cooled.

REGAL MUSHROOMS

*Use teriyaki sauce for a slightly sweet flavor, or soy
sauce for a saltier version. Delicious either way.*

½ cup dry white wine
¼ cup teriyaki or soy sauce
1 pound mushrooms, washed and
   halved

½ stick (¼ cup) butter
¼ cup chopped onion
¼ cup toasted almonds

- Whisk together wine and teriyaki or soy sauce.
- Pour over mushrooms, cover, and marinate in refrigerator for 2 to 3 hours.
- Drain mushrooms, reserving marinade.
- In large skillet, melt butter and sauté mushrooms and onion until tender. Add marinade and almonds to skillet and simmer 5 to 10 minutes.

⇢ Mushroom Tips ⇠

Don't peel mushrooms – that's where the flavor is!

*Cook mushrooms, especially wild mushrooms,
as soon as you can. They dry out and lose
their flavor as they age.*

SAVORY ROASTED NEW POTATOES

Yield: 6-8 servings

16 egg-size new red potatoes, cut
    into large bite-size pieces
1 teaspoon minced fresh garlic
½ teaspoon paprika
2 tablespoons minced fresh rosemary

½ teaspoon salt
¼ teaspoon freshly ground black
    pepper
1 tablespoon Worcestershire sauce
¼ cup olive oil

- Preheat oven to 375°. Spray 9x13-inch baking dish with nonstick spray.
- Place potatoes in prepared dish and sprinkle with garlic, paprika, rosemary, salt, and pepper. Toss to mix well.
- In small bowl, whisk together Worcestershire and olive oil; drizzle mixture over potatoes. Toss again to coat.
- Bake in lower half of oven at 375°, stirring occasionally, for 45 to 55 minutes or until browned and tender.

OVERNIGHT COMPANY POTATOES

Rich mashed potatoes that you don't have to do at the last minute.

Yield: 8-10 servings

5-7 pounds potatoes, peeled and cut
    into chunks
½ (8-ounce) package cream cheese,
    softened
12 ounces sour cream

1 stick (½ cup) butter, softened
1 packet dry Italian dressing mix
Salt and black pepper to taste
Seasoned salt

- Cook potatoes in water until tender, drain well, and mash.
- Add cream cheese, sour cream, butter, dressing mix, salt, and pepper to mashed potatoes, stirring well to mix.
- Spray 9x13-inch baking dish with nonstick spray. Pour potatoes into prepared dish and sprinkle with seasoned salt.
- Cover and refrigerate overnight or up to 24 hours.
- When ready to bake, preheat oven to 325°. Bake, covered with foil, at 325° for 25 minutes.

CREAMY SCALLOPED POTATOES

Yield: 8 servings

1 large clove garlic, minced
1 shallot, chopped
½ teaspoon red pepper flakes
3 tablespoons butter
1¼ cups milk
1¼ cups heavy cream
½ teaspoon salt

¼ teaspoon freshly ground black
   pepper
2½ pounds small red potatoes,
   unpeeled, cut into ⅛-inch
   slices
1 cup shredded Gruyère cheese
½ teaspoon paprika

- Preheat oven to 350°. Spray 8x12-inch baking dish with nonstick spray.
- In large Dutch oven, sauté garlic, shallot, and red pepper flakes in butter about 2 minutes.
- Add milk, cream, salt, and pepper, stirring well.
- Add potatoes to milk mixture, stirring gently to coat potatoes well. Bring to boil over medium heat, stirring occasionally to prevent scorching.
- When mixture begins to boil, spoon into prepared dish. Sprinkle with cheese and paprika.
- Bake, uncovered, at 350° for 45 minutes or until bubbly and golden brown. Allow to sit 15 minutes before serving.

CALIFORNIA SWEET POTATO BAKE

Looks pretty and tastes good too.

Yield: 8-10 servings

4 medium sweet potatoes
½ cup light brown sugar
1 tablespoon cornstarch
¼ teaspoon salt
1 cup orange juice

3 tablespoons cooking sherry
¼ cup white seedless raisins
½ stick (¼ cup) butter
2 tablespoons chopped pecans

- Preheat oven to 350°. Spray 9x13-inch baking dish with nonstick spray.
- Simmer potatoes in water or cook in microwave until tender. Peel, slice, and arrange in prepared dish.
- Stir together brown sugar, cornstarch, salt, juice, sherry, and raisins in saucepan. Bring to boil, reduce heat, and simmer until thickened.
- Add butter and pecans to sugar mixture and pour over potatoes.
- Bake, uncovered, at 350° for 20 minutes.

To cook sweet potatoes quickly, scrub potatoes, prick with a fork, and put in the microwave on paper towels. Cook on High until tender, about 12 to 14 minutes. To peel cooked potatoes easily, submerge hot potatoes in cold water – the peels will blister off.

PUREFOY HOTEL
SWEET POTATO PUDDING

Our family's traditional Thanksgiving sweet potatoes — the grated texture makes all the difference. We always grate the potatoes by hand, but a food processor will also do the job in a pinch.

Yield: 8 servings

2-3 large raw sweet potatoes, peeled and grated (best when grated by hand with coarse grater) to make 4 cups grated potatoes
4 eggs, beaten well
½ cup granulated sugar
1 cup brown sugar

1 stick (½ cup) butter, melted
2 cups whole milk
1 teaspoon fresh lemon zest
4 teaspoons fresh lemon juice
1 teaspoon cinnamon
¼ teaspoon nutmeg

- Preheat oven to 350°. Spray 3-quart casserole dish with nonstick spray.
- Place grated potatoes in large bowl. Add beaten eggs and mix well.
- Add both sugars and mix well.
- Stir in melted butter, milk, lemon zest, lemon juice, cinnamon, and nutmeg. Mix very well.
- Pour into prepared dish and bake, uncovered, at 350° for 30 minutes. Remove from oven, stir well, and bake another 45 to 60 minutes or until set throughout and brown and crusty around the edges. Baking time depends on moisture in potatoes.

When a recipe calls for both lemon juice and zest, pour the lemon juice over the zest to keep it moist and flavorful.

SWEET POTATO CARROT PURÉE

*A 1-pound bag of "baby" carrots may be used
instead of regular carrots — no slicing needed.*

Yield: 8 servings

1 pound carrots, peeled and sliced into chunks	4 large sweet potatoes, baked until fork tender
2½ cups water	1 cup crème fraîche (see recipe below)
1 tablespoon sugar	
1½ sticks (¾ cup) butter, softened, divided	½ teaspoon freshly grated nutmeg
	Salt and black pepper to taste

- Preheat oven to 350°. Spray 9x13-inch baking dish with nonstick spray.
- In saucepan, combine carrots, water, sugar, and 2 tablespoons butter. Bring to boil over medium heat. Reduce heat and cook until water has evaporated and carrots begin to sizzle and are tender.
- Scrape out flesh of potatoes.
- Combine carrots and potatoes in food processor. Add remaining butter and crème fraîche. Process until very smooth. Add nutmeg and season to taste with salt and pepper.
- Spoon mixture into prepared dish and bake, uncovered, at 350° for 30 minutes or until hot.

For crème fraîche: (must be made the day before)

½ cup heavy cream	½ cup sour cream

- Whisk heavy cream and sour cream together. Cover loosely with plastic wrap and let stand on counter (not in refrigerator) overnight until thickened.
- Refrigerate for at least 4 hours before using. Makes 1 cup.

179

SPINACH SPOON BREAD

Our tester recommends heating the milk for the white sauce in the microwave before whisking it in — the sauce will be less likely to separate.

Yield: 6 servings

For white sauce:

2 tablespoons butter

2 tablespoons all-purpose flour

1 cup milk

Salt, white pepper, and paprika to taste

For bread:

1 (10-ounce) package frozen chopped spinach, thawed and drained well

1 (8-ounce) container sour cream

1 (8½-ounce) package cornbread mix

2 eggs

1 stick (½ cup) butter, melted

- Preheat oven to 350°. Spray 8x8-inch or 9x9-inch baking dish with nonstick spray.
- Prepare white sauce by melting butter in small saucepan over medium-high heat. Add flour slowly, whisking constantly. Add milk, continuing to whisk until sauce thickens. Add salt, pepper, and paprika to taste.
- For bread, stir together spinach, sour cream, cornbread mix, eggs, and melted butter in large bowl. Add white sauce and mix well.
- Pour into prepared dish and bake, uncovered, at 350° for 1 hour.

To thaw and cook frozen spinach quickly, put the whole package in the microwave and cook on High about 4 minutes. Open the box and press out excess moisture in a strainer.

SPINACH ORZO

A different and delicious side dish.

Yield: 8 servings

2 teaspoons margarine
½ cup coarsely shredded carrots
2 cloves garlic, chopped
4 cups reduced-sodium chicken broth
2 cups uncooked orzo (12 ounces)

3 cups shredded fresh spinach or one 10-ounce package frozen chopped spinach, thawed and well drained
3 tablespoons Parmesan cheese
Salt and black pepper
1 teaspoon dried basil

- Melt margarine in 3-quart saucepan.
- Cook carrots and garlic in margarine about 2 minutes until carrots are just tender.
- Stir in broth and orzo and bring to boil. Reduce heat and simmer, uncovered, 15 to 20 minutes, stirring occasionally, until broth is absorbed.
- Stir in spinach, Parmesan, salt, pepper, and basil. Continue cooking until spinach is tender and mixture is heated through.

ZUCCHINI CASSEROLE

Two different testers raved about this recipe. Better try it!

Yield: 6-8 servings

8-10 medium zucchini, sliced
2 tablespoons butter
⅓ cup chopped onion
½ cup sour cream

Salt and black pepper to taste
1 teaspoon dried dill
¾ cup grated Parmesan cheese

- Preheat oven to 350°. Spray 1½-quart baking dish with nonstick spray.
- Steam sliced zucchini until tender and drain well.
- Melt butter in small skillet and sauté onion until translucent.
- Stir together drained zucchini, onion, sour cream, salt, pepper, and dill. Pour into prepared dish and cover with Parmesan.
- Bake, uncovered, at 350° for 30 minutes or until bubbly.

GREEK-STYLE SQUASH

Yield: 10-12 servings

Butter-flavored nonstick cooking spray

2½ pounds yellow squash, sliced, or three 10-ounce packages frozen sliced yellow squash, thawed

1 large onion, chopped

1½-2 teaspoons salt, divided

1 cup water

1 (15-ounce) container ricotta cheese

1 cup cottage cheese

½ cup grated Parmesan cheese

½ teaspoon white pepper

1 (16-ounce) package frozen phyllo pastry, thawed

- Preheat oven to 350°. Spray 9x13-inch baking dish with butter-flavored nonstick spray.
- Keep phyllo covered with slightly damp dishtowel until ready to use.
- Combine squash, onion, 1 teaspoon salt, and water in large saucepan or Dutch oven. Bring to boil over medium heat. Reduce heat and simmer 5 to 7 minutes or until squash is tender. Drain and set aside.
- While squash is cooking, stir together ricotta, cottage cheese, Parmesan, remaining salt, and pepper in medium bowl.
- Place 1 phyllo sheet on flat surface (wax paper on countertop works well). Coat sheet with cooking spray. Layer 5 more sheets over first sheet, spraying each with cooking spray. Place phyllo in prepared baking dish, letting excess pastry fall over sides of dish.
- Spoon half of squash mixture and half of cheese mixture over phyllo in dish.
- Repeat layers with 6 more sheets of phyllo (sprayed and layered as above) and remaining squash mixture and cheese mixture.
- Coat remaining phyllo with cooking spray and place on top of casserole. Using scissors, trim overhanging edges of phyllo around dish.
- Bake, uncovered, at 350° for 40 minutes or until golden brown.

SOUTHERN SQUASH CASSEROLE

A lighter version of yummy squash casserole.

Yield: 6 servings

5-6 medium yellow squash, sliced
1 egg, beaten
1 small onion, diced
2 tablespoons butter, cut into small
  pieces

½ cup shredded Cheddar cheese
½ cup cracker crumbs
Salt and black pepper to taste

- Preheat oven to 350°. Spray 8x8-inch baking dish with nonstick spray.
- Place squash in a large saucepan, cover with water, and boil until tender.
- Drain squash well and mash with fork. Add egg, onion, butter, cheese, and cracker crumbs. Season with salt and pepper to taste. Mix well.
- Pour into prepared dish and bake at 350° for 35 to 40 minutes.

The best squash look firm and glossy with brightly-colored skins. Small to medium-sized squash have the best texture and flavor. Summer squash may be refrigerated in a perforated bag in the vegetable drawer for up to 5 days.

FAVORITE SQUASH CASSEROLE

*So delicious that it's worth the calories. Squash may be
mashed in the blender, but we like it chunky.*

Yield: 6-8 servings

2½ pounds yellow summer squash or
zucchini, thickly sliced

1   medium sweet onion, coarsely
chopped

1   (10¾-ounce) can condensed
cream of chicken soup

1   (8-ounce) container sour cream

2   carrots, peeled and grated
Salt and black pepper to taste

1   stick (½ cup) butter

1   (8-ounce) package Pepperidge
Farm herb stuffing mix

- Preheat oven to 350°. Spray 9x13-inch baking dish with nonstick spray.
- In large saucepan, cook squash and onion in boiling salted water until tender; do not overcook. Drain very well and return to saucepan.
- Mash squash lightly with potato masher. Drain well again and return to saucepan.
- Mix soup, sour cream, carrot, salt, and pepper in medium bowl. Fold into mashed, drained squash.
- Melt butter in medium saucepan. Stir stuffing mix into melted butter, mixing well.
- Spread about ⅔ of stuffing mixture on bottom of prepared dish. Fill with squash mixture and top with remaining stuffing.
- Bake, uncovered, at 350° for 30 minutes until browned and bubbly.

Squash comes in winter and summer varieties. Summer squash, including zucchini, crookneck, and pattypan, is softer, more fragile, and more perishable. The varieties of winter squash include pumpkin, acorn, and butternut.

SOUTHERN OKRA & TOMATOES

Add a little water for a "stewier" dish.

Yield: 4 servings

3 tablespoons butter
1 cup fresh okra, cut into ½-inch slices (may use frozen)
¼ cup chopped green bell pepper
½ cup chopped onion

4 fresh tomatoes, peeled and quartered (may use canned)
1 teaspoon salt
¼ teaspoon black pepper

- Melt butter in large skillet. Add okra, bell pepper, and onion. Sauté over medium-low heat until onion is tender.
- Add tomatoes, salt, and pepper. Cook over low heat until tender.

Okra should be refrigerated in a brown paper bag. It doesn't keep well and should be used within 1 to 2 days. Choose fresh pods no longer than your little finger for the best texture and flavor.

TOMATO PIE

*The best summer meal ever may be this pie, fresh green
beans, corn on the cob, and iced tea! The pie can be made
early in the day, baked, and then reheated at serving time.*

Yield: 6-8 servings

1 package of 2 refrigerated pie
crusts (the folded kind, not
already in a pan)

4-6 fresh tomatoes, peeled, seeded,
sliced thickly, and drained

6 ounces Cheddar cheese,
shredded, divided

½ cup mayonnaise

2-3 tablespoons lemon juice

¼ cup sliced fresh basil leaves

½ teaspoon salt

¼ teaspoon lemon pepper
seasoning

- Preheat oven to 425°. Unfold one pie crust and fit into deep-dish pie plate.
- Arrange tomatoes in pie crust. Sprinkle with half of cheese.
- Whisk together mayonnaise, lemon juice, basil, salt, and lemon pepper. Spread mixture over cheese and tomatoes and sprinkle with remaining cheese.
- Place other pie crust over filling, pressing into edges of bottom crust. Cut slits in top crust.
- Place pie on baking sheet and bake at 425° for 20 to 30 minutes until brown and bubbly.

Fresh tomatoes are easy to peel if you cut a small "X" in the base of the tomato and drop it into boiling water for 10 to 15 seconds. Remove tomato from water with tongs and hold it under cold water. The peel will slip right off. To seed, cut in half horizontally and scoop out seeds with a teaspoon or your finger.

CARSON'S TOMATO PIE

A great alternative to a mayonnaise-based pie.

Yield: 6-8 servings

1   refrigerated pie crust
12 ounces mozzarella cheese,
    shredded
    Freshly ground black pepper to
    taste

12 leaves fresh basil, chopped
3   large tomatoes, sliced
¼   cup olive oil

- Preheat oven to 475°.
- Place pie crust in 9-inch pie plate.
- Add mozzarella cheese and top with pepper and basil.
- Add tomatoes in 2 or 3 layers. Drizzle olive oil over tomatoes and top with more fresh pepper.
- Bake at 475° for 40 to 45 minutes. Cover with foil if necessary to prevent over-browning.
- Let sit for 5 to 10 minutes before cutting.

To prevent a soggy tomato pie, salt tomato slices and let them stand for 30 minutes to draw out excess moisture. Blot dry before using.

RATATOUILLE TART

Don't let this long recipe scare you — it is time-consuming but not difficult, and the results are absolutely wonderful.

Yield: 6 servings

12 tablespoons olive oil, divided
1 large eggplant, peeled and cut into ½-inch pieces
1 large onion, chopped
1 green bell pepper, chopped
3 large cloves garlic, minced
1 teaspoon dried thyme
Salt and black pepper to taste

3 tablespoons tomato paste
10 sheets phyllo, thawed if frozen
12 teaspoons Parmesan cheese, divided
1½ cups shredded mild provolone cheese (6 ounces)
4-5 small plum tomatoes, sliced ¼-inch thick
2-3 small zucchini, sliced ¼-inch thick

- Heat 6 tablespoons olive oil in large skillet. Add eggplant, onion, bell pepper, garlic, and thyme. Season generously with salt and pepper. Sauté until vegetables begin to soften, about 10 minutes.
- Reduce heat to low, cover, and cook until eggplant is very soft, about 10 more minutes.
- Uncover skillet and add tomato paste. Cook until liquid evaporates, about 3 minutes.
- Place mixture in strainer set over bowl and cool completely. Discard liquid in bowl and transfer mixture to bowl. Cover and refrigerate. May be made ahead to this point; drain again before continuing with recipe.
- Preheat oven to 350°. Brush 9-inch tart pan with removable bottom with 1 to 2 teaspoons olive oil.
- Stack phyllo sheets on work surface. Using sharp knife and 11-inch round pan or plate as guide, cut sheets into 11-inch rounds.
- Transfer 1 sheet to prepared tart pan. Brush with olive oil and sprinkle with 1 teaspoon Parmesan cheese. Top with next sheet, brush with oil, and sprinkle with 1 teaspoon Parmesan. Continue until all sheets are used.
- Spoon eggplant mixture into phyllo shell. Sprinkle provolone cheese over eggplant.
- Arrange tomato and zucchini slices in concentric, overlapping circles on top of cheese. Brush with olive oil, season with salt and pepper, and sprinkle with remaining 2 teaspoons (or additional) Parmesan cheese.
- Bake, uncovered, at 350° for 1 hour or until crust is golden and zucchini is tender. Cool to room temperature before serving.
- May be prepared up to 4 hours ahead. Let stand at room temperature until served.

TOMATOES ROCKEFELLER

Yield: 12 servings

12 thick tomato slices
2 (10-ounce) packages frozen chopped spinach, cooked and drained
1 cup fresh bread crumbs
1 cup seasoned dry bread crumbs
1 cup finely chopped green onions
6 eggs, slightly beaten
1½ sticks (¾ cup) butter, melted
½ cup grated Parmesan cheese
1 teaspoon dried thyme
¾ teaspoon salt
½ teaspoon minced garlic

- Preheat oven to 350°. Lightly spray 9x13-inch baking dish with nonstick spray.
- Arrange tomato slices in one layer in prepared dish (may need two dishes, depending on size of tomatoes) and set aside.
- Squeeze any excess liquid from spinach and combine with fresh and dry bread crumbs, green onions, eggs, butter, Parmesan, thyme, salt, and garlic.
- Mound spinach mixture on tomato slices.
- Bake, uncovered, at 350° for 15 minutes or until spinach mixture is set.

※ *Tomato Tidbits* ※

Never refrigerate tomatoes. Eat ripe tomatoes within a day or two. Most tomatoes at the grocery store are under-ripe. To ripen tomatoes, put them in a closed paper bag, not on a sunny window sill. To speed ripening, add an apple to the bag.

ROASTED SUMMER VEGETABLES

You may add ½ to 1 pound of quartered fresh mushrooms to this dish.

Yield: 4-6 servings

1 small eggplant, cut into ¼-inch-
 thick slices
4 plum tomatoes, halved
1 green bell pepper, quartered
1 red bell pepper, quartered
1 large purple onion, cut into wedges

1 bunch green onions, sliced
2 garlic bulbs, separated into
 cloves and peeled
2 tablespoons Creole seasoning
2½ tablespoons olive oil
¼ cup shredded fresh basil

- Preheat oven to 400°.
- Toss together eggplant, tomatoes, green and red bell peppers, purple and green onions, garlic, Creole seasoning, olive oil, and basil in large roasting pan.
- Bake at 400° for 20 to 30 minutes or until tender, stirring every 10 minutes.

❖ Goat Cheese Sauce ❖

Combine 3 ounces cream cheese, 3 ounces goat cheese, and 1/4 cup mayonnaise in a saucepan. Heat over medium heat until smooth, stirring to blend well. Stir in 1/4 cup milk and 1 tablespoon chopped chives. Serve over asparagus, broccoli, or potatoes.

SUMMER VEGETABLE SKILLET
Yield: 8 servings

½ stick (¼ cup) butter
4 zucchini, sliced
1 medium onion, chopped
½ cup chopped green bell pepper
2 medium ripe tomatoes, peeled and
   sliced

1½ cups fresh corn kernels
½ teaspoon dried dill
   Salt and black pepper to taste
2 cups shredded Cheddar cheese

- Melt butter in large skillet. Add zucchini, onion, and bell pepper and sauté for 3 to 5 minutes.
- Add tomatoes and corn, reduce heat to medium, and cook an additional 5 minutes or until vegetables are tender.
- Season with dill, salt, and pepper. Sprinkle with cheese, cover, and simmer 10 minutes or until cheese is melted.

EASY VEGETABLE CASSEROLE
Yield: 12 servings

2 (16-ounce) cans shoe peg corn,
   drained
2 (16-ounce) cans French-style green
   beans, drained
1 cup chopped celery
1 cup chopped onion
1 cup chopped green bell pepper
1 cup grated sharp Cheddar cheese

1 (8-ounce) container sour cream
1 (10½-ounce) can condensed cream
   of celery soup
   Pepperidge Farm herb stuffing mix
1 (2-ounce) package sliced almonds
½ stick (¼ cup) butter, melted,
   optional

- Preheat oven to 350°. Spray 9x13-inch baking dish with nonstick spray.
- Stir together corn, green beans, celery, onion, bell pepper, cheese, sour cream, and soup.
- Pour into prepared dish and sprinkle stuffing mix and almonds on top.
- Drizzle with melted butter, if desired, and bake, uncovered, for 30 to 45 minutes or until bubbly.

BAKED APRICOTS

Yield: 6-8 servings

2 (1-pound) cans apricot halves, drained
¾ cup dark brown sugar

20-25 Ritz crackers, crushed
¾-1 stick (6-8 tablespoons) butter, melted

- Preheat oven to 350°. Spray 1½-quart baking dish with nonstick spray.
- Chop apricots into chunks and stir in brown sugar.
- Layer half of apricots in prepared dish, then half of crushed crackers. Repeat layers.
- Drizzle with melted butter.
- Bake, uncovered, at 350° for 30 minutes.

An easy way to crush crackers: put them in a heavy Ziploc bag and roll over the bag with a rolling pin. No mess!

PINEAPPLE CASSEROLE

Sweet and delicious with ham, pork, or chicken.

Yield: 4-6 servings

1 stick (½ cup) butter, softened
1 cup sugar
1 (20-ounce) can crushed pineapple, undrained

5-6 slices white bread, cubed
3 eggs
Dash of salt

- Preheat oven to 400°. Spray 8x8-inch baking dish with nonstick spray.
- Cream butter and sugar together until fluffy.
- Stir in pineapple, bread cubes, eggs, and salt. Mix well and pour into prepared dish.
- Bake, uncovered, at 400° for 45 to 60 minutes.

CRANBERRY APPLE BAKE

An old favorite - unbeatable with turkey or for brunch.

Yield: 8-10 servings

3 cups chopped unpeeled apples
  (Granny Smiths work well)
2 cups fresh cranberries
1 cup sugar
½ cup all-purpose flour, divided

1½ cups quick-cooking oats
  (not instant)
½ cup brown sugar, firmly packed
1 stick (½ cup) butter or
  margarine, melted
½ cup chopped pecans

- Preheat oven to 350°. Spray 9x13-inch baking dish with nonstick spray.
- Toss together apples, cranberries, sugar, and 2 tablespoons flour in large bowl. Pour into prepared dish.
- In same bowl, stir together remaining flour, oats, brown sugar, butter, and pecans. Spoon on top of apples and cranberries.
- Bake, uncovered, at 350° for 40 to 45 minutes or until bubbly and browned on top.

Brown sugar should be stored in a heavy plastic bag in a cool, dry place. To prevent brown sugar from hardening after opening, add a ribbon of orange zest to the bag and keep it tightly sealed.

COLD SPICED FRUIT

Find someone to open all those cans for you, and this practically makes itself. Looks beautiful and tastes so refreshing — a wonderful brunch or buffet side dish. Doubles easily.

Yield: 15 servings

2 unpeeled oranges, thinly sliced and seeded

1 (20-ounce) can pineapple chunks in pineapple juice

1 (16-ounce) can sliced peaches in light syrup

1 (16-ounce) can apricot halves in light syrup

1 (29-ounce) can pear halves in light syrup

1 cup sugar

½ cup white vinegar

3 sticks cinnamon

5 whole cloves

1 (3-ounce) package cherry Jello powder

- Cut orange slices in half, place in large saucepan, and cover with water. Bring to boil, reduce heat, and simmer gently until rind is tender but not mushy. Drain well and set aside.

- Drain pineapple, peaches, apricots, and pears well, reserving all of pineapple juice and half of peach and apricot juices (pear juice may be discarded).

- In same saucepan, stir together reserved juices, sugar, vinegar, cinnamon sticks, cloves, and Jello. Bring to boil, reduce heat, and simmer, uncovered, for 30 minutes.

- While juice mixture is simmering, gently combine all fruits (don't forget the oranges). Pour hot juice mixture over fruit.

- Cover and refrigerate at least 24 hours.

- Do not drain before serving, but serve with a slotted spoon.

Extra
Credits

PASTA

Pasta with Sausage & Chicken 195

Vermicelli with
Sausage & Vegetables 196

Spinach Pasta with
Salmon Cream Sauce 197

Linguine with Clam Sauce 198

Pasta Artichoke Raphael 199

Penne Pasta & Spinach 200

Spinach & Peanut Pesto over Pasta . . . 201

Patty's Garden Tomato Pasta 202

Summertime Pasta 203

Cannelloni with Two Sauces 204

Spaghetti Carbonara 205

Spaghetti Casserole 206

Manicotti with
Cheese & Spinach Stuffing 207

Fresh Spinach Lasagna 208

Special Lasagna 209

Mom's Kid-Approved Lasagna 210

Company Lasagna 211

Sausage Lasagna with Vegetables 212

Austrian Noodles with Walnuts 213

Orzo with Basil & Mushrooms 214

Noodles with Peanut Sauce 215

Homemade Tomato Sauce 216

RICE

Very Yummy Rice 217

Bill Neal's Hoppin' John 217

Cheesy Chile Rice 218

Gretchen's Nutty Wild Rice 218

California Rice Casserole 219

Savory Tomato Rice 220

Lemon Rice with Pine Nuts 221

Gallo Pinto
(Costa Rican Rice & Beans) 222

PASTA WITH SAUSAGE & CHICKEN

Yield: 4 servings

3 tablespoons olive oil

2 skinless, boneless chicken breast halves, cut into 1-inch pieces

⅓ cup dry white wine

1 pound hot Italian sausage, casings removed

2 cups chopped onion

1 red bell pepper, sliced into matchstick strips

1 (14½-ounce) can diced tomatoes, undrained

2 tablespoons tomato paste

1¼ cups chicken broth

1 tablespoon chopped fresh garlic

1 tablespoon chopped fresh rosemary

Salt and black pepper to taste

12 ounces farfalle pasta

1½ cups freshly grated Parmesan cheese, divided

¼ cup chopped fresh Italian parsley

- Heat oil in large, heavy skillet over medium-high heat. Add chicken and sauté until cooked through, about 5 minutes.
- With slotted spoon, transfer chicken to bowl. Add wine to skillet and boil 3 minutes or until reduced to 2 tablespoons, scraping up browned bits. Pour wine over chicken in bowl.
- Add sausage, onion, and bell pepper to same skillet and cook 10 minutes or until sausage browns, breaking up with spoon.
- Add chicken, tomatoes, tomato paste, chicken broth, garlic, and rosemary, stirring to blend and heat through. Season with salt and pepper.
- While other ingredients are cooking, cook pasta in large pot of boiling salted water until just tender.
- Drain pasta and return to pot. Stir in chicken and sausage mixture, 1 cup of cheese, and parsley.
- Transfer to serving bowl and serve with remaining cheese.

VERMICELLI WITH SAUSAGE & VEGETABLES

This is so easy, and can be doubled to feed a crowd.

Yield: 4-6 servings

4 tablespoons butter, divided
½ cup chopped green bell pepper
½ cup chopped onion
½ pound fresh mushrooms, sliced
1 pound Polish sausage, sliced
2 cups sliced zucchini, broccoli florets, or peas

1 (14½-ounce) can diced tomatoes, drained
1 teaspoon garlic powder
1 teaspoon oregano
1 teaspoon Italian seasoning
1 (8-ounce) package vermicelli, uncooked
1 cup grated Parmesan cheese

- Melt 3 tablespoons butter in large skillet over medium-low heat. Add bell pepper, onion, and mushrooms. Sauté 8 to 10 minutes or until tender.
- Add sausage, zucchini, tomatoes, garlic powder, oregano, and Italian seasoning to skillet, mix well.
- Cook 10 minutes or until hot and thoroughly blended.
- While sauce is heating, cook vermicelli according to package directions. Drain and toss with remaining 1 tablespoon butter.
- Stir Parmesan cheese into sauce and serve over hot buttered vermicelli.

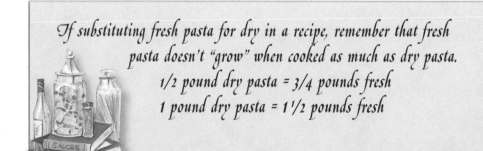

If substituting fresh pasta for dry in a recipe, remember that fresh pasta doesn't "grow" when cooked as much as dry pasta.
1/2 pound dry pasta = 3/4 pounds fresh
1 pound dry pasta = 1 1/2 pounds fresh

SPINACH PASTA WITH SALMON CREAM SAUCE

Next time you grill or poach salmon, cook enough for leftovers so you can make this!

Yield: 6 servings

2 cups heavy cream
½ stick (¼ cup) butter, divided
1 teaspoon salt
  Pinch of freshly grated nutmeg
2 tablespoons salt
1 pound fresh spinach pasta,
  narrower noodles preferred

1 tablespoon grated Parmesan cheese
1½-2 cups flaked cooked salmon, all skin and bones removed
⅓ cup chopped fresh dill (or 1 tablespoon dried)
Additional Parmesan and fresh dill sprigs for garnish

- Bring cream and 2 tablespoons butter to simmer in small saucepan. Add 1 teaspoon salt and nutmeg. Continue simmering until reduced by one-third.
- Bring 4 quarts of water to boil in large pot. Add 2 tablespoons salt and drop in noodles.
- While pasta is cooking, stir Parmesan, salmon and dill into cream and remove from heat. Remember — fresh pasta is ready in 2 to 3 minutes at the most!
- Drain pasta, return it to hot pot, and toss with remaining 2 tablespoons butter until butter is melted.
- Divide pasta equally among 6 heated plates and spoon salmon cream sauce over each portion. Sprinkle with Parmesan, garnish with sprigs of fresh dill, and serve at once.

LINGUINE WITH CLAM SAUCE

An easy and delicious alternative to tomato sauce.

Yield: 4-6 servings

1 (16-ounce) package linguine
1 stick (½ cup) butter or margarine
2 cloves garlic, minced
2 (6½-ounce) cans minced clams, drained
1 tablespoon chopped fresh basil (or ½ teaspoon dried)

2 teaspoons chopped fresh oregano (or ½ teaspoon dried)
½ teaspoon salt
¼ teaspoon black pepper
½ cup chopped fresh parsley
1 cup grated Parmesan cheese

- Cook linguine according to package directions. Drain and keep warm.
- Melt butter in skillet. Add garlic and sauté until tender.
- Add clams, basil, oregano, salt, and pepper. Cook over low heat for 5 minutes, stirring constantly.
- Pour sauce over hot cooked linguine, add parsley, and toss gently.
- Place on platter and top with Parmesan cheese.

When mincing garlic, sprinkle on a little salt so the pieces won't stick to your knife or cutting board.

PASTA ARTICHOKE RAPHAEL

Yield: 4 servings

1 (6½-ounce) jar artichokes
marinated in oil
1 onion, chopped
2 cloves garlic, minced
1 tablespoon olive oil
½ teaspoon dried oregano
½ teaspoon dried basil

1 teaspoon black pepper
½ teaspoon salt
Pinch of red pepper flakes
1 (28-ounce) can diced tomatoes
1 pound pasta
¼ cup grated Parmesan cheese, plus
additional for garnish

- Drain and chop artichokes, reserving liquid.
- In saucepan, sauté onion and garlic in olive oil.
- Add artichoke liquid, oregano, basil, pepper, salt, and red pepper flakes to onion. Cook about 10 minutes. Add tomatoes and simmer 30 minutes.
- While sauce is simmering, cook pasta until just tender.
- Add artichokes and Parmesan to tomato mixture and reduce heat to low. Simmer briefly until blended.
- Toss drained pasta with tomato and artichoke mixture. Sprinkle with additional Parmesan, if desired.

The sauce should dictate what shape of pasta to use: for thinner sauce, use longer pasta – for thicker sauce, use shorter pasta. Orzo and pastina are the exceptions – they are best served in a light broth or sauce.

PENNE PASTA & SPINACH

So versatile — tasty hot, at room temperature, or cold,
and may be served as a main or side dish.

Yield: 8 main dish servings

1 pound penne pasta
6 tablespoons olive oil
⅔ cup pine nuts
3-5 cloves garlic, chopped

2 (10-ounce) packages frozen chopped spinach, thawed and drained
1 (28-ounce) can diced tomatoes, undrained
1 pound feta cheese, crumbled

- Cook pasta according to package directions. Drain but do not rinse.
- Meanwhile, heat olive oil in skillet and add pine nuts and garlic. Sauté until nuts are lightly browned. Add spinach and cook 3 minutes.
- Add tomatoes and heat thoroughly.
- Pour sauce over pasta and toss well. Sprinkle with feta cheese.

To get the smell of garlic off your fingers, rub your fingers on a stainless steel spoon. No one will ever know!

SPINACH & PEANUT PESTO OVER PASTA

*This pesto may also be spread over chicken breasts and
baked, then served over pasta. By itself, the pesto freezes well
— great to have in the freezer for a quick pasta dinner.*

Yield: 4 main dish servings or 8 side dish servings

2 cups tightly packed fresh spinach
leaves, coarsely chopped
1 cup dry roasted peanuts
2 cloves garlic, halved
¼ teaspoon salt
¼ teaspoon freshly ground black
pepper

½ cup peanut oil
½ cup water
1 (16-ounce) package linguini,
uncooked
¼ cup dry roasted peanuts, coarsely
chopped

- Position knife blade in food processor bowl. Add spinach, 1 cup peanuts, garlic, salt, and pepper. Process until smooth, stopping once to scrape down sides.
- With processor running, gradually add peanut oil and water through food chute in a slow, steady stream. Process pesto mixture until smooth.
- Cook linguine according to package directions and drain.
- Spoon pesto over hot linguine and toss gently. Sprinkle with chopped peanuts and serve immediately.

*When buying spinach, remember that one pound
fresh spinach yields about 1½ cups cooked spinach.*

PATTY'S GARDEN TOMATO PASTA

Must be made with real summer tomatoes! Tastes great warm or cold.

Yield: 4-6 servings

2¾ pounds ripe summer tomatoes, peeled, seeded, and chopped

⅓ cup olive oil

2 tablespoons plus 2 teaspoons minced garlic

1 cup chopped fresh cilantro

¼ cup minced red onion or Vidalia onion

2 tablespoons plus 2 teaspoons fresh lime juice

4 teaspoons minced, seeded jalapeño peppers

4 teaspoons tomato paste

2¾ teaspoons chili powder

12 ounces corkscrew pasta

6 ounces crumbled feta cheese

Salt to taste

- Place tomatoes in large bowl.
- Heat oil and sauté garlic over high heat for 2 to 3 minutes until golden.
- Strain oil and pour hot oil over tomatoes. You may add a teaspoon or two of the garlic if desired. Toss to blend.
- Add cilantro, onion, lime juice, peppers, tomato paste, and chili powder. Cover and let stand at room temperature. May be prepared several hours ahead to this point.
- At serving time, cook pasta in salted water until just tender. Drain and toss with tomato mixture.
- Add crumbled cheese and toss. Season to taste with salt.
- Serve immediately while warm. May also be chilled for an excellent pasta salad.

SUMMERTIME PASTA

The taste of summer in a bowl of pasta.

Yield: 8 servings

½ cup corn kernels, fresh or canned (fresh is better, of course!)
4 large tomatoes, peeled, seeded, and chopped
1 cup fresh basil leaves, chopped
4 cloves garlic
½ cup olive oil
½ teaspoon salt
½ teaspoon black pepper
2 tablespoons olive oil
2 teaspoons salt, or more to taste
1½ pounds linguine
Freshly grated Parmesan cheese

- In non-metal bowl, stir together corn, tomatoes, basil, garlic, ½ cup oil, ½ teaspoon salt, and pepper. Cover and set aside for at least 2 hours at room temperature.
- Bring large pot of water to boil. Add 2 tablespoons olive oil and 2 teaspoons salt. Stir in linguine and cook until just tender. Drain and toss with tomato mixture.
- Serve at room temperature, sprinkled with Parmesan cheese.

When buying fresh basil, choose evenly-colored leaves with no sign of wilting. Wrap in barely-damp paper towels and refrigerate in plastic bags for up to 4 days. Or store a bunch of basil, stems down, in a glass of water with a plastic bag over the leaves. This works for parsley, dill, and watercress, too! Refrigerate for up to a week, changing the water every 2 days.

CANNELLONI WITH TWO SAUCES

A lot of trouble — but worth it! Freezes well.

Yield: 6-8 servings

For cannelloni:

4 cloves garlic
1 medium onion
2 tablespoons butter
2 tablespoons olive oil
1 pound ground beef
1 (10-ounce) package frozen chopped spinach, thawed and drained

5 tablespoons grated Parmesan cheese
½ teaspoon dried oregano
Salt and black pepper to taste
2 tablespoons cream
2 eggs, beaten
1 package cannelloni pasta, cooked and drained

For tomato sauce:

1 small onion, chopped
2 tablespoons olive oil
2 (14½-ounce) cans diced tomatoes, undrained
3 tablespoons tomato paste

1 teaspoon dried basil
1 teaspoon sugar
½ teaspoon salt
Black pepper to taste

For cream sauce:

½ stick (¼ cup) butter
¼ cup all-purpose flour
1 cup milk
1 cup heavy cream

1 teaspoon salt
White pepper to taste
Parmesan cheese and butter for top of dish

- Preheat oven to 350°. Spray 9x13-inch baking dish with nonstick spray.
- To prepare cannelloni, blend garlic and onion in blender. Add small amount of water if necessary.
- Heat butter and olive oil in skillet. Add onion and garlic and cook for about 5 minutes. Add meat and brown well.
- Add spinach to skillet and cook until almost all moisture is out. Add Parmesan cheese, oregano, salt, and pepper. Cool.
- Whisk cream and eggs together and stir into meat mixture.
- Stuff cannelloni tubes with mixture, using a pastry bag if desired for easier filling.

CANNELLONI WITH TWO SAUCES *(continued)*

- For tomato sauce, blend onion in blender. Heat olive oil and cook onion in oil until tender.
- Blend tomatoes and add to onions. Add tomato paste, basil, sugar, salt, and pepper. Simmer, partly covered, for 30 minutes while preparing cream sauce.
- For cream sauce, melt butter in skillet and whisk in flour. Cook for 2 minutes, then add milk and cream, whisking constantly until thick. Add salt and white pepper.
- To assemble casserole, glaze bottom of prepared dish with tomato sauce. Arrange stuffed cannelloni in single layer, cover with cream sauce, and top with tomato sauce. Sprinkle with about 3 tablespoons Parmesan cheese and dot with butter.
- Bake, uncovered, at 350° for 30 to 45 minutes or until bubbly.

SPAGHETTI CARBONARA

Use more bacon for an even heartier meal.

Yield: 6-8 servings

1 pound spaghetti	8 slices bacon, cooked and crumbled
3 eggs, beaten	¼ cup chopped fresh parsley
1 cup grated Parmesan cheese, divided	¼ teaspoon dried basil
	1 clove garlic, crushed
½ cup half-and-half	½ stick (¼ cup) butter, cut into chunks

- Cook spaghetti in large pot of boiling, salted water until just tender. Prepare other ingredients while spaghetti is cooking.
- Stir together eggs and ½ cup cheese; set aside.
- Heat half-and-half and stir in bacon, parsley, basil, and garlic.
- In large serving bowl, combine hot drained spaghetti, egg mixture, cream mixture, and butter. Toss until butter is melted and all ingredients are blended.
- Top with remaining cheese and serve immediately.

SPAGHETTI CASSEROLE

Rich, delicious, and easy — a great family supper dish. Must be made 3 to 6 hours ahead.

Yield: 6-8 servings

1   (8-ounce) package spaghetti, uncooked
1½ pounds ground beef
1   (26-ounce) jar spaghetti sauce
1   (24-ounce) container cottage cheese

¼ cup sour cream
1   (8-ounce) package cream cheese, softened
    Grated Parmesan cheese
2   tablespoons butter, cut into small pieces

- Spray 9x13-inch baking dish with nonstick spray.
- Cook spaghetti according to package directions; drain.
- While spaghetti is cooking, brown ground beef in large skillet and drain. Return to skillet, add spaghetti sauce, and simmer 10 minutes.
- In bowl, stir together cottage cheese, sour cream, and cream cheese until thoroughly combined.
- Layer spaghetti, cheese mixture, and meat sauce in prepared dish. Sprinkle with Parmesan cheese and dot with butter.
- Cover and refrigerate 3 to 6 hours.
- Preheat oven to 350°, uncover casserole, and bake, uncovered, at 350° for 30 to 45 minutes.

Don't salt water until it comes to a boil. Salted water has a higher boiling point, so it will take longer.

MANICOTTI WITH
CHEESE & SPINACH STUFFING

Yield: 4 servings

1 pound ricotta cheese
8 ounces mozzarella cheese, shredded
1 (10-ounce) package frozen chopped spinach, cooked, drained, and squeezed dry
1 egg, well beaten
1 tablespoon dried parsley flakes
¼ teaspoon black pepper
1 teaspoon salt
   Dash of nutmeg
8 manicotti shells, boiled until just tender and drained
1 (16-ounce) jar spaghetti sauce
¼ cup grated Parmesan cheese

- Preheat oven to 350°. Spray 9x13-inch baking dish with nonstick spray.
- In large bowl, combine ricotta cheese, mozzarella cheese, spinach, egg, parsley, pepper, salt, and nutmeg.
- Fill manicotti shells with mixture.
- Spread half of spaghetti sauce in bottom of prepared dish.
- Arrange stuffed manicotti in single layer over sauce. Cover with remaining sauce.
- Cover with foil and bake at 350° for 30 minutes. Uncover, sprinkle with Parmesan cheese, and bake, uncovered, an additional 10 minutes.

When covering a pan of something cheesy or sticky with foil, spray one side of the foil with nonstick spray and put that side down over the dish.

FRESH SPINACH LASAGNA

A light, fresh-tasting lasagna, perfect for summer. Don't tell anyone it contains good-for-you tofu until after they taste it! Try the Homemade Tomato Sauce recipe on page 216 if you want to make your own.

Yield: 6-8 servings

1 pound soft tofu
½ cup grated Parmesan cheese
2 eggs
3 cloves garlic, minced
2 tablespoons minced fresh basil (or
   2 teaspoons dried)
2 tablespoons minced fresh thyme
   (or 2 teaspoons dried)
2 tablespoons minced fresh oregano
   (or 2 teaspoons dried)

½ teaspoon salt
⅛ teaspoon black pepper
4 cups tomato sauce, homemade or
   store-bought
1 (8-ounce) package no-boil lasagna
   noodles
4 ounces (2 cups) fresh baby
   spinach leaves (found with
   bagged salads at supermarket)
2 cups shredded mozzarella cheese

- Preheat oven to 375°. Spray 9x13-inch baking dish with nonstick spray.
- In medium bowl, mix tofu, Parmesan cheese, eggs, garlic, basil, thyme, oregano, salt, and pepper.
- Spread 1 cup tomato sauce in bottom of prepared dish. Arrange 1 layer of uncooked noodles over sauce.
- Spread half of tofu mixture over noodles. Top with half of spinach leaves, another cup of tomato sauce, and one-third of mozzarella.
- Repeat layers (noodles, tofu, spinach, sauce, and mozzarella).
- Top with remaining noodles, sauce, and mozzarella. You may not need all noodles in package.
- Cover with aluminum foil and bake at 375° for 30 to 35 minutes. Uncover and let stand 5 minutes before serving.

SPECIAL LASAGNA

Great for family dinners or entertaining.

Yield: 10-12 servings

1 (8-ounce) package lasagna noodles	¼ cup Parmesan cheese
1 pound ground beef	½ teaspoon dried oregano
¼-½ medium onion, chopped	1 teaspoon black pepper, divided
1 (6-ounce) can tomato paste	½ cup water
1 (8-ounce) can tomato sauce	1 (8-ounce) package shredded mozzarella cheese
½ cup sliced mushrooms	1 (16-ounce) container creamed cottage cheese
1 clove garlic, crushed	
1 teaspoon chopped fresh basil	1 cup chopped fresh spinach
1 teaspoon dried parsley	1 egg
1 teaspoon salt, divided	½ cup salami, chopped (optional)

- Spray 9x13-inch baking dish with nonstick spray.
- Cook lasagna noodles as directed on package. Drain and reserve (spread out on waxed paper to prevent sticking, if desired).
- Brown ground beef and onion in large skillet. Drain and return to skillet.
- Add tomato paste, tomato sauce, mushrooms, garlic, basil, parsley, and ½ teaspoon salt to skillet. Simmer gently for one hour.
- In bowl, stir together Parmesan, oregano, ½ teaspoon pepper, water, and mozzarella.
- In another bowl, stir together cottage cheese, spinach, egg, remaining ½ teaspoon each salt and pepper, and salami if using.
- Preheat oven to 350°.
- Layer half of noodles, half of meat sauce, half of Parmesan mixture, and half of cottage cheese mixture in prepared dish. Repeat layers with remaining ingredients.
- Bake at 350° for 30 minutes.

MOM'S KID-APPROVED LASAGNA

Yield: 8 servings

10 ounces lasagna noodles
2 pounds ground chuck
1 clove garlic, minced
1 tablespoon dried parsley
1 tablespoon dried basil
½ teaspoon salt
1 (14½-ounce) can diced tomatoes, undrained
2 (6-ounce) cans tomato paste

3 cups cottage cheese
2 eggs, beaten
½ cup grated Parmesan cheese
½ teaspoon black pepper
2 tablespoons chopped fresh parsley
8 ounces mozzarella cheese, shredded
8 ounces American cheese, thinly sliced

- Cook noodles in salted water and drain. Rinse in cold water.
- Brown ground chuck in large skillet. Add garlic, dried parsley, basil, salt, tomatoes, and tomato paste.
- Simmer for 30 minutes.
- Preheat oven to 375°. Spray 9x13-inch baking dish with nonstick spray.
- In bowl, mix cottage cheese, eggs, Parmesan cheese, pepper, and fresh parsley.
- In prepared dish, layer half of noodles, half of cottage cheese mixture, half of mozzarella and American cheeses (reserve some mozzarella to sprinkle on top), and half of meat sauce. Repeat with remaining ingredients in same order.
- Sprinkle with reserved mozzarella. Cover with foil and bake at 375° for 30 to 45 minutes, uncovering for last 10 minutes or so.

To clean crusty, baked-on pans like lasagna dishes, fill the pan with water, add a Bounce dryer sheet, and soak overnight. In the morning, you can just wipe it out with no scrubbing.

COMPANY LASAGNA

Try ground beef in this recipe for a milder taste, extra-hot sausage
for a spicy dish, or any combination you like. We tested lots of
lasagna recipes, and this one got especially great reviews.

Yield: 10 servings

3 tablespoons olive oil
1 large onion, chopped
2 cloves garlic, minced
1 (28-ounce) can Italian-style stewed
   tomatoes
1 (6-ounce) can tomato paste
1 teaspoon sugar
1 tablespoon fresh oregano
   (or 1 teaspoon dried)
1 tablespoon fresh basil
   (or 1 teaspoon dried)
1 teaspoon salt

1 pound mild sausage
8 ounces hot sausage
1 (16-ounce) container cottage
   cheese or low-fat cottage
   cheese, drained
½ cup grated Parmesan cheese
1 egg, beaten
½ cup plus 1 tablespoon chopped
   fresh parsley, divided
6 lasagna noodles, cooked
12 ounces mozzarella cheese, thinly
   sliced

- Preheat oven to 350°. Spray deep 9x13-inch baking dish with nonstick spray.
- Heat olive oil in large skillet and sauté onion and garlic until tender. Stir in tomatoes, tomato paste, sugar, oregano, basil, and salt. Simmer, uncovered, until thickened.
- While sauce is simmering, brown all sausage in medium skillet, stirring until crumbly; drain well. Add sausage to tomato sauce and mix well.
- Stir together cottage cheese, Parmesan cheese, egg, and ½ cup parsley in bowl until thoroughly blended.
- Spread thin layer of sausage mixture in prepared dish. Layer half of noodles, half of cottage cheese mixture, half of mozzarella cheese, and half of remaining sausage mixture.
- Layer remaining noodles, cottage cheese mixture, sausage mixture, and mozzarella cheese. Sprinkle with 1 tablespoon parsley.
- Cover with foil and bake at 350° for 35 minutes or until bubbly.

May be prepared ahead and refrigerated or frozen.

SAUSAGE LASAGNA WITH VEGETABLES

You don't have to cook those lasagna noodles first!

Yield: 6-8 servings

For sauce:

1 cup chopped onions
1 pound sweet Italian sausage,
   casings removed
2 tablespoons olive oil
3 large cloves garlic, minced
2 large carrots, grated
½ cup chopped fresh basil

2 teaspoons dried oregano
½ teaspoon dried crushed red pepper
1 (28-ounce) can crushed tomatoes
   with added purée
1 (14½-ounce) can diced tomatoes,
   undrained
1 cup water
   Salt and black pepper to taste

For filling:

1 (10-ounce) package frozen
   chopped spinach, thawed and
   squeezed dry
2 (15-ounce) containers ricotta cheese

¾ cup freshly grated Parmesan
   cheese (about 2 ounces)
2 large eggs
   Salt and black pepper to taste

12 lasagna noodles, uncooked
4   cups grated mozzarella cheese

1 cup freshly grated Parmesan
   cheese

- For sauce (sauce may be prepared ahead and frozen), sauté onion and sausage in hot oil until sausage is brown and onion is translucent. Use large spoon to break up sausage into bite-size pieces.
- Add garlic, carrots, basil, oregano, and red pepper. Continue cooking until garlic and carrots are tender.
- Stir in crushed and diced tomatoes and water. Bring to boil, reduce heat, and simmer, uncovered, at least 30 minutes.
- Season to taste with salt and pepper.
- For filling, combine spinach, ricotta, Parmesan, eggs, salt, and pepper in large bowl, using hands if necessary to mix thoroughly.
- Preheat oven to 375°. Spray deep 9x13-inch baking dish with nonstick spray.
- Spread 1¼ cups of sauce in bottom of prepared dish.
- Arrange 3 uncooked noodles over sauce. Spread 1½ cups of filling evenly over noodles. Sprinkle with 1 cup mozzarella and ¼ cup Parmesan.

SAUSAGE LASAGNA WITH VEGETABLES *(continued)*

- Repeat layers of sauce, noodles, filling, and cheeses two more times.
- Top with last 3 noodles. Spoon remaining sauce on top and sprinkle with remaining cheeses.
- Spray large piece of foil with nonstick spray. Cover lasagna with foil, sprayed side down.
- Bake, covered, at 375° for 40 minutes. Remove foil, increase temperature to 400°, and bake 20 more minutes or until noodles are tender and sauce is bubbly. Let stand about 15 minutes before serving.

AUSTRIAN NOODLES WITH WALNUTS
Yield: 4-6 servings

1 (8-ounce) package wide egg noodles
½ stick (¼ cup) unsalted butter
2 cloves garlic, minced
¼ cup fresh bread crumbs

½ cup very finely chopped walnuts (chop by hand or in food processor)
¾ teaspoon salt
¼ cup finely chopped fresh dill

- Cook noodles according to package directions.
- While noodles are cooking, melt butter over low heat in large skillet. Add garlic and sauté for 2 minutes or until tender.
- Stir in bread crumbs and walnuts and cook for 2 more minutes or until lightly toasted.
- Drain cooked noodles, return to cooking pot, and pour butter mixture over noodles. Add salt and dill and toss well to mix.

ORZO WITH BASIL & MUSHROOMS

A wonderful side with any meat, but also makes a great meatless main dish.

Yield: 6 side dish servings

2 tablespoons butter
⅓ cup sliced green onions
4 cloves garlic, minced or chopped
4 cups sliced mushrooms
2 tablespoons olive oil
2 cups orzo pasta, uncooked

4 cups chicken broth
3 tablespoons chopped fresh basil
　(or 1 tablespoon dried)
1 teaspoon salt
½ teaspoon black pepper
½ cup grated Parmesan cheese

- Melt butter in skillet and sauté green onions, garlic, and mushrooms until tender. Set aside.
- In medium saucepan, heat olive oil and orzo for 2 minutes. Add broth to orzo and bring to boil. Reduce heat, cover, and simmer for 15 minutes or until liquid is absorbed.
- Stir in basil, salt, pepper, and mushroom mixture. Heat for 2 to 3 minutes until blended and heated through.
- Sprinkle with Parmesan cheese and serve hot.

☀ *Herb Hints* ☀
Pick fresh herbs in the morning, just after the dew has dried.
Always snip fresh herbs with scissors.
Three units of fresh herbs = 1 unit dried herbs.

NOODLES WITH PEANUT SAUCE

Yield: 6-10 servings

⅔ cup chunky Smuckers (or other natural) peanut butter
¼ cup very hot tap water
4 teaspoons hot chili oil or hot pepper flakes (adjust to taste)
6 tablespoons light soy sauce

6-8 tablespoons sesame oil
Ground ginger to taste
1 (8-ounce) package angel hair or fettuccine
3-4 green onions, sliced

- While pasta water is coming to a boil, whisk together peanut butter, hot water, chili oil, soy sauce, sesame oil, and ginger until blended and pourable.
- Cook noodles until just tender. Drain and rinse with cold water to stop cooking.
- Pour peanut sauce over noodles and toss well to mix. Sprinkle with green onions.
- Serve at room temperature.

HOMEMADE TOMATO SAUCE

Canned tomatoes make this easy, but the taste is fresh.
Well worth the 10 minutes it takes to get it in the pot!

Yield: about 8 cups

3 tablespoons olive oil
1 large onion, finely chopped
1 large carrot, finely chopped
1 large celery stalk, finely chopped

3 (28-ounce) cans whole tomatoes, undrained
1 tablespoon salt
2 teaspoons dried oregano
1 teaspoon sugar

- In large saucepan over medium heat, cook olive oil, onion, carrot, and celery until soft but not browned.
- Add undrained tomatoes, salt, oregano, and sugar.
- Simmer, partly covered, over low heat for 45 minutes, breaking up tomatoes with wooden spoon and stirring occasionally.

Freezes well.

VERY YUMMY RICE

*An old favorite that still can't be beat — perfect
with any kind of beef for a dinner party.*

Yield: 8 servings

½ stick (¼ cup) butter
1 large onion, chopped
2 cups uncooked converted rice
2 cans beef consommé

8 ounces sharp Cheddar cheese, grated
2 (4-ounce) cans mushrooms with
   liquid
1 cup slivered almonds, toasted
   (optional)

- Preheat oven to 325°. Spray 1½-quart casserole dish with nonstick spray.
- Heat butter in large skillet and sauté onion until tender. Add uncooked rice and simmer for 5 minutes.
- Pour rice mixture, consommé, cheese, and undrained mushrooms into prepared dish. Stir well.
- Cover tightly and bake at 325° for 1 hour.
- Fluff rice with fork and stir in almonds just before serving.

BILL NEAL'S HOPPIN' JOHN

*An essential part of any New Year's Day gathering.
Brings you good luck all year and tastes great too!*

Yield: 4-6 servings

1 (16-ounce) can black-eyed peas,
   drained and rinsed
2 cups hot cooked rice
1 cup chopped fresh tomato (use
   plum tomatoes in winter)

½ cup finely chopped scallions
½ teaspoon salt
¼ teaspoon black pepper
½ cup shredded Cheddar cheese
   (optional)

- Combine peas and rice in large skillet or saucepan. Mix lightly over medium-low heat.
- Sprinkle with tomato, scallions, salt, and pepper.
- Cover and heat through.
- Serve topped with cheese, if desired. Recipe may be doubled.

CHEESY CHILE RICE

Rich with a kick — wonderful side dish for a Mexican meal.

Yield: 8-10 servings

1 (24-ounce) container sour cream
3 (4-ounce) cans mild green chiles, drained, seeded and chopped
3 cups cooked rice
Salt and black pepper to taste

12 ounces Monterey Jack cheese, shredded
½ cup shredded Cheddar or grated Parmesan cheese

- Preheat oven to 350°. Spray 9x13-inch baking dish with nonstick spray.
- Stir together sour cream and chiles until thoroughly blended.
- Season cooked rice with salt and pepper. Stir rice into sour cream mixture.
- Place half of rice mixture in prepared dish. Top with Monterey Jack cheese.
- Cover cheese with remaining rice mixture and sprinkle with Cheddar or Parmesan.
- Bake, uncovered, at 350° for 30 to 40 minutes.

GRETCHEN'S NUTTY WILD RICE

Yield: 6-8 servings

1 cup uncooked wild rice
5½ cups chicken broth
1 cup pecan halves, coarsely chopped
1 cup dried cranberries or currants
2 green onions, thinly sliced

Zest of 1 large orange
⅓ cup fresh orange juice
¼ cup olive oil
1 teaspoon salt
2 tablespoons sugar
3-4 tablespoons orange juice concentrate

- Cook rice in chicken broth according to package directions. Rice is done when it "pops" open. Drain any remaining liquid.
- In bowl, stir together pecans, cranberries, green onions, orange zest, orange juice, olive oil, salt, sugar, and concentrate. Pour over rice and toss well.
- Cover and let stand for 2 hours or more to blend flavors.
- May be served at room temperature or reheated (may need to add ½ cup additional chicken broth to reheat).

CALIFORNIA RICE CASSEROLE

This can be made early in the day and refrigerated before baking, so it works well for entertaining. Bring to room temperature before putting in the oven.

Yield: 6-8 servings

½ stick (¼ cup) butter
1 cup chopped onion
4 cups cooked rice, cooled
1 (8-ounce) container sour cream
1 cup cottage cheese
½ teaspoon salt

⅛ teaspoon black pepper
1 (4-ounce) can chopped green chiles, drained well
1 (4-ounce) can chopped black olives, drained well
2 cups shredded Cheddar cheese

- Preheat oven to 375°. Spray 9x13-inch baking dish with nonstick spray.
- Melt butter in large skillet. Add onion and sauté 5 minutes. Remove from heat.
- Stir in cooked rice, sour cream, cottage cheese, salt, pepper, chiles, and olives.
- Spoon half of rice mixture into prepared baking dish. Top with 1 cup Cheddar cheese. Repeat layers.
- Bake, uncovered, at 375° for 25 to 30 minutes.

White rice may be stored in an airtight container for up to a year. Brown rice, however, should be used within 6 months – it contains oils that could become rancid.

SAVORY TOMATO RICE

An all-microwave dish if you cook the bacon in the microwave first. Easy to do while your cooktop and oven are occupied with the rest of dinner!

Yield: 4-6 servings

4 strips bacon, cooked until crisp
1 (14½-ounce) can diced tomatoes, undrained
¾ cup uncooked rice
⅓ cup chili sauce
1 small green bell pepper, chopped (optional)

1 small onion, finely diced
1 teaspoon brown sugar
½-1 teaspoon salt
⅛ teaspoon freshly ground black pepper
½ teaspoon Worcestershire sauce
2 cups hot water

- Crumble bacon into 2-quart microwave-safe baking dish with lid.
- Add tomatoes, rice, chili sauce, bell pepper if using, onion, brown sugar, salt, pepper, Worcestershire, and hot water. Stir well and cover.
- Microwave on high, covered, for 23 to 25 minutes, stirring every 8 minutes.
- Allow to stand 5 to 10 minutes before serving.

LEMON RICE WITH PINE NUTS

A simple, yet elegant side dish for a dinner party.
Use fresh herbs, if possible, for best color and flavor.

Yield: 6-8 servings

3   cups chicken broth
1½ cups uncooked white rice
¼   cup pine nuts
3   tablespoons butter
1   small onion, minced
¼   cup fresh lemon juice

1   tablespoon chopped fresh dill
      (or 1 teaspoon dried)
1½ teaspoons chopped fresh mint
      (or 1 teaspoon dried)
      Salt and freshly ground black
      pepper to taste

• Place chicken broth and rice in large saucepan and bring to boil. Reduce heat to low, cover, and simmer 15 to 18 minutes. Remove from heat and set aside.

• Toast pine nuts in oven or toaster oven, watching carefully (takes just a few minutes in 350° oven).

• In medium saucepan, melt butter over medium heat. Add onion and cook until translucent, about 5 minutes.

• Add cooked rice, toasted pine nuts, lemon juice, dill, and mint. Season with salt and pepper, toss well, and heat thoroughly to serve.

Pine nuts, also called piñon nuts or pignoli, really do come from inside a pine cone! The labor-intensive process of removing them from the cones makes them expensive. They should be stored in an airtight container in the refrigerator, where they will keep for about 3 months, or in the freezer for up to 9 months.

GALLO PINTO
(COSTA RICAN RICE & BEANS)

From a CLS alumna living in Costa Rica. There, this dish is served with eggs for breakfast, or with tortillas, tomato, avocado, or meat any time. Chop the whole onion and bell pepper — you'll use half for the rice and half for the beans.

For rice:

1 tablespoon oil
½ medium onion, chopped
½ large red bell pepper, chopped

3 cups uncooked rice
6 cups water
1 teaspoon salt

For beans:

1 tablespoon butter
2 cloves garlic, chopped
½ onion, chopped
½ large red bell pepper, chopped
2 cans black beans, undrained
2 cups water

¼ cup lizano sauce (Costa Rican pepper sauce)
1 teaspoon sugar
Dash of salt
½ cup fresh cilantro, chopped

- Heat oil in large saucepan and sauté onion and bell pepper until tender.
- Add rice and sauté briefly (less than 1 minute). Add water and salt, cover, and cook on medium to medium-high heat for 20 minutes. Stir after first 10 minutes. Remove from heat and set aside.
- To prepare beans, melt butter in large skillet. Add garlic, onion, and bell pepper and sauté for 3 minutes over medium heat.
- Add undrained beans and water, and reduce heat to medium-low.
- Add lizano sauce, sugar, and salt. Cook for 5 to 10 minutes, adding water if necessary to keep beans moist.
- Add rice mixture and cilantro to beans in skillet and toss to mix.

Extra
Curricular

EGGS

CHEESE

BRUNCH

BREADS

Spicy Apple Bread 223

One-Pan Banana Bread 224

Blueberry Bread 224

Pineapple Bread 225

Pumpkin Raisin Bread & Muffins 226

Strawberry Bread 227

Granddaddy Johnson's
    Oatmeal Bread 228

Jalapeño Corn Bread 229

Apple Cheddar Muffins 230

Morning Glory Muffins 231

Pumpkin Muffins 232

Annie Mae's One-Hour
    Buttermilk Rolls 233

Easy Biscuits 234

Sweet Potato Biscuits 235

Garlic Knots 235

BRUNCHES

Baked Eggs & Cheese 236

Never-Fail Breakfast Soufflé 237

Posner's Famous Spinach Quiche 238

Spring Frittata 239

Vegetable Frittata with
    Herbs & Goat Cheese 240

New York Brunch Wrap 241

Rio Grande Grits Casserole 242

Cinnamon Sour Cream
    Coffee Cake 243

Skillet Coffee Cake 244

Blueberry Brunch Cake 245

Better-than-Bought
    Cinnamon Rolls 246

Butterscotch Monkey Bread 247

Banana Pancakes 248

Apple Pizzas 249

Overnight French Toast 250

William of Orange French Toast 251

Cranberry Maple Sauce 252

SPICY APPLE BREAD

A chunky, filling bread — great for breakfast or snacks.

Yield: 2 loaves

3 cups all-purpose flour	1¼ cups vegetable oil
1½ teaspoons baking soda	4 eggs, beaten
½ teaspoon baking powder	4 teaspoons vanilla extract
1½ teaspoons salt	3 cups chopped, peeled apples
2 teaspoons cinnamon	½ cup raisins (optional)
1 teaspoon ground cloves	½ cup chopped walnuts (optional)
2½ cups sugar	

- Preheat oven to 325°. Grease bottom only of 2 loaf pans.
- In large bowl, whisk together flour, baking soda, baking powder, salt, cinnamon, and cloves.
- Add sugar, oil, eggs, and vanilla. Beat on low speed with electric mixer for 2 minutes.
- Add apples, raisins, and walnuts. Stir until well blended.
- Divide batter evenly between prepared pans.
- Bake at 325° for 1 hour.
- Cool in pans on wire racks for 10 minutes. Remove from pans and cool completely before slicing. Loaves are easier to cut after being in the refrigerator for 1 day.

ONE-PAN BANANA BREAD

The easiest banana bread recipe ever!

Yield: 1 loaf

⅓ cup vegetable oil
1½ cups mashed ripe bananas
    (about 3 large bananas)
½ teaspoon vanilla extract
3 eggs

2⅓ cups Bisquick (regular or
    low-fat)
1 cup sugar
½ cup chopped nuts

- Preheat oven to 350°. Grease 5x9-inch loaf pan.
- Combine all ingredients in loaf pan and stir with fork until moistened.
- Beat vigorously with fork for 1 minute.
- Bake at 350° for 55 to 65 minutes.
- Cool in pan 5 minutes, then loosen with knife and remove.
- Freezes well.

BLUEBERRY BREAD

Yield: 1 loaf

1½ cups all-purpose flour
½ cup old-fashioned oats
⅔ cup sugar
2¼ teaspoons baking powder
½ teaspoon salt
2 eggs, beaten

1 cup mashed banana (about 2 large
    bananas)
⅓ cup cooking oil
½ cup chopped nuts (optional)
1 cup blueberries
1 tablespoon sugar for sprinkling

- Preheat oven to 350°. Grease and flour 8x4½-inch loaf pan.
- Whisk together flour, oats, sugar, baking powder, and salt in bowl.
- Beat eggs in separate bowl and add mashed banana and oil.
- Add egg mixture to dry ingredients and mix.
- Add nuts, if using, and blueberries. Mix gently.
- Pour into prepared pan. Sprinkle sugar on top.
- Bake at 350° for 40 to 45 minutes. Cool in pan for 10 minutes before turning out.

JALAPEÑO CORN BREAD
Yield: 6-8 servings

2¼ cups plain cornmeal (to use self-rising, see note below)

2-3 tablespoons all-purpose flour

1 teaspoon salt

1 teaspoon baking soda

1¼ cups buttermilk

⅔ cup salad oil

2 eggs, beaten

1 (6-ounce) can cream-style corn

3-4 tablespoons chopped jalapeño pepper

½ cup chopped green bell pepper

½-¾ cup chopped onion

½ pimento pepper, chopped

6 slices bacon, fried and crumbled (optional)

- Preheat oven to 375°. Grease 9x13-inch metal baking pan or large cast iron skillet. Put pan in oven to heat while mixing batter.
- Stir together cornmeal, flour, salt, baking soda, buttermilk, oil, eggs, corn, jalapeños, bell pepper, onion, pimento, and bacon if using, in order listed.
- Pour batter into heated pan and bake at 375° for 40 minutes.

Note: If using self-rising cornmeal, omit salt, soda, and flour.

No buttermilk? Here are some substitutes: put 1 tablespoon lemon juice or white vinegar in a measuring cup and fill with milk to make 1 cup; let stand 5 minutes. Or whisk together 1 cup plain yogurt, 1 cup whole milk, and 1¾ teaspoons cream of tartar.

APPLE CHEDDAR MUFFINS

From the King's Arms Tavern in Williamsburg.

Yield: 16 muffins

2 cups all-purpose flour
1 tablespoon baking powder
¼ teaspoon baking soda
½ teaspoon cinnamon
½ teaspoon salt
½ stick (¼ cup) butter, softened

¼ cup sugar
2 large eggs
1 (8-ounce) container sour cream
2 apples, peeled, cored, and finely chopped
½ cup shredded Cheddar cheese

- Preheat oven to 425°. Spray sixteen 2½-inch muffin cups with nonstick spray.
- In large bowl, whisk together flour, baking powder, baking soda, cinnamon, and salt.
- In separate large bowl, cream butter and sugar until light and fluffy. Beat in eggs, one at a time. Stir in sour cream.
- Add butter mixture to dry ingredients all at once and stir to blend. Do not overmix batter, or muffins will be tough.
- Stir in apples and cheese.
- Spoon batter into prepared muffin cups, filling each about half full. Bake at 425° for 15 to 20 minutes, or until toothpick inserted in center comes out clean.
- Turn hot muffins out of cups and serve at once.

If all muffin cups in the pan are not filled, put water or ice cubes in the empty cups to keep the pan from buckling.

ANNIE MAE'S ONE-HOUR BUTTERMILK ROLLS

Yield: 2+ dozen

2 tablespoons yeast
¼ cup warm water (105°-115°)
   Pinch of sugar
1½ cups lukewarm buttermilk (see note)

½ cup shortening, melted and cooled to lukewarm
3 tablespoons sugar
4½ cups all-purpose flour
½ teaspoon baking soda
1 teaspoon salt

- Line 2 large baking sheets with parchment.
- Sprinkle yeast over warm water with pinch of sugar.
- Stir buttermilk, shortening, and 3 tablespoons sugar into yeast mixture.
- In separate bowl, whisk together flour, baking soda, and salt.
- Stir dry ingredients into buttermilk mixture. Beat until smooth and let stand for 10 minutes.
- Roll dough and shape into crescent rolls. Place on prepared baking sheets.
- Cover rolls with dishtowels and let rise for 30 minutes.
- While rolls are rising, preheat oven to 400°.
- Bake at 400° for 15 to 20 minutes until lightly browned.

Note: You may substitute 6 tablespoons "Saco Buttermilk Blend" powder and 1½ cups lukewarm water for the buttermilk. Add powder to flour mixture and add water with shortening and sugar.

EASY BISCUITS

Surprise your family with hot homemade biscuits!
Also great for luncheons and brunches.

Yield: 24 mini biscuits

2 cups Bisquick
1 (8-ounce) container sour cream

1 stick (½ cup) butter, melted

- Preheat oven to 450°. Grease mini-muffin tins.
- Mix Bisquick, sour cream, and melted butter. Spoon batter into muffin tins.
- Bake at 450° for 8 to 10 minutes.

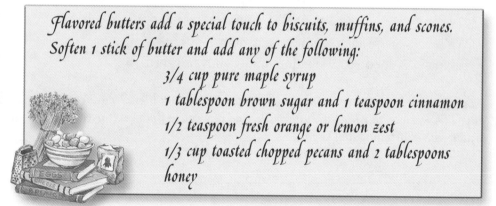

Flavored butters add a special touch to biscuits, muffins, and scones.
Soften 1 stick of butter and add any of the following:
> *3/4 cup pure maple syrup*
> *1 tablespoon brown sugar and 1 teaspoon cinnamon*
> *1/2 teaspoon fresh orange or lemon zest*
> *1/3 cup toasted chopped pecans and 2 tablespoons honey*

NEVER-FAIL BREAKFAST SOUFFLÉ

Wonderful to have in the refrigerator for overnight guests. Be sure to use good-quality baked ham — the deli will shred it for you.

Yield: 8 servings

16 slices white bread
1 pound baked ham, shredded
1 pound sharp Cheddar cheese,
   shredded
4 eggs

3 cups 2% or whole milk
½ teaspoon dry mustard
   Dash of salt
½ stick (¼ cup) butter
2 cups crushed corn flake cereal

- Spray 9x13-inch baking dish with nonstick spray.
- Line prepared dish with 8 slices of bread. Top with shredded ham and cheese, then cover with remaining 8 slices of bread. Poke holes in top layer of bread with fork.
- Beat together eggs, milk, dry mustard, and salt until thoroughly blended. Pour mixture over bread - pour slowly to allow it to soak in!
- Cover tightly with foil and refrigerate overnight.
- When ready to cook, preheat oven to 325°.
- In skillet, melt butter and sauté crushed corn flakes until lightly browned. Sprinkle over soufflé.
- Bake, uncovered, at 325° for 45 minutes or until all liquid is absorbed and soufflé is firm in center.

POSNER'S FAMOUS SPINACH QUICHE
Yield: 8 servings

1 (10-ounce) package frozen
   chopped spinach
1 (9-inch) frozen pie crust
2 eggs, beaten
1 (8-ounce) container sour cream

1 teaspoon salt
   Black pepper to taste
1 (2½-ounce) can French fried
   onions
2 cups shredded Cheddar cheese

- Preheat oven to 350°.
- Cook spinach according to package directions. Drain well.
- Prick pie crust with fork and bake at 350° for 7 to 8 minutes.
- Beat eggs with sour cream.
- Stir in spinach, salt, pepper, onions, and cheese. Mix well and pour into pie crust.
- Increase oven temperature to 375°.
- Bake at 375° for 40 minutes or until center is set and crust is golden brown.

Note: May substitute chopped broccoli for the spinach.

SPRING FRITTATA

Tastes fresh — makes a delicious luncheon with a green salad, good bread, and pinot grigio or chardonnay. Use a food processor for easy shredding of vegetables.

Yield: 6-8 servings

4   large eggs, lightly beaten
3   cups shredded zucchini
2   cups shredded carrots
1½ cups all-purpose flour
¾   cup mayonnaise
1   cup shredded Cheddar cheese
    (4-ounce block)

½ cup grated Parmesan cheese
¼ cup chopped onion
1 tablespoon chopped fresh basil
  Freshly ground black pepper to
  taste

- Preheat oven to 375°. Grease quiche pan or deep-dish pie plate.
- Stir together eggs, zucchini, carrots, flour, mayonnaise, Cheddar and Parmesan cheeses, onion, basil, and pepper. Mix well and pour into prepared pan.
- Bake at 375° for 30 to 35 minutes or until set.

Frittata is the Italian version of the French omelet. The "filling" ingredients are mixed in with the eggs, rather than folded inside, and the whole mixture is cooked in a skillet or pie pan.

VEGETABLE FRITTATA WITH HERBS & GOAT CHEESE

This has lots of ingredients and instructions, but is really very easy.
Makes a wonderful brunch or light supper.

Yield: 6 servings

For vegetables:

1 tablespoon olive oil
2 medium red-skinned potatoes, sliced ⅛-inch thick
1 medium onion, halved and thinly sliced
1 red bell pepper, cut into strips
1 yellow bell pepper, cut into strips

1 tablespoon chopped fresh marjoram (or 1 teaspoon dried)
2 teaspoons minced fresh rosemary (or ¾ teaspoon dried, crushed)
½ teaspoon salt
¼ teaspoon dried rubbed sage

For frittata:

9 large eggs
1 tablespoon chopped fresh dill (or 1 teaspoon dried)
¾ teaspoon salt

½ teaspoon black pepper
4 ounces goat cheese, crumbled, divided
2 teaspoons olive oil

- Heat 1 tablespoon oil in 12-inch nonstick ovenproof skillet over medium-low heat. Add potatoes, onion, red and yellow bell peppers, marjoram, rosemary, salt, and sage. Cook 5 minutes, stirring occasionally.
- Cover skillet and cook 15 minutes or until potatoes are tender, stirring occasionally.
- Remove from heat and cool mixture in skillet 5 minutes. Vegetables may be prepared up to 2 hours ahead. Let stand at room temperature.
- To prepare frittata, preheat oven to 350°.
- Whisk eggs, dill, salt, and pepper in large bowl to blend.
- Mix in 3 ounces of goat cheese (reserving 1 ounce).
- Remove several slices of potato and bell pepper from vegetable mixture and reserve for garnish. Stir remaining vegetable mixture into egg mixture.
- Wipe skillet clean with paper towel and add 2 teaspoons oil. Heat over medium-high heat, coating bottom with oil.
- Pour egg and vegetable mixture into skillet, stirring vegetables to distribute

VEGETABLE FRITTATA WITH HERBS & GOAT CHEESE (*continued*)

throughout. Arrange reserved vegetables on top and sprinkle with remaining 1 ounce cheese.

- Cook on stove until sides begin to set, about 2 minutes. Transfer skillet to oven and bake until set in center, about 15 minutes.
- Run spatula around edge frittata to loosen. Slide out onto platter.
- Serve hot, or cover loosely with foil and let stand at room temperature up to 2 hours. Cut into wedges to serve.

NEW YORK BRUNCH WRAP

Yield: 4 main course servings or 10-12 appetizer servings

4 **small taco-size flour tortillas**	4 **paper-thin slices red onion**
½ **(8-ounce) package cream cheese, softened**	2 **tablespoons coarsely chopped fresh dill**
4 **ounces thinly-sliced smoked salmon (about 8 slices)**	1 **tablespoon drained capers**
2 **plum tomatoes, finely chopped**	1 **lemon**
	Freshly ground black pepper to taste

- Heat tortillas, one at a time, on grill or in hot skillet, turning until soft and pliable, 5 to 15 seconds each. Or heat in microwave, stacked in a moist microwave-safe paper towel, about 10 seconds per tortilla.
- Spread one-fourth of cream cheese on each tortilla, leaving ½-inch border.
- Top with even layer of smoked salmon (1 ounce each), tomatoes, onion, dill, and capers. Top with generous squeeze of lemon juice and dash of pepper.
- Roll tightly, pressing firmly to seal.
- Slice off end pieces, then cut each in half or thirds for a meal or 6 to 8 slices for appetizers. If preparing for appetizers, refrigerate about 15 minutes before slicing. Slice cold, then let stand at room temperature, tightly covered, for 30 to 60 minutes before serving.

To make ahead, seal in wax paper, foil, or plastic wrap and refrigerate. Rolls keep well for a day.

RIO GRANDE GRITS CASSEROLE

Not your mother's grits casserole!

Yield: 12 servings

4 cups water
1 cup quick-cooking grits
1 teaspoon garlic salt
½ pound smoked sausage or kielbasa
1 tablespoon vegetable oil
1 cup chopped onion
1 cup chopped green bell pepper
2 cloves garlic, minced

1¾ cups salsa
1 can black beans, rinsed and drained
2 cups shredded Cheddar cheese, divided
Sour cream
Chopped cilantro

- Preheat oven to 350°. Spray 9x13-inch baking dish with nonstick spray.
- In large saucepan, bring water to boil. Gradually stir in grits and garlic salt. Reduce heat, cover, and cook 5 minutes.
- Cut sausage in half lengthwise, then crosswise into ¼-inch slices. Heat oil in large skillet and add sausage, onion, bell pepper, and garlic. Cook until onion is tender.
- Stir in salsa and beans.
- Spoon half of grits into prepared dish. Top with half of sausage mixture and one cup of cheese. Repeat layers.
- Bake at 350° for 20 to 25 minutes.
- Serve with sour cream and chopped cilantro.

Freeze extra chopped onion and bell pepper for future use. Keep for up to 2 months.

CINNAMON SOUR CREAM COFFEE CAKE

Moist and delectable — great for brunch or to take on a weekend out of town.

Yield: 1 Bundt cake

For batter:

1 package Duncan Hines Butter Recipe Golden cake mix (in the red box)
¾ cup vegetable oil

4 eggs, beaten
1 (8-ounce) container sour cream
½ cup sugar

For topping:

6 tablespoons (light or dark) brown sugar, firmly packed

1½ cups chopped pecans
1 tablespoon cinnamon

- Preheat oven to 325°. Generously grease and flour Bundt pan.
- Combine cake mix, oil, eggs, sour cream, and sugar. Beat according to cake mix package directions.
- To make topping, mix brown sugar, pecans, and cinnamon in small bowl.
- Sprinkle ¼ of topping in bottom of prepared pan. Cover with ⅓ of cake batter. Layer twice more and top with remaining topping.
- Bake at 325° for 1 hour. Let cool in pan 20 to 30 minutes, then turn out onto serving plate.

SKILLET COFFEE CAKE
Yield: 10-12 servings

1½ sticks (¾ cup) butter, melted
1½ cups sugar
2   eggs
1½ cups all-purpose flour

½ teaspoon salt
1 teaspoon almond flavoring
Slivered almonds
Sugar

- Preheat oven to 350°. Line large iron skillet with foil (leave excess foil on either side for later use).
- Stir together melted butter and sugar in large bowl.
- Beat in eggs, one at a time.
- Add flour, salt, and almond flavoring; mix well.
- Pour batter into prepared skillet. Cover top with slivered almonds and sprinkle with sugar.
- Bake at 350° for 30 to 40 minutes.
- Remove cake, still in foil, from skillet. When cool, wrap tightly in foil to store.

Do not try to peel foil while cake is still warm — it will stick.

BLUEBERRY BRUNCH CAKE
Yield: 1 9-inch coffee cake

1¼ cups all-purpose flour, divided
1 cup sugar, divided
2 teaspoons baking powder
1 egg
½ cup milk
⅓ cup vegetable oil

1 tablespoon lemon juice
1 cup blueberries
¼ teaspoon cinnamon
½ cup chopped pecans
2 tablespoons butter, softened

- Preheat oven to 350°. Spray 9-inch square baking pan with nonstick spray.
- Whisk together 1 cup flour, ½ cup sugar, and baking powder.
- In separate small bowl, stir together egg, milk, oil, and lemon juice. Pour into dry ingredients and mix well.
- Pour batter into prepared pan and sprinkle blueberries on top.
- Mix together remaining ¼ cup flour, remaining ½ cup sugar, cinnamon, pecans, and butter until crumbly. Sprinkle on top of blueberries.
- Bake at 350° for 40 minutes.

Eat more blueberries! They are the number one source of antioxidants in the produce aisle. Antioxidants fight free radicals, thereby helping prevent cancers, high cholesterol, and aging skin.

BETTER-THAN-BOUGHT CINNAMON ROLLS

Rolls may also be baked in 9x9-inch square baking pans, which hold 9 rolls each.
Use disposable foil pans and give as Christmas presents to your very favorite people.

Yield: 48 rolls

For dough:

2 packages active dry yeast (be sure to use fresh yeast)
4 cups warm water (105°-115°)
1 cup instant dry milk powder
½ cup sugar

1 cup canola oil
1 tablespoon salt
2 teaspoons baking powder
1 teaspoon baking soda
10 cups bread flour (or more)

For filling:

2 cups sugar
2 tablespoons cinnamon

2 sticks (1 cup) butter, melted

For glaze:

1 box confectioners' sugar

½-¾ cup orange juice

- In large mixer bowl, beat together yeast, warm water, dry milk, sugar, oil, salt, baking powder, and baking soda. You do not have to dissolve yeast in warm water before mixing.
- Stir in flour, 1 cup at a time, to make soft dough. You may need to add more flour - dough should be soft but not sticky.
- Place dough in very large, lightly greased bowl, spray top with nonstick spray or brush with oil, and cover with plastic wrap. Let rise in refrigerator at least 4 hours or overnight.
- Meanwhile, mix together 2 cups sugar, cinnamon, and melted butter for filling.
- After rising time, punch dough down and divide it into 4 equal pieces.
- For each quarter of dough, knead briefly and roll into a 9x14-inch rectangle. Spread with one-fourth of filling. Roll up, starting at long edge, and slice into 12 pieces.
- Butter four 9x13-inch baking pans. Place 12 rolls in each pan, not quite touching. Cover loosely with waxed paper and let rise in pans for 30 to 40 minutes.

BETTER-THAN-BOUGHT CINNAMON ROLLS (*continued*)

- While rolls are rising, preheat oven to 375°.
- Bake at 375° for 13 to 15 minutes, until golden brown.
- Mix together confectioners' sugar and orange juice for glaze.
- Let rolls cool slightly, then top with glaze while rolls are still warm. (If glaze is poured on while rolls are too hot, it soaks in and can make rolls soggy.)

To give as gifts or make ahead, bake rolls as directed, cool, and wrap well. Package glaze in small Ziploc bags. At serving time, warm rolls and cut off corner of bag to drizzle on glaze.

BUTTERSCOTCH MONKEY BREAD

So easy and so yummy! Must be prepared the night before.

Yield: 8-10 servings

½ cup chopped pecans
22 frozen dough balls (dinner rolls)
1 (3-ounce) package butterscotch pudding mix (not instant)

1 stick (½ cup) butter
¾ cup brown sugar
¾ teaspoon cinnamon

- Night before serving: grease large Bundt pan generously with nonstick spray. Sprinkle bottom of pan with pecans.
- Arrange 14 dough balls around bottom of pan and 8 dough balls on top around center ring.
- Sprinkle pudding mix over dough balls.
- Melt together butter, brown sugar, and cinnamon in small saucepan. Pour mixture over dough and cover. Put in oven (not turned on) to rise overnight.
- Morning of serving: remove pan from oven, uncover, and preheat oven to 350°.
- Bake at 350° for 30 minutes, covering with foil for last few minutes if getting too brown.
- Cool for a few minutes before removing from pan — don't leave in pan too long, as bread will stick to pan.

BANANA PANCAKES

Yield: 12 pancakes

6 tablespoons butter, divided	1 cup milk
1½ cups all-purpose flour	2 eggs
2 tablespoons sugar	½ teaspoon vanilla extract
2½ teaspoons baking powder	Maple syrup and sliced bananas
¼ teaspoon salt	for serving
1 very ripe banana, peeled	

- Melt 4 tablespoons butter and set aside to cool.
- In medium bowl, whisk together flour, sugar, baking powder, and salt until well blended.
- In separate bowl, mash banana until almost smooth.
- Add milk, eggs, and vanilla; stir until well blended.
- Pour banana mixture and reserved melted butter into flour mixture. Blend gently with fork until batter is just blended and a little lumpy.
- Grease griddle with remaining 2 tablespoons butter. Using about ¼ cup batter for each pancake, cook pancakes on hot griddle.
- Serve warm with syrup and sliced bananas.

APPLE PIZZAS

One of the few "hot breakfast" treats easy enough to put together on school mornings. Children actually hurry downstairs when they smell these baking!

Yield: 4 servings (2 "pizzas" each)

1 (8-count) roll refrigerated flaky biscuits

1 apple, finely chopped (may peel or not)

Cinnamon sugar

Squeeze margarine

- Preheat oven as directed on biscuit package.
- On ungreased cookie sheet, gently press each biscuit with fingers into flattened round. Press about 1 tablespoon chopped apple lightly into each biscuit.
- Sprinkle generously with cinnamon sugar and drizzle margarine on top.
- Bake as directed on biscuit package.

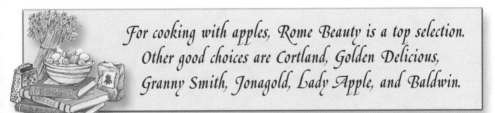

For cooking with apples, Rome Beauty is a top selection. Other good choices are Cortland, Golden Delicious, Granny Smith, Jonagold, Lady Apple, and Baldwin.

OVERNIGHT FRENCH TOAST

Yield: 6 servings

4 eggs
1 cup milk
2 tablespoons orange juice
1 tablespoon sugar
1 teaspoon cinnamon

½ teaspoon vanilla extract
1 loaf French bread, sliced
½ stick (¼ cup) butter or margarine
  Syrup and confectioners' sugar
  (optional)

- Stir together eggs, milk, orange juice, sugar, cinnamon, and vanilla. Beat until well blended.
- Spray 9x13-inch baking dish with nonstick spray and arrange bread in prepared dish.
- Pour egg mixture over bread, turning to coat both sides.
- Cover and refrigerate overnight.
- Melt butter in skillet and cook bread until lightly browned on both sides. Serve immediately with syrup or confectioners' sugar.

WILLIAM OF ORANGE FRENCH TOAST

*Tested by an entire book club when prepared and served by
one member's husband, William. We're still talking about it!*

Yield: 4 servings (2 slices each)

3 tablespoons freshly grated orange
  zest
2 cups fresh orange juice
¼ cup sugar
¼ teaspoon vanilla extract
2 tablespoons Triple Sec liqueur

For sauce:
3 tablespoons unsalted butter
2 tablespoons sweet orange
  marmalade

6 large eggs
½ cup half-and-half
  Pinch of salt
8 (1-inch thick) diagonal slices challah
  or good-quality Italian bread
3 tablespoons unsalted butter,
  melted

1 tablespoon Triple Sec

- In large bowl, whisk together zest, orange juice, sugar, vanilla, Triple Sec, eggs, half-and-half, and salt.
- Arrange bread slices in single layer in 9x13-inch glass baking dish. Pour mixture over bread, turning slices to coat. Refrigerate, covered, for 4 hours or overnight.
- Preheat oven to 400°. Brush large rimmed baking sheet with melted butter.
- Using a slotted spatula, remove bread from dish and arrange in single layer on baking sheet, leaving at least 2 inches between slices.
- Bake at 400° in middle of oven for 5 minutes. Rotate pan and bake 5 minutes more. Remove pan, turn bread slices over, and bake 5 minutes more. Rotate pan once again and bake 5 minutes more or until bread is puffed and golden.
- While bread is baking (between all that rotating and turning over), prepare sauce. Cook butter, marmalade, and Triple Sec over low heat in small saucepan, stirring, until butter is melted.
- Place 2 slices toast on each plate and drizzle with sauce. Top with maple syrup, if desired.

CRANBERRY MAPLE SAUCE

A new taste for pancakes, waffles, and French toast.

Yield: 2½ cups

2 (12-ounce) packages fresh
   cranberries
1½ cups pure maple syrup

1 cup brown sugar
½ cup water
¾ teaspoon maple extract

- Combine cranberries, syrup, brown sugar, water, and extract in large saucepan. Bring to boil, stirring often.
- Reduce heat to medium and simmer until cranberries pop, stirring often, about 12 minutes.
- Transfer to bowl and cool completely. Cover and chill.
- May be made up to 5 days before serving.

Maple-flavored syrup should not be substituted for pure maple syrup. Maple-flavored syrup is corn syrup with a small amount of pure maple syrup added and will not give foods the same flavor as pure maple syrup. Pure maple syrup must be refrigerated after opening.

SWEETS & TREATS

Double Chocolate Mousse Cake 253

Chocolate Chocolate
Chocolate Cake 254

Leah's Chocolate Cake 255

Black Russian Cake 256

Turtle Cake 257

Apricot Nectar Cake 258

Banana Cake 259

Glazed Poppy Seed Cake 260

Incredible Cheesecake 261

Amaretto Cheesecake 262

Chocolate Angel Nut Pie 263

Pumpkin Hazelnut Cheesecake 264

Chocolate Cheesecake 265

Decadent Chocolate Cream Pie 266

Coconut Caramel Pies 267

Mom Coles's Chocolate Pie 268

New England Pecan Pie 269

Summertime Peach Pie 270

Sally's Pear Pie 270

Raspberry Cream Pie 271

Frozen Strawberry
Margarita Pie 272

Sugarless Apple Pie 273

Chocolate Toffee Cookies 274

Sunshine Crisps 275

Gram's Brown Edge Cookies 275

Dried Cranberry &
White Chocolate Biscotti 276

Cornflake Cookies 277

Georgia's Cookies 278

Coconut Cups 278

Honey's Ginger Snaps 279

Butterscotch
Cream Cheese Bars 280

Lynn's Famous Brownies 281

Caramel Graham
Fudge Brownies 282

Raspberry Walnut Brownies 283

Viorenes 284

Apricot Brownies 285

Blueberry Gingerbread 286

Date Bars 287

Easy Lemon Squares 288

Pecan Squares 289

Raisin Bars 290

Red Rock Ranch
Mixed Berry Crisp 291

Lemon Semifreddo 292

Grandma Mary's
Soda Cracker Dessert 293

Grandma K's Apple Pudding 293

Strawberry Angel Food Delight 294

Angel Food Trifle 295

Pretzel Salad 296

Easy Russian Cream with Berries 296

Classic Crème Brûlée 297

Light & Luscious 298

Oreo Sundae Dessert 299

Lemon Ice Cream 299

Summertime Peach Ice Cream 300

Everlasting Ice Cream 300

Microwave Fudge Sauce 301

Lemon Sauce 301

Devonshire Cream 302

DOUBLE CHOCOLATE MOUSSE CAKE

Very elegant, but not at all complicated — and may be made the day before serving.

Yield: 8-10 servings

For cake:

2 (8-ounce) packages semisweet chocolate squares (16 1-ounce squares)
4 sticks (2 cups) butter
1 cup sugar

1 cup half-and-half
1 tablespoon vanilla extract
½ teaspoon salt
8 eggs

For glaze:

1 (6-ounce) package semisweet chocolate chips
2 tablespoons butter

3 tablespoons milk
2 tablespoons white corn syrup

- Preheat oven to 350°. Grease 10-inch springform pan.
- In 3-quart saucepan over low heat, combine chocolate, butter, sugar, half-and-half, vanilla, and salt until chocolate melts and mixture is smooth, stirring constantly. Remove from heat and let cool slightly.
- In large bowl, beat eggs slightly.
- Slowly beat chocolate mixture into eggs (be sure chocolate has cooled somewhat, to avoid scrambling eggs).
- Pour into prepared pan and bake at 350° for 45 minutes. Cake is done when toothpick inserted 2 inches from edge comes out clean.
- Cool cake completely on wire rack.
- When cake is cool, remove sides of pan, wrap cake in plastic wrap, and refrigerate until well chilled (at least 6 hours).
- When cake is cold, prepare glaze. In 2-quart saucepan over low heat, heat chocolate chips and butter until chocolate melts and mixture is smooth.
- Remove pan from heat. Beat milk and corn syrup into chocolate mixture.
- Spread warm glaze over top and down sides of cake.
- Refrigerate if not serving immediately. To serve, garnish with whipped cream.

CHOCOLATE CHOCOLATE CHOCOLATE CAKE

*An extra-rich and extra-chocolatey cake! Be sure
to use good-quality cocoa and chocolate chips.*

Yield: 1 3-layer cake

For cake:

3 cups all-purpose flour
2 cups sugar
½ cup unsweetened cocoa powder
2 teaspoons baking soda
1 teaspoon salt

2 cups cold water
1 cup corn oil
1 tablespoon vanilla extract
1½ cups semisweet chocolate chips, divided

For frosting:

1¼ sticks unsalted butter, softened
5 cups confectioners' sugar, divided
6-8 tablespoons whole milk

1¼ teaspoons vanilla extract
¾ cup plus 3 tablespoons unsweetened cocoa powder

- Preheat oven to 350°. Butter and flour three 9-inch round cake pans.
- Sift flour, sugar, cocoa, baking soda, and salt into medium bowl and whisk together until combined.
- In large bowl, stir together water, corn oil, and vanilla.
- Add dry ingredients to water mixture and whisk until combined.
- Divide batter evenly into 3 prepared pans. Sprinkle each pan of batter with ½ cup chocolate chips.
- Bake at 350° for about 25 minutes or until cake tester comes out clean. Cool on racks for 15 minutes, then remove from pans and cool completely before assembling.
- To prepare frosting, with electric mixer, beat butter in large bowl until fluffy.
- Gradually beat in 3 cups confectioners' sugar.
- Add 6 tablespoons milk and vanilla; beat well.
- Add cocoa and remaining confectioners' sugar. Beat until thoroughly blended, adding remaining 2 tablespoons milk if needed to thin to spreading consistency.
- To assemble, place 1 cake layer, chocolate chips side up, on serving plate. Spread with ⅔ cup frosting. Top with second layer, chips side up, and spread

with ⅔ cup frosting. Top with third layer, chips side DOWN. Spread remaining frosting over sides and top of cake.

- May be made a day ahead and stored at room temperature.

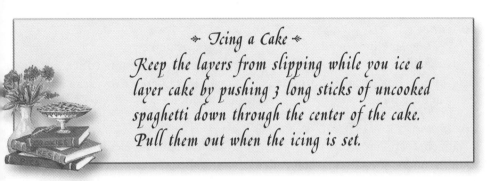

⊹ Icing a Cake ⊹
Keep the layers from slipping while you ice a layer cake by pushing 3 long sticks of uncooked spaghetti down through the center of the cake. Pull them out when the icing is set.

LEAH'S CHOCOLATE CAKE

This recipe is foolproof, and it freezes well.

Yield: 1 Bundt cake

1 box Pillsbury German chocolate cake mix
1 (3-ounce) box instant chocolate pudding mix
1 cup water
4 eggs, beaten

½ cup vegetable oil
1 (12-ounce) package semisweet chocolate chips
1 cup chopped pecans (optional)
Powdered sugar or chocolate sauce (optional)

- Preheat oven to 325°. Spray Bundt cake pan with nonstick spray.
- Combine cake mix, pudding mix, water, eggs, oil, chocolate chips, and pecans, if using. Beat well and pour into prepared pan.
- Bake at 325° for 1 hour. Remove from pan while still warm.
- Dust with powdered sugar or drizzle with chocolate sauce before serving, if desired.

BLACK RUSSIAN CAKE

Delicious served plain or with ice cream or
whipped cream. A light but very flavorful cake!

Yield: 1 Bundt cake

For cake:

1 box Duncan Hines devil's food cake mix

1 (3-ounce) box instant chocolate pudding mix

4 eggs, beaten

¾ cup prepared strong coffee

¾ cup mixed crème de cacao and Kahlúa

For topping:

1 cup confectioners' sugar

2 tablespoons prepared strong coffee

2 tablespoons Kahlúa

2 tablespoons crème de cacao

Sifted confectioners' sugar for garnish

- Preheat oven as directed on cake mix box. Grease and flour Bundt cake pan.
- Combine cake mix, pudding mix, eggs, ¾ cup coffee, and ¾ cup crème de cacao and Kahlúa. Beat for 4 minutes.
- Pour into prepared pan and bake 45 to 50 minutes.
- Remove cake from pan while still warm and poke holes in top of cake for topping.
- Mix confectioners' sugar and 2 tablespoons each coffee, Kahlúa, and crème de cacao in saucepan over medium-high heat.
- Let mixture come to boil and remove from heat.
- Pour hot topping over warm cake. When cake has cooled, sift confectioners' sugar over cake to garnish.

TURTLE CAKE

Gooey caramel, chocolate, and nuts inside a chocolate cake — yum!

Yield: 1 9x13-inch cake

1 box chocolate cake mix (moist type) plus ingredients needed to make cake

1 (12- to 14-ounce) package caramels

½ cup evaporated milk

1 cup semisweet chocolate chips

1 cup chopped pecans

- Preheat oven to 350°. Grease and flour 9x13-inch baking pan.
- Mix cake mix according to directions on box. Pour half of batter into prepared pan. Bake at 350° for 20 minutes.
- While cake is baking, unwrap caramels and melt with evaporated milk over low heat, stirring constantly. Pour this mixture over baked cake.
- Sprinkle chocolate chips and pecans over caramel. Pour on remaining cake batter and bake again at 350° for 25 minutes.
- Cool completely before cutting, or refrigerate if not serving immediately.

⤞ *Decorate a Cake with Elegant Chocolate Leaves* ⤝

Select clean, unblemished rose or other non-poisonous leaves. Brush melted chocolate evenly over each leaf with a small, soft brush. Let set in refrigerator, then very gently peel the leaf off to reveal its imprint in chocolate.

APRICOT NECTAR CAKE

A very pretty cake — lovely for luncheons or showers.

Yield: 1 Bundt cake

For cake:

1 box yellow cake mix
1 (3-ounce) package apricot Jello
    powder (use peach or mixed-fruit
    flavor if you can't find apricot)

1 (9-ounce) can apricot nectar
¾ cup oil
4 eggs

For glaze:

1 cup confectioners' sugar
2 tablespoons butter, softened

½ cup lemon juice

- Preheat oven to 350°. Grease and flour Bundt pan.
- Combine cake mix, Jello powder, nectar, oil, and eggs in large mixing bowl. Beat at medium speed for 3 minutes.
- Pour into prepared pan and bake at 350° for 1 hour.
- Remove cake from pan while still hot.
- For glaze, whisk together confectioners' sugar, butter, and lemon juice in saucepan over low heat, mixing well. Add more confectioners' sugar if thicker glaze is preferred.
- Drizzle over hot cake.

If cakes or muffins want to stick to the bottom of their pans, place the hot pans on a cold, damp towel for about 30 seconds before removing.

BANANA CAKE

Yield: 1 9x13-inch cake

For cake:

6 medium bananas, puréed
2 cups sugar
2 sticks (1 cup) butter, softened
2 eggs
¼ teaspoon salt

2 cups all-purpose flour
1 teaspoon cinnamon
1 teaspoon nutmeg
1 tablespoon baking soda

For frosting:

1 cup confectioners' sugar
1 (3-ounce) package cream cheese, softened

2 tablespoons milk
½ teaspoon vanilla extract

- Preheat oven to 350°. Spray 9x13-inch baking pan with nonstick spray.
- With electric mixer, beat together bananas and sugar.
- Beat in butter until creamy. Add eggs and salt, blending well.
- In separate bowl, whisk together flour, cinnamon, nutmeg, and baking soda.
- Add dry ingredients to banana mixture and beat for 1 to 2 minutes.
- Pour batter into prepared pan and bake at 350° for 45 to 50 minutes. Let cool before frosting.
- For frosting, beat together confectioners' sugar, cream cheese, milk, and vanilla until smooth. Spread on completely cooled cake. Store cake in refrigerator.

❖ Cake Cutting ❖

For a clean, well-defined cut, heat the blade of a thin, sharp knife by running it under hot water and drying it before cutting. Serrated knives work well with angel food cakes.

GLAZED POPPY SEED CAKE

Very easy and delicious — perfect with coffee.

Yield: 2 loaf cakes

For cake:

3 cups all-purpose flour	1½ teaspoons baking powder
2⅓ cups sugar	1½ cups milk
3 eggs	1½ teaspoons vanilla extract
1½ tablespoons poppy seeds	1½ teaspoons butter flavoring
1 cup plus 2 tablespoons oil	1½ teaspoons almond extract
1½ teaspoons salt	

For glaze:

¼ cup orange juice	½ teaspoon almond extract
¾ cup sugar	

- Preheat oven to 325°. Grease and flour 2 loaf pans.
- In large bowl of electric mixer, beat together flour, sugar, eggs, poppy seeds, oil, salt, baking powder, milk, vanilla, butter flavoring, and almond extract.
- Pour evenly into prepared pans.
- Bake at 325° for 1 hour or until cake tester inserted in center comes out clean.
- Cool for 10 minutes in pans before glazing.
- While cake is cooling, prepare glaze. Whisk together orange juice, sugar, and almond extract until sugar is dissolved. Pour over cakes in pans.

INCREDIBLE CHEESECAKE
Yield: 12 servings

For crust:
2 cups chocolate wafer crumbs
1 stick (½ cup) butter, melted

1 teaspoon cinnamon

For first layer:
4 (8-ounce) packages cream cheese,
    softened
1 cup sugar

1 tablespoon lemon juice
2 teaspoons vanilla extract
1 egg

For second layer:
2 cups sour cream
¼ teaspoon almond extract

½-¾ cup sugar

- Do not preheat oven.
- Mix crumbs, melted butter, and cinnamon and press into 10-inch springform pan (smaller pan will be too small).
- To make first layer, beat together cream cheese, sugar, lemon juice, vanilla, and egg until thoroughly blended. Pour into prepared crust.
- Place in cold oven and turn heat to 350°. Bake for 50 minutes.
- Remove cake and let cool while making second layer. Blend together sour cream, almond extract, and sugar. Spread over first layer.
- Return to 350° oven and bake 10 minutes more.
- Cool thoroughly, then refrigerate until serving.

Don't crack the cheesecake! Cheesecakes crack when they are over-cooked. The simplest way to avoid cracking is to shorten the cooking time. Dental floss, wrapped around your fingers and held tightly, works well to cut cheesecake!

AMARETTO CHEESECAKE

The fresh lime juice adds a tangy kick to this dessert.

Yield: 10-12 servings

For crust:

13 (5x2½-inch) cinnamon crisp graham crackers

1 stick (½ cup) butter, melted

¼ cup sugar

For filling:

4 (8-ounce) packages cream cheese, softened

1½ cups sugar

1½ tablespoons fresh lime juice

2 teaspoons almond extract

Pinch of salt

4 eggs

For topping:

1 (16-ounce) carton sour cream

¼ cup sugar

1 teaspoon almond extract

- Preheat oven to 350°. Spray 9-inch springform pan with nonstick spray.
- Crush crackers in food processor. Mix crumbs with melted butter and sugar. Press into prepared pan and chill in refrigerator.
- For filling, combine cream cheese and sugar in large mixing bowl and beat with electric mixer until creamy.
- Add lime juice, almond extract, and salt, beating well.
- Add eggs, one at a time, beating between additions.
- Pour filling into crust. Bake at 350° for 45 minutes or until browned.
- Remove from oven, leaving oven on, and let stand 10 minutes.
- For topping, whisk together sour cream, sugar, and almond extract. Mix well and spread over cake. Bake at 350° for 10 minutes.
- Cool to room temperature, then refrigerate 4 to 5 hours before serving.

CHOCOLATE ANGEL NUT PIE

The crunchy meringue crust is a wonderful complement to the creamy chocolate. Should not be prepared more than a day ahead.

Yield: 8 servings

For meringue shell:

2 egg whites
¼ teaspoon cream of tartar

½ cup sugar
½ cup finely chopped walnuts

For filling:

¾ cup semisweet chocolate chips
3 tablespoons hot water
1 teaspoon vanilla extract

1 cup heavy cream, whipped
Additional whipped cream (lightly sweetened, if desired) for topping

- Preheat oven to 275°. Generously grease 9-inch pie plate.
- Beat egg whites with cream of tartar until foamy.
- Beat in sugar, 1 tablespoon at a time, beating well between additions. Continue beating until stiff and glossy. Do not underbeat.
- Pile into pie plate, pressing meringue up sides of pan to form shell. Sprinkle with walnuts.
- Bake at 275° for 1 hour or until delicately browned and crisp to touch. Cool completely.
- To make filling, melt chocolate chips in double boiler.
- Stir in water and cook until thickened. Remove from heat.
- Cool slightly and add vanilla, then fold in whipped cream.
- Turn into meringue shell and refrigerate until set.
- Garnish each slice with whipped cream before serving.

Make decorative chocolate curls using a citrus zester. Spread melted chocolate evenly over a cool surface, and let stand until just set. Pull the zester across the surface to remove small curls.

PUMPKIN HAZELNUT CHEESECAKE

*When you're in charge of Thanksgiving dessert,
wow your crowd with this luscious cheesecake!*

Yield: 12 servings

For crust:

2 cups gingersnap cookie crumbs
1/4 cup brown sugar, firmly packed

5 tablespoons unsalted butter,
   melted and cooled

For filling:

4 (8-ounce) packages cream cheese,
   softened
1 1/3 cups brown sugar, firmly packed
1 1/3 cups canned solid pack pumpkin
   purée (not pie filling)

1 tablespoon vanilla extract
1 1/2 teaspoons cinnamon
1/4 teaspoon allspice
5 large eggs, at room temperature

For topping:

1 cup hazelnuts
1/4 cup brown sugar, firmly packed

1/4 cup unsalted butter
1/4 cup heavy cream

- Preheat oven to 350°. Spray 9-inch springform pan with nonstick spray.
- In food processor with metal blade, process gingersnap crumbs and brown sugar.
- Add melted butter and mix until crumbs stick together.
- Spray hands with nonstick spray and press crumbs on bottom and up sides of prepared pan. Bake crust in middle of oven at 350° for 10 minutes. Remove from oven and cool.
- For filling, beat cream cheese and brown sugar in large bowl on medium speed of electric mixer until well blended.
- Add pumpkin, vanilla, cinnamon, and allspice.
- Add eggs, one at a time, beating well after each addition.
- Pour into crust and spread to edges.
- Bake at 350° for 55 to 65 minutes or until cake puffs and center is almost set. Place on rack to cool - this will take 1 to 2 hours.
- When you take cake out of oven, place hazelnuts on baking sheet and roast at 350° for 10 minutes. Set aside.

PUMPKIN HAZELNUT CHEESECAKE (*continued*)

- When cake has cooled, prepare topping. In heavy saucepan over medium heat, combine brown sugar, butter, and cream. Stir until sugar dissolves, then bring to boil.
- Add hazelnuts and boil about 2 minutes, stirring occasionally, until mix coats nuts.
- Spoon topping over cooled cake and let cool.
- Cover with foil and refrigerate overnight or up to 4 days.
- To serve, remove foil, run a knife around sides to loosen, release sides, and slice in wedges.

CHOCOLATE CHEESECAKE
Yield: 12 servings

1 box chocolate cake mix, divided
1 tablespoon vegetable oil
4 eggs, well beaten, divided
2 (8-ounce) packages cream cheese, softened
½ cup sugar

1½ cups skim milk
1 teaspoon vanilla extract
1 (8-ounce) container whipped topping
1 chocolate candy bar, shaved

- Preheat oven to 300°. Spray 9x13-inch baking dish with nonstick spray.
- Remove 1 cup cake mix and set aside. Pour remaining cake mix into large mixing bowl. Add oil and 1 well-beaten egg. Stir well until mixture is crumbly.
- Press mixture into bottom and up sides of prepared dish. Set aside.
- In same bowl, beat cream cheese and sugar until smooth.
- Add 3 well-beaten eggs and reserved cake mix. Beat at medium speed for 1 minute.
- Add milk and vanilla; beat at low speed until smooth.
- Pour into crust and bake at 300° for 55 to 65 minutes or until center is firm.
- Cool cheesecake in pan for about 15 minutes, then spread whipped topping over top. Garnish with shaved chocolate. Chill thoroughly before serving.

DECADENT CHOCOLATE CREAM PIE

A very swanky chocolate pie.

Yield: 10 servings

For crust:

16 Oreo cookies, broken up

For filling:

2½ cups half-and-half
   Pinch of salt
⅓ cup sugar, divided
2 tablespoons cornstarch
6 large egg yolks
6 tablespoons cold unsalted butter,
   cut into pieces

For topping:

1 cup heavy cream
1 tablespoon sugar

2 tablespoons unsalted butter,
   melted

6 ounces semisweet chocolate,
   chopped (Callebaut or Hershey's
   Special Dark)
1 ounce unsweetened chocolate,
   chopped (Callebaut or Hershey's
   unsweetened)
1 teaspoon vanilla extract

½ teaspoon vanilla extract

- Preheat oven to 350°.
- Process Oreos in food processor until fine crumbs form. Add melted butter and mix well.
- Press into bottom and up sides of 9-inch glass pie plate. Refrigerate 15 to 20 minutes to firm, then bake at 350° for 10 minutes. Cool on rack.
- For filling, combine half-and-half, salt, and 3 tablespoons sugar in heavy saucepan. Bring to simmer over medium heat, stirring constantly.
- Stir together remaining sugar and cornstarch in small bowl, then sprinkle over egg yolks in medium bowl. Removing the chalazae (strands attached to yolks) before beating yolks will prevent lumps.
- Whisk egg yolks until thick and glossy and sugar has begun to dissolve, about 2 minutes.
- Drizzle about ½ cup of simmering half-and-half over yolks, whisking constantly, then whisk yolk mixture back into half-and-half in saucepan, still whisking constantly. Mixture begins to thicken within 30 seconds.

DECADENT CHOCOLATE CREAM PIE (continued)

- Return to simmer, whisking constantly, until 3 to 4 bubbles burst on surface and mixture is thick and glossy - this doesn't take long.
- Remove from heat and whisk in butter and both chocolates until melted. Stir in vanilla and pour into baked crust.
- Press plastic wrap onto surface and refrigerate for 3 hours.
- To prepare topping, whip cream until soft peaks form. Fold in sugar and vanilla. Swirl on top of pie before serving.

COCONUT CARAMEL PIES

Yield: 2 pies

½ stick (¼ cup) butter or margarine
1 (7-ounce) package flaked coconut
½ cup chopped pecans
1 (8-ounce) package cream cheese, softened
1 (14-ounce) can sweetened condensed milk

1 (16-ounce) container whipped topping
2 (9-inch) pie crusts, baked
1 (12-ounce) jar caramel ice cream topping

- Melt butter in large skillet. Add coconut and chopped pecans. Cook until golden brown, stirring often. Set aside.
- With electric mixer, beat cream cheese and condensed milk until smooth. Fold in whipped topping.
- Layer one-fourth of cream cheese mixture in each pie crust.
- Drizzle one-fourth of caramel topping on each pie. Sprinkle one-fourth of coconut mixture evenly over topping. Repeat layers.
- Cover and freeze until firm. Let stand at room temperature about 5 minutes before serving.

MOM COLES'S CHOCOLATE PIE

*You can turn this into a butterscotch pie by substituting
brown sugar for white and leaving out the cocoa.*

Yield: 2 pies

For pie:

6   egg yolks, beaten (large or extra
      large eggs)
1¾ cups sugar
½   cup all-purpose flour
4   heaping tablespoons
      unsweetened cocoa powder

1   (12-ounce) can evaporated milk
1½ cups water
5   tablespoons butter
1½ tablespoons vanilla extract
2   pie crusts, baked

For meringue:

6   egg whites   ½ cup sugar

- Preheat oven to 450°.
- Place beaten egg yolks in heavy saucepan with sugar, flour, and cocoa. Slowly stir in milk and water. Stir well until smooth.
- Add butter and cook over medium heat, stirring constantly, until mixture thickens.
- Remove from heat and add vanilla. Pour into baked pie crusts.
- For meringue, beat egg whites with electric mixer until frothy.
- Add sugar slowly, beating to stiff peaks.
- Spread over chocolate mixture in pie crust.
- Bake at 450° for 5 minutes or until meringue is lightly browned.
- Cool pies and chill in refrigerator before serving.

NEW ENGLAND PECAN PIE

An easy pecan pie — try it warm with Devonshire Cream (page 302).

Yield: 2 pies

¼ cup all-purpose flour
2 dashes salt (less than ¼ teaspoon)
1 cup sugar
6 eggs
2 sticks (1 cup) butter, softened

2 cups light corn syrup
2 teaspoons vanilla extract
2 cups chopped pecans
2 (9-inch) deep-dish pie crusts, unbaked

- Preheat oven to 375°.
- Whisk together flour, salt, and sugar.
- In separate bowl, beat together eggs, butter, syrup, and vanilla. Add flour mixture to egg mixture and beat well.
- Spread 1 cup pecans into each pie crust. Pour half of mixture into each crust over pecans.
- Bake at 375° for 10 minutes, then reduce heat to 350° and bake for 50 more minutes. You may need to cover edges with aluminum foil for second half of baking if crust is getting too brown.
- Serve warm or store in refrigerator.

You'll find honey, corn syrup, and molasses much easier to measure if you uncap the bottle and microwave for 30 to 45 seconds on High. That's for a 12-ounce bottle – smaller amounts take even less time.

SUMMERTIME PEACH PIE

Yield: 1 deep-dish pie

4 large fresh ripe peaches, peeled
   and thinly sliced
1 unbaked deep-dish pie crust
5 tablespoons butter, softened
1 cup sugar

1 egg
⅓ cup all-purpose flour
½ teaspoon almond extract
1 tablespoon vanilla extract

- Preheat oven to 300°.
- Arrange peaches in bottom of pie crust.
- Cream butter and sugar in food processor or electric mixer.
- Add egg, flour, almond extract, and vanilla. Mix well and spread mixture over peaches in shell.
- Bake at 300° for 1 hour.

SALLY'S PEAR PIE

To make equally delicious pear tarts, dice pear halves and put in tart shells with the filling. Makes about 8 to 10 tarts.

Yield: 6-8 servings

1 stick (½ cup) butter, softened
1 cup sugar
½ cup all-purpose flour
1 teaspoon vanilla extract
   Juice of ½ lemon

1 egg
1 (16-ounce) can pear halves, well
   drained
1 (9-inch) deep-dish unbaked pie
   crust

- Preheat oven to 350°.
- Beat together butter, sugar, flour, vanilla, and lemon juice.
- Add egg and beat well.
- Put pears, cut-side down, in pie crust.
- Spoon filling over pears.
- Bake at 350° for 30 to 40 minutes.

Especially good served warm with vanilla ice cream.

RASPBERRY CREAM PIE

A beautiful and elegant pie.

Yield: 8 servings

For crust:

33 vanilla wafers, crushed
⅓ cup chopped pecans

3-4 tablespoons butter, melted

For filling:

1 (8-ounce) package cream cheese, softened
⅔ cup confectioners' sugar

2 tablespoons Grand Marnier or Triple Sec
1 teaspoon vanilla extract
1 cup heavy cream, whipped

For topping:

1 cup sugar
3 tablespoons water, divided

2½ cups frozen raspberries
2 tablespoons cornstarch

- Preheat oven to 350°.
- Combine wafer crumbs, pecans, and butter for a crust. Mix well, press into pie plate, and bake at 350° about 20 minutes or until brown. Cool.
- To prepare filling, combine cream cheese, confectioners' sugar, Grand Marnier or Triple Sec, and vanilla. Beat well, then fold in whipped cream.
- Pour into cooled crust. Cover and refrigerate.
- In saucepan, bring sugar, 1 tablespoon water, and raspberries to slow boil.
- In small bowl, whisk together 2 tablespoons cold water and cornstarch until smooth.
- Add cornstarch mix to boiling raspberries. Stir until glossy and slightly thickened. Remove from heat and cool.
- Top pie filling with raspberries. Cover and refrigerate until serving time.

Whipping Cream: A few drops of lemon juice added to whipping cream will help it whip faster and better.

FROZEN STRAWBERRY MARGARITA PIE

Yield: 1 pie

1¼ cups crushed pretzels
¼ cup sugar
10 tablespoons butter or margarine, melted
1 (14-ounce) can sweetened condensed milk

1½ cups crushed or puréed strawberries
⅓ cup lime juice
1 (8-ounce) container whipped topping, thawed
Additional whipped topping and fresh strawberries for garnish

- Mix pretzels, sugar, and melted butter in 10-inch pie plate. Press mixture into bottom and up sides of pie plate and refrigerate.
- Stir together condensed milk, strawberries, and lime juice in large bowl until well blended.
- Gently fold in whipped topping and pour into crust.
- Freeze 6 hours or overnight until firm.
- Before serving, let stand at room temperature 15 minutes. Garnish with additional whipped topping and strawberries.

SUGARLESS APPLE PIE

Yield: 1 pie

For crust:

1 stick (½ cup) margarine, melted
½ cup finely chopped pecans

1 cup all-purpose flour

For filling:

2 tablespoons cornstarch
1 teaspoon apple pie spice
1 (12-ounce) can unsweetened
   apple juice concentrate

4 cups peeled and sliced Golden
   Delicious apples (about 3 large
   apples)

- Preheat oven to 350°.
- Mix margarine, pecans, and flour until thoroughly blended. Press into 10-inch pie plate.
- Bake at 350° for 20 to 25 minutes or until lightly browned.
- In saucepan, combine cornstarch, apple pie spice, and apple juice concentrate. Cook over medium heat until hot, but not boiling.
- Add apples and cook until apples are tender. Let apple filling cool.
- Pour into pie crust and refrigerate until firm.

❧ *Feathering Cream* ❧

Flood a plate with chocolate sauce or fruit purée, then carefully spoon drops of heavy cream onto it at regular intervals around the edges of the plate. Draw the tip of a toothpick through each drop to make a chain of feathered heart shapes.

CHOCOLATE TOFFEE COOKIES

No one who tastes this can believe it starts with saltines!

Yield: 3 dozen pieces

1 sleeve saltine crackers
  (35 crackers)
2 sticks (1 cup) butter
1 cup brown sugar, firmly packed

1 (12-ounce package) semisweet or
  milk chocolate chips, or a
  combination
1 cup chopped pecans

- Preheat oven to 350°. Line 10x15-inch jelly roll pan with foil and spray foil with nonstick spray.
- Place saltines in single layer to cover bottom of pan, breaking crackers to fit if necessary (may need more than 1 sleeve).
- Combine butter and brown sugar in saucepan. Bring to boil and boil 3 minutes, stirring occasionally, until thoroughly blended.
- Pour butter mixture over crackers and spread to edges.
- Bake at 350° for 20 minutes - no longer!
- Remove pan from oven and immediately cover with chocolate chips. When chocolate melts, spread to edges with spatula. Sprinkle with pecans.
- Refrigerate at least 30 minutes, then break into bite-size pieces. Store covered in refrigerator.

To soften brown sugar, place in a microwave-safe dish and add a wedge of apple. Cover tightly and microwave on High for 30 seconds. Remove apple and stir.

SUNSHINE CRISPS
Yield: about 3 dozen squares

1½-2 packages plain or cinnamon graham crackers
2 sticks (1 cup) butter
1 cup brown sugar
1 cup chopped nuts (any combination of pecans, walnuts, and almonds)

- Preheat oven to 350°. Line 15x10-inch jelly roll pan with foil and spray with nonstick spray.
- Cover bottom of prepared pan with graham crackers.
- Melt butter in saucepan and add brown sugar.
- Add nuts and boil for 2 minutes, stirring constantly.
- Pour hot mixture evenly over graham crackers.
- Bake at 350° for 10 minutes.
- Cut into squares while still warm.

GRAM'S BROWN EDGE COOKIES
Yield: about 3 dozen cookies

½ cup shortening
½ cup sugar
1 egg, beaten
¾ cup all-purpose flour
½ teaspoon vanilla extract
Pinch of salt

- Preheat oven to 350°. Lightly spray cookie sheet with nonstick spray.
- Cream shortening and sugar in electric mixer.
- Stir in egg, flour, vanilla, and salt. Beat well.
- Roll into balls the size of large marbles and place 2 inches apart on prepared cookie sheet.
- Bake at 350° for 6 minutes or until edges are brown.

DRIED CRANBERRY &
WHITE CHOCOLATE BISCOTTI

Worth the effort!

Yield: about 3 dozen cookies

2½ cups all-purpose flour
1 teaspoon baking powder
½ teaspoon salt
1½ cups sugar
1 stick (½ cup) unsalted butter
2 large eggs

½ teaspoon almond extract
1½ cups dried cranberries
1 (6-ounce) package white chocolate chips
1 egg white

- Preheat oven to 350°. Line large, heavy baking sheet with parchment paper.
- Whisk together flour, baking powder, and salt in medium bowl.
- Using electric mixer, beat sugar, butter, whole eggs, and almond extract in large bowl until well blended.
- Stir in flour mixture, dried cranberries, and white chocolate.
- Divide dough in half. With floured hands, shape each half into a log about 2½ inches wide, 9 inches long, and 1 inch high.
- Transfer both logs to prepared sheet, spacing evenly.
- Whisk egg white in small bowl until frothy. Brush logs with egg white glaze on top and sides.
- Bake logs at 350° for about 35 minutes until golden brown.
- Cool completely on baking sheet on wire rack, leaving oven on.
- Transfer logs to work surface, discarding parchment. Using serrated knife, slice logs on diagonal into ½-inch thick slices.
- Arrange slices on same baking sheet and return to oven.
- Bake 10 minutes, turn biscotti over, and continue to bake 5 more minutes. Cool before serving.

CORNFLAKE COOKIES

A light, crisp cookie.

Yield: 3-4 dozen cookies

2 sticks (1 cup) butter, softened
1 cup sugar
1½ cups all-purpose flour
1 teaspoon cream of tartar

1 teaspoon baking soda
1½ cups crushed corn flakes cereal
   (plain, not frosted)

- Preheat oven to 350°.
- Cream butter and sugar until fluffy.
- In separate bowl, whisk together flour, cream of tartar, and baking soda.
- Combine two mixtures and add corn flakes. Mix well.
- Drop by tablespoonfuls onto ungreased cookie sheets.
- Bake at 350° for 10 to 12 minutes or until edges are slightly browned. Remove gently (they are delicate) from cookie sheet to cool.

✦ *Baking Cookies* ✦
Use shiny baking sheets; dark pans absorb more heat and can cause over-browning.

GEORGIA'S COOKIES

Easy, rich, and delicious. And they contain Special K,
so they must be good for you — right?

Yield: 24 squares or more

1 cup sugar
1 cup light Karo syrup
1 cup peanut butter
6 cups Special K cereal

1 (6-ounce) package chocolate chips
1 (6-ounce) package butterscotch
  chips

- Spray 9x13-inch baking dish with nonstick spray.
- Mix sugar and syrup together in large saucepan and cook over low heat until sugar is dissolved.
- Mix in peanut butter.
- Stir in cereal and mix well.
- Press into prepared dish.
- Melt chocolate and butterscotch chips together in saucepan. Pour over cereal mixture.
- Refrigerate briefly until firm, but not so long that chocolate hardens and makes cutting difficult. Cut into small squares.

COCONUT CUPS

Try these when you need a pick-up dessert for a buffet supper party.

Yield: 20 cups

1 (14-ounce) package flaked coconut
1 (12-ounce) package Hershey's
  Skor toffee bits
1 cup slivered almonds

1 (14-ounce) can sweetened
  condensed milk
5 boxes small phyllo cups (4 cups to
  a box)

- Preheat oven to 375°.
- Combine coconut, Skor bits, almonds, and condensed milk; mix very well.
- Spoon into phyllo cups and arrange cups on cookie sheets.
- Bake at 375° for 10 minutes or until tops are lightly browned.

May be prepared 1 day ahead and stored in sealed container.

HONEY'S GINGER SNAPS

A great choice when you need a lot of cookies.
Dough must be refrigerated overnight.

Yield: 8-10 dozen cookies

3 sticks (1½ cups) margarine
½ cup molasses
2 cups sugar
2 eggs
4 cups all-purpose flour

4 teaspoons baking soda
2 teaspoons cinnamon
1 teaspoon ground cloves
1 teaspoon ginger
1 cup sugar for coating

- Melt margarine, remove from heat, and add molasses, 2 cups sugar, and eggs.
- In separate bowl, whisk together flour, baking soda, cinnamon, cloves, and ginger.
- Add dry ingredients gradually to margarine mixture, mixing well.
- Cover and refrigerate dough overnight.
- When ready to bake, preheat oven to 350°.
- Roll dough into small balls, roll in sugar to coat, and place on ungreased cookie sheets.
- Bake at 350° for 8 to 10 minutes.

An apple wedge placed in an airtight container will soften cookies that have hardened.

BUTTERSCOTCH CREAM CHEESE BARS

Worth every calorie!

Yield: 24 bars

2 cups butterscotch chips
5 tablespoons butter
2 cups graham cracker crumbs
1 cup chopped pecans
1 (8-ounce) package cream cheese, softened

1 (14-ounce) can sweetened condensed milk
1 egg
1 teaspoon vanilla extract

- Preheat oven to 350°. Spray 9x13-inch baking pan with nonstick spray.
- Combine butterscotch chips and butter in saucepan and cook over low heat until smooth, stirring constantly.
- Remove from heat and stir in graham cracker crumbs and pecans.
- Press half of crumb mixture into bottom of prepared pan.
- Beat cream cheese in mixer bowl until fluffy. Add condensed milk, egg, and vanilla. Beat until smooth and blended.
- Spread cream cheese mixture over crumb layer in pan. Top with remaining crumb mixture.
- Bake at 350° for 25 to 30 minutes or until tester comes out clean.
- Cool to room temperature on wire rack, then refrigerate, covered, before cutting into bars.

LYNN'S FAMOUS BROWNIES

Yield: 24-30 squares

For brownies:

4 (1-ounce) squares unsweetened chocolate
2 sticks (1 cup) butter
4 eggs

1¾ cups sugar
2 teaspoons vanilla extract
½ teaspoon salt
1 cup all-purpose flour

For frosting:

6 tablespoons butter
1 cup sugar

6 tablespoons whole milk or half-and-half
1½ cups semisweet chocolate chips

- Preheat oven to 350°. Spray 9x13-inch baking pan with nonstick spray.
- In large saucepan, melt chocolate and butter. Remove from heat and let cool briefly.
- Add eggs, one at a time, beating well after each addition.
- Add sugar, vanilla, salt, and flour; beat well.
- Pour into prepared pan and bake at 350° for 20 to 25 minutes. Be ready to frost brownies as soon as they come out of the oven.
- A few minutes before brownies finish baking, prepare frosting by combining butter, sugar, and milk in small saucepan. Bring to boil and boil for 30 seconds.
- Remove from heat and stir in chocolate chips, blending until melted and smooth.
- Immediately pour frosting over hot brownies. Let cool before cutting into squares.

CARAMEL GRAHAM FUDGE BROWNIES

With so many goodies in this recipe, it can't miss!

Yield: 24 bars

1 box Pillsbury Traditional fudge brownie mix, divided
1½ cups graham cracker crumbs
½ cup sugar
1 stick (½ cup) margarine or butter, melted
1 (14-ounce) package caramels, unwrapped

⅓ cup evaporated milk
¾ cup peanut butter chips
¾ cup semisweet chocolate chips
1 cup chopped pecans or walnuts, divided
¼ cup water
¼ cup oil
1 egg

- Preheat oven to 350°.
- In medium bowl, combine 1½ cups brownie mix, graham cracker crumbs, sugar, and melted margarine. Mix well and press mixture into bottom of ungreased 9x13-inch baking pan.
- In medium saucepan, combine caramels and evaporated milk. Cook over medium heat until caramels are melted, stirring constantly.
- Carefully spread melted caramel mixture over crust.
- Sprinkle with peanut butter chips, chocolate chips, and ¾ cup chopped nuts.
- In same bowl, combine remaining brownie mix, water, oil, and egg. Beat 50 strokes by hand.
- Carefully spoon batter evenly over nuts.
- Sprinkle with remaining ¼ cup nuts.
- Bake at 350° for 33 to 38 minutes or until center is set.
- Cool completely, then cut into bars.

RASPBERRY WALNUT BROWNIES

A delicious blend of chocolate, raspberry, and walnut flavors.

Yield: 12 bars

For brownies:

3 (1-ounce) squares unsweetened chocolate
½ cup shortening
3 eggs
1½ cups sugar

1½ teaspoons vanilla extract
¼ teaspoon salt
1 cup all-purpose flour
1½ cups chopped walnuts
⅓ cup raspberry jam

For glaze:

1 ounce unsweetened chocolate
2 tablespoons butter
2 tablespoons light corn syrup

1 cup confectioners' sugar
1 teaspoon vanilla extract

- Preheat oven to 325°. Generously grease 8x8-inch baking pan.
- Melt chocolate with shortening in double boiler over warm water. Cool slightly.
- Blend together eggs, sugar, vanilla, and salt. Stir in chocolate mixture, then flour. Fold in walnuts.
- Turn into prepared pan. Bake at 325° for about 40 minutes.
- Spoon jam over hot brownies and spread carefully. Let cool.
- Prepare glaze by melting 1 ounce chocolate in small saucepan. Blend in butter and syrup. Add confectioners' sugar, then vanilla, and mix well.
- Spread glaze over brownies and cut into 12 bars when completely cool.

For easier pouring, coat measuring cups and utensils with nonstick spray before measuring corn syrup or honey.

VIORENES

Timing is the key to these wonderful brownies. The icing "sets up" as it cools, but it is hard to wait that long for a taste.

Yield: 16-24 brownies

For brownies:
1 stick (½ cup) butter
2 (1-ounce) squares unsweetened chocolate
¾ cup all-purpose flour, sifted
1 cup sugar

2 eggs, beaten
1 cup chopped pecans
1 teaspoon vanilla extract
Miniature marshmallows to cover baked brownies

For icing:
½ stick (¼ cup) butter
⅓ cup evaporated milk (about half of a 5-ounce can)

1 cup sugar
½ cup semisweet chocolate chips

- Do not preheat oven. Grease and flour 8-inch baking pan.
- Melt butter and chocolate in saucepan over medium-low heat.
- Remove from heat and stir in flour, sugar, eggs, pecans, and vanilla. Mix well and pour into prepared pan.
- Place in cold oven, turn heat to 250°, and bake 40 to 45 minutes. Do not overbake - brownies should be fudgy.
- Remove from oven, cover with miniature marshmallows, and pour icing over marshmallows.
- Start preparing icing while brownies are baking. Combine butter, evaporated milk, and sugar in small saucepan.
- As soon as brownies come out of oven, bring mixture to boil. Boil gently for 3 minutes. Take off heat and stir in chocolate chips until melted and smooth.
- Immediately pour hot icing over hot marshmallow-covered brownies. Icing hardens quickly, so work fast! Let cool completely before cutting into small squares.

APRICOT BROWNIES

*For a new twist on a "brownie sundae," cut into large squares
and serve warm with vanilla ice cream and caramel sauce.*

Yield: 32-40 small squares

1	stick (½ cup) butter, softened	Scant ½ teaspoon salt
2	cups light brown sugar, firmly	1½ teaspoons vanilla extract
	packed	½ cup pecans, chopped (optional)
2	eggs	¾ cup dried apricots, chopped and
1¼	cups all-purpose flour	dusted with flour
2	teaspoons baking powder	

- Preheat oven to 350°. Spray 9x13-inch pan with nonstick spray.
- Cream butter and brown sugar.
- Add eggs one at a time, mixing well after each addition.
- In separate bowl, sift flour with baking powder and salt.
- Add dry ingredients to butter mixture, mixing well.
- Add vanilla, pecans if using, and apricots. Mix well.
- Spread batter into prepared pan.
- Bake at 350° for 25 to 30 minutes, then turn heat down to 275° and bake an additional 18 to 20 minutes or until golden brown. Do not overbake!

Store all-purpose white flour in a cool, dry place for up to 6 months and self-rising flour for up to 3 months. Whole wheat and other flours with a higher fat content should be used within 2 months, so buy smaller amounts of those. If the temperature is above 75° or humidity is high, store flour in a heavy plastic bag in the refrigerator to prevent mold and insects. Bring refrigerated flour to room temperature before baking to avoid a heavy texture in the finished product.

BLUEBERRY GINGERBREAD

Try this with lemon sauce (see page 301) or with more blueberries and sweetened whipped cream. If there are any leftovers, it makes a great breakfast treat.

Yield: 8-10 servings

½ cup oil
1 cup sugar
½ teaspoon salt
3 tablespoons molasses
1 egg
2 cups all-purpose flour
½ teaspoon ginger

1 teaspoon cinnamon
½ teaspoon nutmeg
1 teaspoon baking soda
1 cup blueberries
1 cup buttermilk
¼ cup sugar for sprinkling on top
  (optional)

- Preheat oven to 350°. Grease and flour 12x7½-inch pan.
- In large bowl of electric mixer, beat together oil, 1 cup sugar, salt, and molasses. Beat in egg.
- In separate bowl, whisk together flour, ginger, cinnamon, nutmeg, and baking soda.
- Add 2 tablespoons of flour mixture to blueberries and toss lightly to dredge berries.
- Add remaining flour mixture to sugar mixture, alternately with buttermilk, beating after each addition.
- Stir in floured blueberries.
- Pour into prepared pan. Sprinkle top with ¼ cup sugar, if desired.
- Bake at 350° for 35 to 40 minutes. May be served warm or cold.

Measure ingredients accurately! Use a glass measure for liquids and metal or plastic measuring cups for solids and dry ingredients.

DATE BARS

This is a very old recipe — a nice alternative to chocolate.

Yield: 24 bars

¾ cup all-purpose flour
1 teaspoon baking powder
Pinch of salt
1 cup dark brown sugar
2 eggs
1 cup chopped pecans

1 cup chopped dates (not the sugary
  kind — buy whole, pitted dates
  and cut up with scissors)
1 teaspoon vanilla extract
  Confectioners' sugar

- Preheat oven to 350°. Spray 8x8-inch or 11x7-inch baking pan with nonstick spray.
- Whisk together flour, baking powder, and salt in large bowl.
- Add brown sugar, eggs, pecans, dates, and vanilla. Mix well and spread into prepared pan.
- Bake at 350° for 30 minutes. Let cool.
- Cut into squares and roll each square in confectioners' sugar.

Store in tightly covered cookie tin.

EASY LEMON SQUARES

Very rich, so may be cut into small squares. A great "finger dessert" for a party.

Yield: 25-30 squares

1 box Duncan Hines lemon cake
  mix
1 stick (½ cup) butter, melted
3 eggs

1 (8-ounce) package cream cheese,
  softened
1 (16-ounce) box confectioners'
  sugar, plus extra for dusting top

- Preheat oven to 350°. Spray 9x13-inch baking pan with nonstick spray. (If using a dark pan, preheat oven to 325°.)
- In mixing bowl, combine cake mix, melted butter, and one egg. Pat dough into prepared pan.
- In same bowl, mix softened cream cheese, 2 eggs, and confectioners' sugar. Beat until creamy.
- Spread cream cheese mixture over dough in pan.
- Bake at 350° for 30 to 35 minutes. (If using dark pan, bake at 325° for 35 to 40 minutes.)
- Allow to cool and dust top with confectioners' sugar before cutting.

PECAN SQUARES

Who wouldn't love a bite of pecan pie for dessert or with coffee?

Yield: 36 squares

For crust:
⅔ cup confectioners' sugar

2 cups all-purpose flour

2 sticks (1 cup) butter, softened

For topping:
⅔ cup (about 11 tablespoons) butter, melted

½ cup honey

3 tablespoons heavy cream

½ cup brown sugar

3½ cups shelled pecans, pieces or halves

- Preheat oven to 350°. Grease 9x13-inch baking pan.
- Sift confectioners' sugar and flour together.
- Cut in butter, using pastry blender or two knives, until fine crumbs form.
- Pat dough into prepared pan.
- Bake at 350° for 25 minutes, or until edges brown and center looks set.
- For topping, stir together melted butter, honey, cream, and brown sugar; mix well.
- Stir in pecans, coating them thoroughly.
- Spread mixture over crust.
- Return to oven and bake 35 minutes more. Cool completely before cutting into squares.

RAISIN BARS
Yield: 24-36 small squares

1	cup raisins	1	teaspoon baking soda
1	cup water	1	teaspoon cinnamon
½	cup canola oil	1	teaspoon nutmeg
1	cup sugar	1	teaspoon allspice
1	egg, beaten	½	teaspoon ground cloves
1¾	cups all-purpose flour		Confectioners' sugar for topping
¼	teaspoon salt		

- Preheat oven to 375°. Grease and flour 9x13-inch or 9x9-inch baking pan.
- Combine raisins and water in saucepan. Bring to boil and remove from heat.
- Stir in oil and cool to lukewarm, then stir in sugar and egg.
- In bowl, whisk together flour, salt, baking soda, cinnamon, nutmeg, allspice, and cloves.
- Add dry ingredients to raisin mixture and beat well.
- Pour into prepared pan.
- Bake at 375° for 20 minutes if using large pan or 25 to 30 minutes for smaller pan.
- When cool, cut into bars and dust with confectioners' sugar.

RED ROCK RANCH
MIXED BERRY CRISP

*Made with frozen berries, so you can make it any
time of year. A winner with our testers.*

Yield: 6-8 servings

2 (12-ounce) packages frozen
   mixed berries (about 6 cups)
¼ cup sugar
1 cup all-purpose flour, divided
1 tablespoon fresh lemon juice
¾ cup old-fashioned oats

⅔ cup light brown sugar
1 teaspoon cinnamon
½ teaspoon ginger
¼ teaspoon nutmeg
¼ teaspoon salt
7 tablespoons cold unsalted butter

- Preheat oven to 375°. Spray 9x9-inch baking dish with nonstick spray.
- Toss together berries, sugar, ¼ cup flour, and lemon juice in bowl until well coated. Pour into prepared pan.
- In same bowl, stir together remaining ¾ cup flour, oats, brown sugar, cinnamon, ginger, nutmeg, and salt.
- Cut butter into pieces and add to flour mixture, rubbing in with fingertips until mixture forms small moist clumps.
- Sprinkle mixture over berries in pan.
- Bake, uncovered, at 375° for 1 hour or until topping is golden brown. Let cool slightly before serving with whipped cream or ice cream.

LEMON SEMIFREDDO

An easy but very elegant dessert.

2 large eggs
½ cup sugar
½ cup honey
1 teaspoon vanilla extract
2 tablespoons lemon extract
   (tablespoons is correct!)

1 cup ricotta cheese
1 cup heavy cream, not whipped
¼ cup balsamic vinegar
¼ cup brown sugar
2 pints strawberries, rinsed,
   trimmed, and sliced

* Whisk together eggs, sugar, honey, vanilla, and lemon extract.
* Add ricotta and mix well.
* Fold in cream. Cover and freeze overnight.
* When ready to serve, whisk together balsamic vinegar and brown sugar until smooth.
* Scoop semifreddo into individual serving bowls, top with sliced strawberries, and drizzle with balsamic mixture.

Semifreddo – Italian for "half cold," semifreddo culinarily refers to various chilled or partially frozen desserts including cake, ice cream, and fruit with custard or whipped cream.

GRANDMA MARY'S SODA CRACKER DESSERT

A funny name for a tasty dessert!

Yield: 6-8 servings

24 soda crackers (saltines), crushed
1 stick (½ cup) butter, melted
4 egg whites
1 cup sugar
1 teaspoon vanilla extract
1 teaspoon white vinegar
1 (21-ounce) can cherry pie filling
Whipped cream or whipped topping
½ cup finely chopped pecans

- Preheat oven to 400°. Spray 9x9-inch baking dish with nonstick spray.
- Mix crushed crackers with melted butter and press into bottom of prepared pan.
- Beat egg whites until stiff. Fold in sugar, vanilla, and vinegar.
- Spread over crust and bake at 400° for 10 minutes. Remove and cool.
- Spread pie filling on top of crust, then top with whipped cream or whipped topping.
- Sprinkle with pecans. Cover and refrigerate until serving time.

GRANDMA K'S APPLE PUDDING

Do you suppose Grandma K and Grandma Mary are related?

Yield: 4-6 servings

4 apples, peeled and sliced
½ cup sugar
1 tablespoon butter, melted
1 cup all-purpose flour
1 teaspoon baking powder
Pinch of salt
½ cup milk

- Preheat oven to 350°. Grease 8x8-inch baking dish.
- Arrange apples in dish.
- Whisk together sugar, butter, flour, baking powder, salt, and milk. Pour over apples.
- Bake at 350° for 15 minutes or until browned.

STRAWBERRY ANGEL FOOD DELIGHT

A light, creamy dessert — perfect after a heavy meal.

Yield: 10-12 servings

1 (5.9-ounce) package instant vanilla pudding mix

2 cups milk, divided

¾ round angel food cake (store-bought or homemade), cut into ½-inch cubes

1 (14-ounce) can sweetened condensed milk

1 (8-ounce) container whipped topping, thawed

1½ pints strawberries, fresh or frozen (thawed if frozen), sliced

Fresh strawberries and mint for garnish

- Whisk pudding mix with 1 cup milk and reserve.
- Line bottom of 9x13-inch pan or trifle bowl with half of cake cubes.
- Whisk together reserved vanilla pudding, remaining 1 cup milk, and condensed milk. Fold in whipped topping.
- Pour one-third of pudding mixture over layer of cake, then arrange layer of strawberries over pudding.
- Repeat with remaining cake cubes, one-third of pudding, and remaining strawberries. Top with remaining pudding.
- Cover with plastic wrap and store in refrigerator until serving time.
- To serve, garnish with fresh strawberries and sprigs of mint.

When your children want popsicles but they ought to eat fruit, fool them with Fruitsicles! Put toothpicks into seedless grapes, pineapple chunks, or the fruit of your (or their) choice. Freeze until hard and hand them out!

ANGEL FOOD TRIFLE

*To save time, use a store-bought angel food cake —
you'll still get credit for the homemade custard!*

Yield: 15 servings

1 (16-ounce) package angel food
  cake mix (plus ingredients
  needed to make cake)
⅓ cup sugar
¼ cup cornstarch
¼ teaspoon salt
2 cups skim milk
¼ cup egg substitute

1 teaspoon lemon zest
¼ cup fresh lemon juice
2 (8-ounce) containers low-fat
  vanilla yogurt
2 cups sliced strawberries
3 kiwis, sliced
2 strawberry fans for garnish

- Prepare cake from mix according to package directions. When cake has cooled, cut into bite-size cubes and set aside.
- Combine sugar, cornstarch, and salt in saucepan. Gradually whisk in milk, blending well. Cook over medium heat until mixture begins to thicken, whisking constantly.
- Remove from heat. Add egg substitute slowly, whisking constantly.
- Return to heat and cook over medium-low heat for 2 minutes, whisking constantly.
- Remove from heat and cool slightly, then stir in lemon zest and lemon juice. Cover and refrigerate until cold.
- Fold yogurt into cold custard mixture.
- To assemble trifle, place one-third of cake pieces in bottom of 16-cup trifle bowl, then spoon one-third of custard over cake.
- Arrange half of strawberry slices and half of kiwi slices around lower edge of bowl and over custard.
- Repeat layers with remaining ingredients, ending with strawberry fans on top.
- Cover and chill 3 to 4 hours. Will not keep much longer than that before serving.

PRETZEL SALAD

The pretzels are in the crust, and it's not a salad — just a delightful dessert.

2½ cups crushed pretzels
1½ sticks (¾ cup) margarine, melted
1 cup sugar
1 (8-ounce) package cream cheese, softened

1 (8-ounce) container whipped topping
1 (6-ounce) box strawberry Jello powder
2 cups boiling water
2 (10-ounce) bags frozen strawberries

- Preheat oven to 325°.
- Stir together pretzels and margarine and press into 9x13-inch baking dish. Bake at 325° for 10 minutes. Refrigerate.
- Beat together sugar and cream cheese. Fold in whipped topping and spread over chilled pretzel crust.
- Mix Jello with boiling water until dissolved. Add frozen strawberries and let thicken in refrigerator for about 10 minutes.
- Pour Jello over cream cheese mixture and return to refrigerator for several hours.

EASY RUSSIAN CREAM WITH BERRIES

This is easy, but sounds (and tastes) so elegant.

Yield: 8 servings

3 pints fresh berries (raspberries, strawberries, blueberries, or combination)
¼ cup Grand Marnier liqueur

2 cups sour cream
¾ cup sugar
1 tablespoon vanilla extract or Grand Marnier

- Wash and drain berries. Place berries in bowl and pour liqueur over. Set aside.
- In separate bowl, whisk together sour cream, sugar, and vanilla until sugar is dissolved.
- To serve, layer drained fruit in 4-cup glass dish and pour cream over top.

Russian cream will keep well for up to 2 weeks in airtight container in refrigerator.

CLASSIC CRÈME BRÛLÉE

So simple, so rich, so beloved by so many!

Yield: 4-6 servings

8 egg yolks	1 teaspoon vanilla extract
⅓ cup sugar	½ cup sifted sugar
2 cups heavy cream	(for caramelized topping)

- Preheat oven to 300°.
- In large bowl, whisk together egg yolks and ⅓ cup sugar until sugar is dissolved and mixture is thick and pale yellow.
- Add cream and vanilla and continue to whisk until well blended.
- Strain into another large bowl, skimming off any foam or bubbles.
- Divide mixture among four 7-ounce or six 5-ounce ramekins or custard cups. Size of ramekins is important — they should be filled up close to top so sugar will caramelize on top.
- Place ramekins in large baking pan containing about 1 inch of water. Bake at 300° for 45 to 50 minutes or until set around edges but still loose in center.
- Remove from oven and leave in water bath until cool.
- Remove ramekins from water bath, cover with plastic wrap, and refrigerate for at least 2 hours, or up to 2 days.
- When ready to serve, sift about 1 tablespoon sugar over each individual custard.
- For best results, use small hand-held torch to melt sugar. If you don't have a torch, place custards under broiler until sugar melts.
- Refrigerate custards for a few minutes before serving.

LIGHT & LUSCIOUS

Yield: 12-15 servings

For crust:

1 stick (½ cup) butter, softened
1 cup all-purpose flour

½ cup finely-chopped pecans
1 tablespoon sugar

For first layer:

1 (8-ounce) package cream cheese,
   softened

1 cup confectioners' sugar
1 (8-ounce) container frozen
   whipped topping, thawed

For second layer:

2 (3-ounce) packages instant
   pudding mix, lemon or chocolate
   flavor
3 cups milk

1 (8-ounce) container frozen
   whipped topping, thawed

- Preheat oven to 400°. Spray 9x13-inch baking dish with nonstick spray.
- Mix together butter, flour, pecans, and sugar.
- Spread mixture with fingers into prepared pan.
- Bake at 400° for 10 minutes or until lightly browned. Cool.
- To make first layer, beat cream cheese and confectioners' sugar together.
- Beat whipped topping into cream cheese mixture until smooth.
- Spread mixture onto cooled crust.
- For second layer, whisk together instant pudding and milk until smooth. Spread over cream cheese layer.
- Refrigerate until pudding is set.
- Top with second container of whipped topping.

May be prepared ahead and refrigerated.

OREO SUNDAE DESSERT
Yield: 10-12 servings

1 package Oreo cookies (smaller package with 2 rows)
1 stick (½ cup) butter, melted
½ gallon vanilla ice cream
1 (5-ounce) can evaporated milk
2 (1-ounce) squares unsweetened chocolate
1 cup sugar
1 (8-ounce) container whipped topping, thawed

- Crush cookies and mix with melted butter. Press into 9x13-inch baking dish. Chill.
- Set out ice cream to soften. Spread softened ice cream over cookie crust and place in freezer.
- Stir together evaporated milk, chocolate, and sugar in medium saucepan. Cook over medium-low heat until blended. Cool and spread over ice cream. Return to freezer.
- When chocolate sauce layer has cooled, cover with whipped topping and freeze until firm.
- Let stand at room temperature several minutes before serving.

LEMON ICE CREAM
So refreshing on a hot summer day.

Juice of 8 lemons (about 1⅔ cups, or 12 ounces bottled juice)
4 cups sugar
2 quarts whole milk (or enough to fill freezer canister ¾ full)
1 pint (2 cups) heavy cream
Zest of 1 orange
Pinch of salt

- Stir together lemon juice, sugar, milk, cream, orange zest, and salt.
- Pour into ice cream freezer and freeze according to appliance instructions.

SUMMERTIME PEACH ICE CREAM

Great way to use peaches that are about to get too ripe!

Yield: 2 quarts

4 cups peeled, diced fresh peaches (6-8 peaches)

1 cup sugar

1 (12-ounce) can evaporated milk

1 (3.75-ounce) package instant vanilla pudding mix

1 (14-ounce) can sweetened condensed milk

4 cups half-and-half

- Stir together peaches and sugar, and let stand 1 hour.
- Process peaches in food processor until smooth.
- Stir together evaporated milk and pudding mix in large bowl. Stir in peaches, condensed milk, and half-and-half.
- Pour mixture into 4-quart ice cream freezer and freeze according to appliance instructions.

To slice soft peaches, freeze them partially – just enough to firm them up for mush-free slicing. This will take about 20 minutes.

EVERLASTING ICE CREAM

An old Alabama recipe — fabulous!

8 ripe peaches, peeled and pitted

3 ripe bananas, peeled

2 cups sugar

Juice of 4 oranges (about 1¼ cups)

Juice of 3 lemons (about ⅔ cup)

1 pint (2 cups) whole milk

1 pint (2 cups) half-and-half

- In large bowl of electric mixer, cream peaches, bananas, and sugar until thoroughly blended.
- Add orange juice, lemon juice, milk, and half-and-half; mix well.
- Pour into ice cream freezer and freeze according to appliance instructions.

MICROWAVE FUDGE SAUCE

It's worth buying an 8-cup microwave-safe measuring cup to make this luscious sauce.

Yield: 4 cups

2 cups sugar
½ cup unsweetened cocoa powder
¼ cup light corn syrup
1 (5-ounce) evaporated milk

1 tablespoon butter
1 teaspoon vanilla extract
⅛ teaspoon salt

- Combine sugar, cocoa, syrup, and evaporated milk in 8-cup microwave measuring cup. Cook in microwave on High for 6 minutes, stirring well every 2 minutes.
- Add butter, vanilla, and salt. Stir very well until thoroughly blended.
- Store in refrigerator and warm in microwave to serve.

LEMON SAUCE

Delicious over gingerbread or pound cake.

Yield: 1¼ cups

½ cup sugar
¼ teaspoon salt
1 tablespoon cornstarch
1 cup boiling water

1 teaspoon lemon zest
2 tablespoons butter
3 tablespoons fresh lemon juice

- Whisk together sugar, salt, and cornstarch in small saucepan.
- Add boiling water, turn heat to medium-low, and cook until clear.
- Add lemon zest and cook 1 more minute.
- Remove from heat and add butter and lemon juice. Stir well to mix.

DEVONSHIRE CREAM

This sauce is wonderful poured over fresh fruit. If beaten to a stiff consistency,
it may be used as a dip for cut fruit or a spread for scones or muffins.

Yield: 15-20 servings with fruit

1 (8-ounce) package cream cheese, softened
1 pint whipping cream

Confectioners' sugar to taste
½ teaspoon vanilla extract

- Beat cream cheese with electric mixer or in food processor.
- Slowly add cream and beat to desired consistency.
- Add confectioners' sugar and vanilla. Beat until blended.

What's the difference between whipping cream and heavy cream? Heavy cream has a higher percentage of milk fat than whipping cream. Whipping cream whips faster —in under 3 minutes for stiff peaks, while heavy cream takes about 5 minutes. Heavy cream is thicker, sweeter-tasting, and more buttery, and also holds its consistency better after whipping. Cooking experts recommend using pasteurized heavy cream if you can find it – or ultrapasteurized heavy cream as a second choice.

Curriculum

A

Ainslie's Chicken Pot Pie 135
Almond Chicken Salad 88
Amaretto Cheesecake 262
Angel Food Trifle 295
Annie Mae's One-Hour
  Buttermilk Rolls 233
Apache Cheese Bread 25

Appetizers *(also see Dips & Spreads)*
  Artichoke Truffles 17
  Bacon-Wrapped Water Chestnuts . . . 14
  Basic Bruschetta 18
  Carolina Shrimp 15
  Dijon Chicken Tidbits 12
  Gougères 9
  Hatcher Crackers 16
  Havarti Cheese Pastry 27
  Hot Crab Bites 10
  Orange Toast 21
  Oven-Dried Grape Tomatoes 20
  Parmesan Glazed Walnuts 20
  Pecan Praline Brie with Fruit 28
  Prissy Pecans 21
  Romano Shrimp
    Stuffed Mushrooms 13
  Salmon Roll-Ups 18
  Spinach Parmesan Toasts 12
  Sun-Dried Tomato Toasts 11
  Tortilla Roll Appetizers 19
  Wing Dings 14

Apple Cheese Ball 32

Apples
  Apple Cheddar Muffins 230
  Apple Lime Salad 80
  Apple Pizzas 249
  Cranberry Apple Bake 193
  Grandma K's Apple Pudding 293
  Sautéed Apple Salad with
    Roquefort & Walnuts 66

Spicy Apple Bread 223
Sugarless Apple Pie 273

Apricots
  Apricot Brownies 285
  Apricot Nectar Cake 258
  Baked Apricots 192

Artichokes
  Artichoke Truffles 17
  Chicken & Artichoke Soup 51
  Light Spinach Artichoke Dip 23
  Pasta Artichoke Raphael 199
  Shrimp, Artichoke &
    Grits Casserole 144

Asparagus
  Asparagus with
    Maple Vinaigrette 167
  Marinated Asparagus 168
  Roasted Asparagus 169

Austrian Noodles with Walnuts 213
Avocado & Corn Salsa 29

B

Baby Back Ribs
  with Peach Sauce 104
Bacon & Tomato Dip 36
Bacon-Wrapped Water Chestnuts 14
Baked Apricots 192
Baked Eggs & Cheese 236
Balsamic Vinaigrette 65

Bananas
  Banana Cake 259
  Banana Pancakes 248
  Everlasting Ice Cream 300
  One-Pan Banana Bread 224

Barbecued Shrimp 146
Basic Bruschetta 18
Beach Weekend Fizzies 39

Beans & Peas

Bill Neal's Hoppin' John 217
Black Bean Salsa 31
Black Beans & Pork over Rice . . . 105
Brown Rice & Red Lentil Soup . . . 54
Casserole à la Nini 97
Chicken Chili 50
Cornbread Casserole 99
Fabulous Mexican Dip 24
Gallo Pinto (Costa Rican
  Rice & Beans) 222
McClellanville Caviar 31
Mexican Chicken & Rice 136
New Year's Day
  Black-Eyed Pea Stew 48
Rio Grande Grits Casserole 242
Taco Soup 45
Tuscan White Bean Soup with
  Prosciutto 53

Beef

Ground

Cannelloni with Two Sauces . . . 204
Casserole à la Nini 97
Cornbread Casserole 99
Enticing Enchiladas 98
Grandmommy's Mazetti 96
Mom's Kid-Approved
  Lasagna 210
Spaghetti Casserole 206
Special Lasagna 209
Taco Cheesecake 100
Taco Soup 45

Roast

Beef & Pork Barbecue 101
Eye of the Round Roast 91
French Dip Sandwiches 95
Julia's Easy Pot Roast 92

Steak

Company Beef Stroganoff 94
Filets with Mushroom Sauce . . . 93

Stew Beef

Football Stew 46
Vegetable Beef Soup 45

Tenderloin

Julie Taylor's Marinated
  Beef Tenderloin 91

Beef & Pork Barbecue 101

Better-than-Bought
  Cinnamon Rolls 246

Beverages

Beach Weekend Fizzies 39
Bourbon Slushes 42
Chocolate Martini 44
Cosmopolitans 41
Cranberry-Apple Limeade 40
Favorite Party Punch 39
Homemade Irish
  Cream Liqueur 44
Mary Ann Little's
  Creek Water Tea 37
Mr. James' Margaritas 41
Old-Fashioned Lemonade 38
Peach Fuzzies 43
Purple Cow Shake 38
Sugar Syrup 38
Swamp Water 43

Bill Neal's Hoppin' John 217
Black Bean Salsa 31
Black Beans & Pork over Rice 105
Black Russian Cake 256
Blue Cheese & Walnut Dip 33

Blueberries

Blueberry Bread 224
Blueberry Brunch Cake 245
Blueberry Gingerbread 286
Easy Russian
  Cream with Berries 296

Bourbon Chicken with Peaches 115

Bourbon Slushes 42

Breads
Annie Mae's One-Hour
Buttermilk Rolls 233
Apple Cheddar Muffins 230
Apple Pizzas 249
Banana Pancakes 248
Better-than-Bought
Cinnamon Rolls 246
Blueberry Bread 224
Blueberry Brunch Cake 245
Butterscotch Monkey Bread 247
Cinnamon Sour Cream
Coffee Cake 243
Easy Biscuits 234
Garlic Knots 235
Granddaddy Johnson's
Oatmeal Bread 228
Jalapeño Corn Bread 229
Morning Glory Muffins 231
One-Pan Banana Bread 224
Overnight French Toast 250
Pineapple Bread 225
Pumpkin Muffins 232
Pumpkin Raisin
Bread & Muffins 226
Skillet Coffee Cake 244
Spicy Apple Bread 223
Strawberry Bread 227
Sweet Potato Biscuits 235
William of
Orange French Toast 251

Broccoli
Broccoli & Cranberry Slaw 70
Broccoli Chowder 57
Broccoli Slaw Salad 69

Brown Rice & Red Lentil Soup 54
Buttermilk Substitutes 229
Butters, Flavored 234

Butterscotch Cream Cheese Bars . . . 280
Butterscotch Monkey Bread 247

C

Cabbage
Broccoli & Cranberry Slaw 70
Hicks Family Reunion
Marinated Slaw 68
Oriental Slaw 72

Cakes *(see Desserts)*
California Rice Casserole 219
California Sweet Potato Bake 177
Cannelloni with Two Sauces 204

Capers
Double Tomato Salad 75
Grape Tomatoes & Capers 75
Sea Bass Roasted with Capers . . . 163
Shrimp & Caper Dip 34

Caramel Graham
Fudge Brownies 282
Carolina Shrimp 15
Carrots, Glazed 171
Carson's Tomato Pie 187
Casserole à la Nini 97

Casseroles
California Rice Casserole 219
Casserole à la Nini 97
Chicken Spectacular 127
Cornbread Casserole 99
Crab Casserole 147
Cranberry Apple Bake 193
Easy Vegetable Casserole 191
Favorite Squash Casserole 184
Grandmommy's Mazetti 96
Incredulada Enchiladas 131
Mexican Chicken & Rice 136

Pineapple Casserole 192
Poppy Seed Chicken 130
Rio Grande Grits Casserole 242
Shrimp, Artichoke
   & Grits Casserole 144
Southern Squash Casserole 183
Spaghetti Casserole 206
Three-Cheese Chicken Pasta 128
Vidalia Onion Casserole 173

Cheese
Apache Cheese Bread 25
Apple Cheddar Muffins 230
Apple Cheese Ball 32
Baked Eggs & Cheese 236
Blue Cheese & Walnut Dip 33
Cheesy Chile Rice 218
Cheesy Corn Dip 22
Chicken Breasts Stuffed with
   Mozzarella & Canadian Bacon . . . 120
Havarti Cheese Pastry 27
Manicotti with Cheese
   & Spinach Stuffing 207
Miss Virginia's
   Blue Cheese Dressing 74
Parmesan Glazed Walnuts 20
Pecan Praline Brie with Fruit 28
Potato Salad with
   Blue Cheese & Walnuts 83
Roasted Roquefort Potatoes 174
Sautéed Apple Salad
   with Roquefort & Walnuts 66
Spinach Parmesan Toasts 12
Swiss & Chive Spread 35
Three-Cheese Chicken Pasta 128
Vegetable Frittata with
   Herbs & Goat Cheese 240
Warm Goat Cheese Salad 76

Cheesy Chile Rice 218
Cheesy Corn Dip 22
Chicago Pasta Salad 87

Chicken *(see Poultry)*
Chicken & Artichoke Soup 51
Chicken & Cranberry Mold 90
Chicken Breasts Stuffed
   with Mozzarella
   & Canadian Bacon 120
Chicken Chili 50
Chicken Lo Mein 134
Chicken Pecan Salad
   with Cranberries 89
Chicken Pot Pie, Ainslie's 135
Chicken Spectacular 127
Chicken-Chutney Croissants 125
Chili, Chicken 50
Chili Maple Glaze 109
Chilled Summer Squash Soup
   with Curry 60

Chocolate *(also see Desserts)*
Caramel Graham
   Fudge Brownies 282
Chocolate Angel Nut Pie 263
Chocolate Cheesecake 265
Chocolate Chocolate
   Chocolate Cake 254
Chocolate Martini 44
Chocolate Toffee Cookies 274
Decadent Chocolate Cream Pie . . 266
Double Chocolate
   Mousse Cake 253
Dried Cranberry &
   White Chocolate Biscotti 276
Georgia's Cookies 278
Leah's Chocolate Cake 255
Lynn's Famous Brownies 281
Microwave Fudge Sauce 301
Mom Coles's Chocolate Pie 268
Oreo Sundae Dessert 299
Raspberry Walnut Brownies 283
Turtle Cake 257
Viorenes 284

Cinnamon Sour Cream
    Coffee Cake 243
Citrus Marinated Turkey Breast 136
Classic Crème Brûlée 297
Coconut Caramel Pies 267
Coconut Cups 278
Cold Spiced Fruit 194
Colorful Crabmeat 34
Company Beef Stroganoff 94
Company Lasagna 211

Condiments & Relishes
(also see Sauces & Seasonings)
    Avocado & Corn Salsa 29
    Black Bean Salsa 31
    Flavored Butters 234
    Lemon Mayonnaise 156
    Mint Butter 113
    Summertime Fresh Peach Salsa . . . 166
    Tomato Cilantro Salsa 160

Corn
    Avocado & Corn Salsa 29
    Cheesy Corn Dip 22
    Jalapeño Corn Bread 229
    Salmon Fillets with
        Sautéed Corn & Spinach 154
Cornbread Casserole 99
Cornflake Cookies 277
Cosmopolitans 41
Crab Casserole 147

Cranberries & Cranberry Juice
    Broccoli & Cranberry Slaw 70
    Chicken & Cranberry Mold 90
    Chicken Pecan Salad
        with Cranberries 89
    Cosmopolitans 41
    Cranberry Apple Bake 193
    Cranberry Maple Sauce 252

Cranberry-Apple Limeade 40
Dried Cranberry &
    White Chocolate Biscotti 276
Raisin Bread-Cranberry
    Stuffing 138
Crawfish Dip 26
Crawfish Étouffée 150
Creamy Almond Chicken 124
Creamy Chicken & Pasta Soup 52
Creamy Scalloped Potatoes 176
Creamy Tomato Basil Soup 55
Creole Chicken Pasta 129

Crock Pot Recipes
    Crock Pot Chicken
        Brunswick Stew 49
    Crock Pot Pork Tenderloin 103
    Slow Cooker Barbecue 102
Crook's Corner Shrimp & Grits 142
Crunchy Romaine Toss 71

D

Date Bars 287
Decadent Chocolate Cream Pie 266

Desserts *(also see Chocolate)*
    Cakes & Cheesecakes
        Amaretto Cheesecake 262
        Apricot Nectar Cake 258
        Banana Cake 259
        Black Russian Cake 256
        Cake Cutting 259
        Chocolate Cheesecake 265
        Chocolate Chocolate
            Chocolate Cake 254
        Double Chocolate
            Mousse Cake 253
        Glazed Poppy Seed Cake 260
        Incredible Cheesecake 261

Leah's Chocolate Cake 255
Pumpkin Hazelnut
  Cheesecake 264
Turtle Cake 257

Cookies & Bars
Apricot Brownies 285
Blueberry Gingerbread 286
Butterscotch Cream
  Cheese Bars 280
Caramel Graham
  Fudge Brownies 282
Chocolate Toffee Cookies 274
Coconut Cups 278
Cornflake Cookies 277
Date Bars 287
Dried Cranberry &
  White Chocolate Biscotti ... 276
Easy Lemon Squares 288
Georgia's Cookies 278
Gram's Brown Edge Cookies .. 275
Honey's Ginger Snaps 279
Lynn's Famous Brownies 281
Pecan Squares 289
Raisin Bars 290
Raspberry Walnut Brownies ... 283
Sunshine Crisps 275
Viorenes 284

Frostings, Icings & Sauces
Devonshire Cream 302
Feathering Cream 273
Frosting 254, 259
Glaze 253, 258, 260
Icing 284
Icing a Cake 255
Lemon Sauce 301
Microwave Fudge Sauce 301
Topping 256

Pies
Chocolate Angel Nut Pie 263
Coconut Caramel Pies 267

Decadent Chocolate
  Cream Pie 266
Frozen Strawberry
  Margarita Pie 272
Mom Coles's Chocolate Pie ... 268
New England Pecan Pie 269
Raspberry Cream Pie 271
Sally's Pear Pie 270
Sugarless Apple Pie 273
Summertime Peach Pie 270

Puddings & Desserts
Angel Food Trifle 295
Classic Crème Brûlée 297
Easy Russian Cream
  with Berries 296
Everlasting Ice Cream 300
Grandma K's Apple Pudding ... 293
Grandma Mary's
  Soda Cracker Dessert 293
Lemon Ice Cream 299
Lemon Semifreddo 292
Light & Luscious 298
Oreo Sundae Dessert 299
Pretzel Salad 296
Red Rock Ranch Mixed
  Berry Crisp 291
Strawberry Angel Food
  Delight 294
Summertime Peach
  Ice Cream 300
Devonshire Cream 302
Dijon Chicken Tidbits 12

Dips & Spreads *(also see Appetizers)*
Apache Cheese Bread 25
Apple Cheese Ball 32
Avocado & Corn Salsa 29
Bacon & Tomato Dip 36
Black Bean Salsa 31
Blue Cheese & Walnut Dip 33
Cheesy Corn Dip 22

Colorful Crabmeat 34
Crawfish Dip 26
Fabulous Mexican Dip 24
Gran's Fresh Tomato Salsa 30
Hearts of Palm Spread 22
Light Spinach Artichoke Dip 23
McClellanville Caviar 31
Salmon Spread 25
Shrimp & Caper Dip 34
Swiss & Chive Spread 35
That Ranch Stuff 27
Vegetable Cheesecake 35
Vidalia Onion Dip 24

Double Chocolate Mousse Cake . . . 253
Double Tomato Salad 75
Dressed Baked Flounder 157
Dried Cranberry &
    White Chocolate Biscotti 276

E

Easy Biscuits 234
Easy Lemon Squares 288
Easy Russian Cream with Berries . . . 296
Easy Vegetable Casserole 191

Eggplant
    Ratatouille Tart 188
    Roasted Summer Vegetables 190

Eggs
    Baked Eggs & Cheese 236
    Never-Fail Breakfast Soufflé 237
    Overnight French Toast 250
    Posner's Famous Spinach Quiche . . 238
    Spring Frittata 239
    Vegetable Frittata with
        Herbs & Goat Cheese 240
    William of Orange
        French Toast 251

Emeril's Wedgie Salad 67
Ensalada Nochebuena
    (Winter Fruit Salad) 77
Enticing Enchiladas 98
Essence 146
Everlasting Ice Cream 300
Eye of the Round Roast 91

F

Fabulous Mexican Dip 24
Favorite Party Punch 39
Favorite Squash Casserole . . . . . . , . 184
Filets with Mushroom Sauce 93

Fish
    Dressed Baked Flounder 157
    Grilled Grouper 158
    Grilled Maple-Mustard Salmon . . 165
    New York Brunch Wrap 241
    Orange Roughy with
        Tomato Cilantro Salsa 160
    Pan-Seared Tuna with Ginger-
        Shiitake Cream Sauce 164
    Red Snapper Joliet Rouge 161
    Salmon Fillets with
        Sautéed Corn & Spinach 154
    Salmon in Ginger Soy Sauce 158
    Salmon Roll-Ups 18
    Salmon Spread 25
    Salmon Topped with
        Fresh Veggies 155
    Salmon with Lemon
        Mayonnaise 156
    Sautéed Red Snapper
        with Tomato Olive Sauce 162
    Sea Bass Roasted with Capers . . . 163
    Spinach Pasta with
        Salmon Cream Sauce 197
    Stuffed Sole or Flounder
        Fillets with Lemon Sauce 159

Flavored Butters 234
Football Stew 46
French Dip Sandwiches 95
Fresh Fruit with Lime Sauce 79
Fresh Mint Vinaigrette 112
Fresh Spinach Lasagna 208
Frogmore Stew 56
Frozen Strawberry Margarita Pie . . . 272
Fruit, Cold Spiced 194
Fruitsicles 294

G

Gallo Pinto (Costa Rican
   Rice & Beans) 222
Garlic Knots 235
Gazpacho 61
Georgia's Cookies 278
Ginger-Shiitake Cream Sauce 164
Glazed Carrots 171
Glazed Poppy Seed Cake 260
Goat Cheese Sauce 190
Gougères 9
Gourmet Quesadillas 132
Grace's Chicken 122
Gram's Brown Edge Cookies 275
Gran's Fresh Tomato Salsa 30
Granddaddy Johnson's
   Oatmeal Bread 228
Grandma K's Apple Pudding 293
Grandma Mary's
   Soda Cracker Dessert 293
Grandmommy's Mazetti 96
Grape Tomatoes & Capers 75
Greek Marinated Vegetable Salad 73
Greek Shrimp over Pasta 145
Greek-Style Squash 182
Green Bean Bundles 169
Green Beans Y'all Won't Believe 170
Gretchen's Nutty Wild Rice 218

Grilling Recipes

Baby Back Ribs
   with Peach Sauce 104
Filets with Mushroom Sauce 93
Grace's Chicken 122
Grilled Grouper 158
Grilled Lamb 111
Grilled Maple-Mustard Salmon . . 165
Grilled Pork Tenderloin
   with Chili Maple Glaze 109
Grilled Spice-Rubbed
   Pork Tenderloin 107
Marinade for Grilled Pork
   or Chicken 110
Marinade for Pork Tenderloin . . . 111
Salmon with
   Lemon Mayonnaise 156
Sweet & Spicy Grilled Chicken . . 125
Uncle Charlie's Grilled
   Barbecue Chicken 126

Grits

Crook's Corner Shrimp & Grits . . . 142
Rio Grande Grits Casserole 242
Shrimp, Artichoke
   & Grits Casserole 144

H

Hatcher Crackers 16
Havarti Cheese Pastry 27
Hearts of Palm Spread 22
Hermione's Couscous Salad 84
Hicks Family Reunion
   Marinated Slaw 68
Homemade Irish Cream Liqueur 44
Homemade Tomato Sauce 216
Honey Mustard Sauce 109
Honey's Ginger Snaps 279
Hot Crab Bites 10
How to Cook a Frozen
   Turkey Breast 137

I

Incredulada Enchiladas 131
Incredible Cheesecake 261

J

Jalapeño Corn Bread 229
Julia's Easy Pot Roast 92
Julie Taylor's Marinated
   Beef Tenderloin 91

L

Lamb

Grilled Lamb 111
Lamb Chops with Mint Butter . . . 113
Spring Lamb with Fresh Mint
   Vinaigrette 112

Leah's Chocolate Cake 255

Lemons

Easy Lemon Squares 288
Lemon Garlic Chicken 117
Lemon Ice Cream 299
Lemon Mayonnaise 156
Lemon Rice with Pine Nuts 221
Lemon Sauce (sweet) 301
Lemon Sauce (savory) 159
Lemon Semifreddo 292
Old-Fashioned Lemonade 38

Light & Luscious 298
Light Caesar Salad 74
Light Spinach Artichoke Dip 23
Linguine with Clam Sauce 198
Lynn's Famous Brownies 281

M

Mahogany Glazed Chicken 121
Manicotti with Cheese
   & Spinach Stuffing 207
Maple Vinaigrette 167
Marinade for Grilled Pork
   or Chicken 110
Marinade for Pork Tenderloin 111
Marinated Asparagus 168
Mary Ann Little's Creek Water Tea . . . 37
McClellanville Caviar 31
Meg's Crabcakes 148

Mexican Recipes

Enticing Enchiladas 98
Fabulous Mexican Dip 24
Gourmet Quesadillas 132
Incredulada Enchiladas 131
Mexican Chicken & Rice 136
Taco Cheesecake 100
Tortilla Torta 133

Microwave Recipes

California Sweet Potato Bake 177
Measuring Honey 269
Microwave Fudge Sauce 301
New York Brunch Wrap 241
Savory Tomato Rice 220
Softening Brown Sugar 274

Mint Butter 113
Miss Virginia's
   Blue Cheese Dressing 74
Mom Coles's Chocolate Pie 268
Mom's Kid-Approved Lasagna 210
Morning Glory Muffins 231
Mr. James' Margaritas 41

Mushrooms

Mushroom Sauce 93
Orzo with Basil & Mushrooms . . . 214
Pan-Seared Tuna with
   Ginger-Shiitake Cream Sauce . . 164
Regal Mushrooms 172
Romano Shrimp
   Stuffed Mushrooms 13

N

Never-Fail Breakfast Soufflé 237
New England Pecan Pie 269
New Year's Day
  Black-Eyed Pea Stew 48
New York Brunch Wrap 241
Noodles with Peanut Sauce 215

Nuts

Almond Chicken Salad 88
Austrian Noodles with Walnuts . . . 213
Blue Cheese & Walnut Dip 33
Chicken Pecan Salad
  with Cranberries 89
Chocolate Angel Nut Pie 263
Coconut Caramel Pies 267
Coconut Cups 278
Creamy Almond Chicken 124
New England Pecan Pie 269
Parmesan Glazed Walnuts 20
Peas & Peanuts Salad 73
Pecan Praline Brie with Fruit 28
Pecan Squares 289
Potato Salad with Blue Cheese
  & Walnuts 83
Prissy Pecans 21
Pumpkin Hazelnut Cheesecake . . 264
Raspberry Walnut Brownies 283
Salad with Spiced Pecans
  & Balsamic Vinaigrette 65
Sautéed Apple Salad
  with Roquefort & Walnuts 66
Spinach & Peanut Pesto
  over Pasta 201
Toasting Nuts 33

O

Okra & Tomatoes, Southern 185
Old-Fashioned Lemonade 38
One-Pan Banana Bread 224

Onions

Vidalia Onion Casserole 173
Vidalia Onion Dip 24

Oranges & Orange Juice

Beach Weekend Fizzies 39
Bourbon Slushes 42
Citrus Marinated Turkey Breast . . 136
Orange-Basil Chicken 118
Orange Toast 21
William of Orange
  French Toast 251

Orange-Basil Chicken 118
Orange Roughy with Tomato
  Cilantro Salsa 160
Orange Toast 21
Oregano Peas 174
Oreo Sundae Dessert 299
Oriental Slaw 72
Orzo with Basil & Mushrooms 214
Oven-Dried Grape Tomatoes 20
Overnight Company Potatoes 175
Overnight French Toast 250
Oysters Mosca 153

P

Pan-Seared Tuna with Ginger-
  Shiitake Cream Sauce 164
Parmesan Chicken with
  Balsamic Butter Sauce 119
Parmesan Glazed Walnuts 20

Pasta

Austrian Noodles with Walnuts . . . 213
Cannelloni with Two Sauces 204
Chicago Pasta Salad 87
Chicken Lo Mein 134
Company Beef Stroganoff 94
Company Lasagna 211
Crab Casserole 147

Creamy Chicken & Pasta Soup 52
Creole Chicken Pasta 129
Fresh Spinach Lasagna 208
Grandmommy's Mazetti 96
Greek Shrimp over Pasta 145
Linguine with Clam Sauce 198
Manicotti with Cheese
    & Spinach Stuffing 207
Mom's Kid-Approved Lasagna ... 210
Noodles with Peanut Sauce 215
Orzo with Basil & Mushrooms ... 214
Pasta Artichoke Raphael 199
Pasta with Sausage & Chicken ... 195
Patty's Garden Tomato Pasta 202
Penne Pasta & Spinach 200
Sausage Tortellini Soup 47
Spaghetti Carbonara 205
Spaghetti Casserole 206
Special Lasagna 209
Spinach & Peanut Pesto
    over Pasta 201
Spinach Pasta with
    Salmon Cream Sauce 197
Summertime Pasta 203
Three-Cheese Chicken Pasta 128
Tortellini & Shells Salad 86
Vermicelli with Sausage &
    Vegetables 196

Patty's Garden Tomato Pasta 202

Peaches
Bourbon Chicken with Peaches .. 115
Everlasting Ice Cream 300
Peach Fuzzies 43
Peach Sauce 104
Summertime Fresh Peach Salsa ... 166
Summertime Peach Ice Cream ... 300
Summertime Peach Pie 270

Pear Pie, Sally's 270

Peas, Oregano 174

Peas & Peanuts Salad 73
Pecan Praline Brie with Fruit 28
Pecan Squares 289
Penne Pasta & Spinach 200

Pies (see Desserts)

Pineapple
Pineapple Bread 225
Pineapple Casserole 192

Poppy Seed Chicken 130

Pork
Bacon
    Bacon & Tomato Dip 36
    Bacon-Wrapped
        Water Chestnuts 14
    Spaghetti Carbonara 205
Chops
    Pork Chops in Honey
        Mustard Sauce 109
Ground
    Grandmommy's Mazetti 96
Ham
    Apache Cheese Bread 25
    Never-Fail Breakfast Soufflé ... 237
    Tuscan White Bean Soup
        with Prosciutto 53
Ribs
    Baby Back Ribs with
        Peach Sauce 104
Roast & Tenderloin
    Beef & Pork Barbecue 101
    Black Beans & Pork
        over Rice 105
    Crock Pot Pork Tenderloin 103
    Grilled Pork Tenderloin
        with Chili Maple Glaze 109
    Grilled Spice-Rubbed
        Pork Tenderloin 107
    Marinade for Grilled Pork
        or Chicken 110

Index

Marinade for
Pork Tenderloin 111

Pork Tenderloin with
Mustard Sauce 108

Provençal Pork Roast 106

Slow Cooker Barbecue 102

Sausage
Company Lasagna 211

Frogmore Stew 56

New Year's Day
Black-Eyed Pea Stew 48

Pasta with Sausage
& Chicken 195

Sausage Lasagna
with Vegetables 212

Sausage Tortellini Soup 47

Vermicelli with Sausage
& Vegetables 196

Pork Chops in Honey
Mustard Sauce 109

Pork Tenderloin with
Mustard Sauce 108

Posner's Famous Spinach Quiche . . . 238

Potatoes
Creamy Scalloped Potatoes 176

Overnight Company Potatoes . . . 175

Potato Salad with Blue Cheese
& Walnuts 83

Potato Soup Plus 56

Red Onion Potato Salad 84

Roasted Potatoes & Green Beans
with Rosemary Vinaigrette 82

Roasted Roquefort Potatoes 174

Savory Roasted New Potatoes . . . 175

Potato Salad with Blue Cheese
& Walnuts 83

Potato Soup Plus 56

Poultry
Ainslie's Chicken Pot Pie 135

Almond Chicken Salad 88

Bourbon Chicken
with Peaches 115

Chicken & Artichoke Soup 51

Chicken & Cranberry Mold 90

Chicken Breasts Stuffed
with Mozzarella
& Canadian Bacon 120

Chicken Chili 50

Chicken Lo Mein 134

Chicken Pecan Salad
with Cranberries 89

Chicken Spectacular 127

Chicken-Chutney Croissants 125

Citrus Marinated
Turkey Breast 136

Creamy Almond Chicken 124

Creamy Chicken & Pasta Soup 52

Creole Chicken Pasta 129

Crock Pot Chicken
Brunswick Stew 49

Dijon Chicken Tidbits 12

Gourmet Quesadillas 132

Grace's Chicken 122

How to Cook a Frozen
Turkey Breast 137

Incredulada Enchiladas 131

Lemon Garlic Chicken 117

Mahogany Glazed Chicken 121

Mexican Chicken & Rice 136

Orange-Basil Chicken 118

Parmesan Chicken with
Balsamic Butter Sauce 119

Pasta with Sausage & Chicken . . . 195

Poppy Seed Chicken 130

Quick & Colorful Cutlets 123

Raspberry-Balsamic
Glazed Chicken 116

Sautéed Chicken with
Grape Tomatoes & Basil 122

Stovetop Cooked Chicken
for Recipes 131

Sweet & Spicy
  Grilled Chicken 125
Teriyaki Turkey Burgers 139
Three-Cheese Chicken Pasta 128
Tipsy Cornish Hens 141
Tortilla Torta 133
Turkey Meat Loaf 140
Uncle Charlie's Grilled
  Barbecue Chicken 126
Wing Dings 14

Pretzel Salad 296
Prissy Pecans 21
Provençal Pork Roast 106

Pumpkin
Pumpkin Hazelnut Cheesecake . . 264
Pumpkin Muffins 232
Pumpkin Raisin
  Bread & Muffins 226

Purefoy Hotel Sweet
  Potato Pudding 178
Purple Cow Shake 38

Q

Quiche, Posner's Famous Spinach . . . 238
Quick & Colorful Cutlets 123

R

Raisin Bars 290
Raisin Bread-Cranberry Stuffing . . . 138
Raspberry Cream Pie 271
Raspberry Walnut Brownies 283
Raspberry-Balsamic
  Glazed Chicken 116
Ratatouille Tart 188
Red Onion Potato Salad 84
Red Rock Ranch Mixed
  Berry Crisp 291
Red Snapper Joliet Rouge 161

Regal Mushrooms 172
Rémoulade Sauce 151

Rice
Bill Neal's Hoppin' John 217
Black Beans & Pork over Rice . . . 105
Brown Rice & Red Lentil Soup . . . 54
California Rice Casserole 219
Cheesy Chile Rice 218
Gallo Pinto (Costa
  Rican Rice & Beans) 222
Gretchen's Nutty Wild Rice 218
Lemon Rice with Pine Nuts 221
Mexican Chicken & Rice 136
Savory Tomato Rice 220
Very Yummy Rice 217
Wild Rice Salad 85

Rio Grande Grits Casserole 242
Roasted Asparagus 169
Roasted Green Beans 171
Roasted Potatoes & Green Beans
  with Rosemary Vinaigrette 82
Roasted Roquefort Potatoes 174
Roasted Summer Vegetables 190
Rob's Manhattan Clam Chowder . . . 59
Romano Shrimp
  Stuffed Mushrooms 13
Rush's Oyster Special 153

S

Salad Dressings
Balsamic Vinaigrette 65
Dressing 62, 63, 64, 68, 69
Maple Vinaigrette 167
Miss Virginia's Blue
  Cheese Dressing 74
That Ranch Stuff 27

Salads
Almond Chicken Salad 88

Index

Apple Lime Salad 80
Broccoli & Cranberry Slaw 70
Broccoli Slaw Salad 69
Chicago Pasta Salad 87
Chicken & Cranberry Mold 90
Chicken Pecan Salad
    with Cranberries 89
Crunchy Romaine Toss 71
Double Tomato Salad 75
Emeril's Wedgie Salad 67
Ensalada Nochebuena
    (Winter Fruit Salad) 77
Fresh Fruit with Lime Sauce 79
Grape Tomatoes & Capers 75
Greek Marinated
    Vegetable Salad 73
Hermione's Couscous Salad 84
Hicks Family Reunion
    Marinated Slaw 68
Light Caesar Salad 74
Oriental Slaw 72
Peas & Peanuts Salad 73
Potato Salad with Blue Cheese
    & Walnuts 83
Red Onion Potato Salad 84
Roasted Potatoes & Green Beans
    with Rosemary Vinaigrette 82
Salad with Spiced Pecans
    & Balsamic Vinaigrette 65
Sautéed Apple Salad with
    Roquefort & Walnuts 66
Strawberry Cheesecake Salad 81
Strawberry Spinach Salad 63
Summer Fruit Salad 78
Sunflower Spinach Salad 62
Tortellini & Shells Salad 86
Warm Goat Cheese Salad 76
Wild Rice Salad 85
Winter Spinach Salad 64

Sally's Pear Pie 270

Salmon Fillets with Sautéed
    Corn & Spinach 154
Salmon in Ginger Soy Sauce 158
Salmon Roll-Ups 18
Salmon Spread 25
Salmon Topped with
    Fresh Veggies 155
Salmon with Lemon Mayonnaise . . . 156
Sandwiches, French Dip 95

Sauces & Seasonings
(also see Condiments & Relishes)

Balsamic Butter Sauce 119
Chili Maple Glaze 109
Cranberry Maple Sauce 252
Cream Sauce 204
Crème Fraîche 179
Essence 146
Fresh Mint Vinaigrette 112
Ginger-Shiitake Cream Sauce 164
Goat Cheese Sauce 190
Homemade Tomato Sauce 216
Honey Mustard Sauce 109
Lemon Sauce 159
Marinade for Grilled Pork
    or Chicken 110
Mushroom Sauce 93
Mustard Sauce 108
Peach Sauce 104
Rémoulade Sauce 151
Tomato Olive Sauce 162
Tomato Sauce 204
White Sauce 144

Sausage Lasagna with Vegetables 212
Sausage Tortellini Soup 47
Sautéed Apple Salad with
    Roquefort & Walnuts 66
Sautéed Chicken with Grape
    Tomatoes & Basil 122
Sautéed Red Snapper with
    Tomato Olive Sauce 162

Savory Roasted New Potatoes 175
Savory Tomato Rice 220
Sea Bass Roasted with Capers 163

Seafood *(also see Fish)*
Clams
   Linguine with Clam Sauce 198
   Rob's Manhattan
     Clam Chowder 59
Crabmeat
   Colorful Crabmeat 34
   Crab Casserole 147
   Grades of Crabmeat 147
   Hot Crab Bites 10
   Meg's Crabcakes 148
   Soft Shelled Crabs in
     Brown Butter 149
Lobster
   Stuffed Lobster Tails 152
Oysters
   Oysters Mosca 153
   Rush's Oyster Special 153
Shrimp & Crawfish
   Barbecued Shrimp 146
   Carolina Shrimp 15
   Crawfish Dip 26
   Crawfish Étouffée 150
   Crook's Corner
     Shrimp & Grits 142
   Frogmore Stew 56
   Greek Shrimp over Pasta 145
   McClellanville Caviar 31
   Romano Shrimp
     Stuffed Mushrooms 13
   Seafood Chowder 58
   Shrimp & Caper Dip 34
   Shrimp, Artichoke & Grits
     Casserole 144
   Shrimp Frederic 143
Seafood Chowder 58

Shrimp & Caper Dip 34
Shrimp, Artichoke
   & Grits Casserole 144
Shrimp Frederic 143
Skillet Coffee Cake 244
Slow Cooker Barbecue 102
Soft Shelled Crabs
   in Brown Butter 149

Soups & Stews
   Broccoli Chowder 57
   Brown Rice & Red Lentil Soup ... 54
   Chicken & Artichoke Soup 51
   Chicken Chili 50
   Chilled Summer Squash Soup
     with Curry 60
   Creamy Chicken & Pasta Soup 52
   Creamy Tomato Basil Soup 55
   Crock Pot Chicken
     Brunswick Stew 49
   Football Stew 46
   Frogmore Stew 56
   Gazpacho 61
   New Year's Day
     Black-Eyed Pea Stew 48
   Potato Soup Plus 56
   Rob's Manhattan
     Clam Chowder 59
   Sausage Tortellini Soup 47
   Seafood Chowder 58
   Taco Soup 45
   Tuscan White Bean Soup
     with Prosciutto 53
   Vegetable Beef Soup 45

Southern Okra & Tomatoes 185
Southern Squash Casserole 183
Spaghetti Carbonara 205
Spaghetti Casserole 206
Special Lasagna 209
Spiced Pecans 65
Spicy Apple Bread 223

Spinach

Cannelloni with Two Sauces 204
Fresh Spinach Lasagna 208
Hermione's Couscous Salad 84
Light Spinach Artichoke Dip 23
Manicotti with Cheese
  & Spinach Stuffing 207
Penne Pasta & Spinach 200
Posner's Famous
  Spinach Quiche 238
Salmon Fillets with Sautéed
  Corn & Spinach 154
Spinach & Peanut Pesto
  over Pasta 201
Spinach Orzo 181
Spinach Parmesan Toasts 12
Spinach Spoon Bread 180
Strawberry Spinach Salad 63
Sunflower Spinach Salad 62
Winter Spinach Salad 64

Spinach Pasta with
  Salmon Cream Sauce 197
Spring Frittata 239
Spring Lamb with
  Fresh Mint Vinaigrette 112

Squash

Chilled Summer Squash Soup
  with Curry 60
Favorite Squash Casserole 184
Greek-Style Squash 182
Southern Squash Casserole 183

Stovetop Cooked Chicken
  for Recipes 131

Strawberries

Angel Food Trifle 295
Easy Russian Cream
  with Berries 296
Frozen Strawberry
  Margarita Pie 272

Pretzel Salad 296
Strawberry
  Angel Food Delight 294
Strawberry Bread 227
Strawberry Cheesecake Salad 81
Strawberry Spinach Salad 63
Summer Fruit Salad 78

Stuffed Lobster Tails 152
Stuffed Sole or Flounder Fillets
  with Lemon Sauce 159
Stuffing, Raisin Bread-Cranberry . . . 138
Sugar Syrup 38
Sugarless Apple Pie 273
Summer Fruit Salad 78
Summer Vegetable Skillet 191
Summertime Fresh Peach Salsa 166
Summertime Pasta 203
Summertime Peach Ice Cream 300
Summertime Peach Pie 270
Sun-Dried Tomato Toasts 11
Sunflower Spinach Salad 62
Sunshine Crisps 275
Swamp Water 43
Sweet & Spicy Grilled Chicken 125

Sweet Potatoes

California Sweet Potato Bake 177
Microwaving Sweet Potatoes 177
Purefoy Hotel Sweet
  Potato Pudding 178
Sweet Potato Biscuits 235
Sweet Potato Carrot Purée 179

Swiss & Chive Spread 35

T

Taco Cheesecake 100
Taco Soup 45
Teriyaki Turkey Burgers 139

That Ranch Stuff 27
Three-Cheese Chicken Pasta 128
Tipsy Cornish Hens 141

Tomatoes
   Bacon & Tomato Dip 36
   Basic Bruschetta 18
   Carson's Tomato Pie 187
   Creamy Tomato Basil Soup 55
   Double Tomato Salad 75
   Gazpacho 61
   Gran's Fresh Tomato Salsa 30
   Grape Tomatoes & Capers 75
   Homemade Tomato Sauce 216
   Orange Roughy with
      Tomato Cilantro Salsa 160
   Oven-Dried Grape Tomatoes 20
   Patty's Garden Tomato Pasta 202
   Peeling Tomatoes 186
   Ratatouille Tart 188
   Roasted Summer Vegetables 190
   Sautéed Chicken with
      Grape Tomatoes & Basil 122
   Sautéed Red Snapper with
      Tomato Olive Sauce 162
   Savory Tomato Rice 220
   Southern Okra & Tomatoes 185
   Sun-Dried Tomato Toasts 11
   Tomato Pie 186
   Tomatoes Rockefeller 189
Tortellini & Shells Salad 86
Tortilla Roll Appetizers 19
Tortilla Torta 133

Turkey *(see Poultry)*
Turkey Meat Loaf 140
Turtle Cake 257
Tuscan White Bean Soup
   with Prosciutto 53

U
Uncle Charlie's Grilled
   Barbecue Chicken 126

V
Veal, Vermouthy 114
Vegetable Beef Soup 45
Vegetable Cheesecake 35
Vegetable Frittata with
   Herbs & Goat Cheese 240
Vermicelli with Sausage
   & Vegetables 196
Vermouthy Veal 114
Very Yummy Rice 217
Vidalia Onion Casserole 173
Vidalia Onion Dip 24
Viorenes 284

W
Warm Goat Cheese Salad 76
Wild Rice Salad 85
William of Orange French Toast 251
Wing Dings 14
Winter Fruit Salad 77
Winter Spinach Salad 64

Z
Zucchini Casserole 181

FAVORITE RECIPES
FROM *A THIRD COURSE*

Recipe Name	Page Number